University of Hertfordshire

Learning and Information Services

College Lane, Hatfield, Hertfordshire, AL10 9AB

For renewal of Standard and One Week Loans,
please visit the website: http://www.voyager.herts.ac.uk

This item must be returned or the loan renewed by the due date.
The University reserves the right to recall items from loan at any time.
A fine will be charged for the late return of items.

4827/KM/DS

of related interest

Receptive Methods in Music Therapy
Techniques and Clinical Applications for Music Therapy Clinicians,
Educators and Students
Denise Grocke and Tony Wigram
Foreword by Cheryl Dileo
ISBN 978 1 84310 413 1

Interactive Music Therapy in Child and Family Psychiatry
Clinical Practice, Research and Teaching
Amelia Oldfield
Foreword by Dr Joanne Holmes
ISBN 978 1 84310 444 5

Microanalysis in Music Therapy
Methods, Techniques and Applications for Clinicians,
Researchers, Educators and Students
Edited by Thomas Wosch and Tony Wigram
Foreword by Barbara Wheeler
ISBN 978 1 84310 469 8

The Individualized Music Therapy Assessment Profile
IMTAP
Holly Tuesday Baxter, Julie Allis Berghofer, Lesa MacEwan, Judy Nelson,
Kasi Peters and Penny Roberts
Foreword by Ronald M. Borczon, MM, MT-BC, Director of the Music
Therapy Program at California State University, Northridge
ISBN 978 1 84310 866 5

Melody in Music Therapy
A Therapeutic Narrative Analysis
Gudrun Aldridge and David Aldridge
ISBN 978 1 85302 755 0

Music Therapy with Children and their Families
Edited by Amelia Oldfield and Clare Flower
ISBN 978 1 84310 581 7

The Music Effect
Music Physiology and Clinical Applications
Daniel J. Schneck and Dorita S. Berger
Foreword by George D. Patrick
Illustrated by Geoffrey Rowland
ISBN 978 1 84310 771 2

Music Therapy Methods in Neurorehabilitation
A Clinician's Manual
Felicity Baker and Jeanette Tamplin
Foreword by Barbara Wheeler with a contribution from Jeanette Kennelly
ISBN 978 1 84310 412 4

Integrated Team Working

Music Therapy as part of Transdisciplinary and Collaborative Approaches

Edited by Karen Twyford and Tessa Watson

Foreword by Julie Sutton

Jessica Kingsley Publishers
London and Philadelphia

First published in 2008
by Jessica Kingsley Publishers
116 Pentonville Road
London Nl 9JB, UK
and
400 Market Street, Suite 400
Philadelphia, PA 19106, USA

www.jkp.com

Library of Congress Cataloging in Publication Data
Twyford, Karen.
    Integrated team working : music therapy as part of transdisciplinary and collaborative approaches / Karen Twyford and Tessa Watson ; foreword by Julie Sutton.
        p. cm.
    Includes bibliographical references (p.   ).
    ISBN 978-1-84310-557-2 (pb : alk. paper) 1. Music therapy. I. Watson, Tessa, 1967- II. Title.
    ML3920.T93 2008
    615.8'5154--dc22

2007042281

British Library Cataloguing in Publication Data
A CIP catalogue record for this book is available from the British Library

ISBN 978 1 84310 557 2

Printed and bound in Great Britain by
Athenaeum Press, Gateshead, Tyne and Wear

Contents

Part 3: Collaborative Work with the Elderly

Case Studies

Acknowledgements

Karen would like to acknowledge her family, friends and colleagues for their support and inspiration to make this possible, especially, Ross, Sarah and Lachy.

Tessa would like to thank Peter Hutchison for his support and good humour, and her colleagues for their willingness to venture into collaborative projects.

Karen and Tessa would like to thank all the chapter and case study authors who have made it such a pleasure to edit this book.

Foreword

What music is produced in teams: improvised, through-composed, with/ without tonality or a score, chaotic, formed, polyphonic, homophonic, internally driven, democratic and autocratic? Playing the same melody, each voice is different, necessary and of value; each identity is respected, as tensions or conflicts are worked on by the group as a whole. In collaborative teamwork music therapists bring depth and detailed awareness of the task at hand, alongside sensitivity to its management. We know how to improvise, about improvisation's complexity, and that this can involve different aspects of functioning – most specifically, at fundamental levels in a person's inner life. Like music, our work is responsive to the moment, aware of, experiencing and contextualising in depth that moment's past, present and future. Our embedded musical selves meet situations that are spoken about using words, involving concepts, images and theoretical systems different from the essentially musical. Our mastery lies in spaces before words and thoughts originate.

Our pioneers gravitated to teamwork: for professional and emotional support and acceptance, to experience belonging when working in isolation, and to educate and inform. This heavy burden can still be part of today's working experience where next-generation pioneers develop a service. Recently, UK therapists were asked to respond to continuing changes in healthcare provision, provoking discourse reminiscent of ongoing dialogue about threats to survival within parts of the psychoanalytic community. Our profession lives into the future through viewing and re-viewing such external demands, retaining its fundamental musical-personal complexity and depth, flexible enough to speak to societal change. Rather than dilute what we do in adopting other frames of reference, we gain from and add much to such collaborations. Are we so certain a psychiatrist cannot think musically, or that by being able to talk from other theoretical perspectives, we lose something of our work? Medical or psychological alliance does not rob us of identity: it strengthens it.

Our work emerges from our art, from the ways we embody our dual identity of musician and therapist. This is essential to our practice and without it our work suffers and can be justifiably criticised. Holding onto music's uniqueness and respecting its intensely private and personal nature, as De Backer notes, we reveal much through our: 'attitude, way of listening, facial expression, way of thinking, and mental presence. This will indicate how much the music therapist is engaged in the music, how he discovers new things, and to what degree he is comfortable with it' (De Backer 2004, p.72).

Music lives only when it crosses the spaces between and within people: therefore musicians know about teamwork. Through repeated experiences of collaborating, negotiating, rehearsing, practising, reflecting, monitoring, and playing, we develop embodied understanding of working things through with others, informed by our personal relationship with music, from an overall appreciation of what music is, through defining and re-defining the act of music-making in many different contexts, to the deeply individual owning of an inner musical self. Our training process engaged the painful loss of a previous musician identity, in order to discover a therapist self and for a new musician within to emerge. Considering the depth and complexity of such collaborative experience and skill, it is extraordinary that we can undervalue our contribution to multidisciplinary teams.

Through working towards shared understandings involving different language systems, spaces open up, that like silences within music, present opportunities for something new to emerge. Music therapists struggle with and add to groups for the benefit of those we work with. Even though challenges are ever-present, our living professional and human engagement with the art of becoming should assure us that the allegedly shaky future of music therapy is already strongly present, safeguarded and in the continued process of becoming.

Ending where we belong, with music, these words speak implicitly about what we bring to collaboration: 'music is not about statements or about being. It's about becoming. It's not the statement of a phrase that's important, but how you get there and how you leave it and how you make the transition to the next phrase.' (Barenboim and Said 2004, p.21)

Dr Julie Sutton, Belfast Health and Social Care NHS Trust

REFERENCES

Barenboim, D., Said, E. W. (2004) Parallels and Paradoxes. Explorations in Music and Society. UK: London, Bloomsbury Publishing

DeBacker, J. (2004) Music and Psychosis. PhD thesis, Denmark: University of Aalborg

Introduction

This book explores the concept of collaborative working in a variety of clinical areas associated with music therapy. Recent research has indicated that collaborative approaches are common amongst music therapists in the UK. However, very little has been written or published about this work and this book is therefore a timely addition to the literature. The book explores the history and theory of collaborative working, providing a substantial exploration of the topic. It also provides understanding of the types and levels of collaborative approaches employed and the consequences resulting from their implementation.

Our intention is that this book is enlightening to music therapists and a range of workers from professions related to music therapy. Of relevance to varied professions is the exploration of the concept of team working and the description of varying levels of collaboration which occur. The diverse casework which is presented in the chapters that follow highlights the potential for combining music therapy with other disciplines and professions and this will be of interest to all those considering employing it with their own approach.

The majority of music therapists are employed as part of a multi-disciplinary team, and their ability to function as active team members is reliant on an ability to collaborate at a variety of levels. Although the notion of collaborating with other professions is considered part of music therapy training, it is questionable how confident newly qualified therapists are in working with colleagues and in utilising the knowledge and expertise of other professionals. The prospect of collaboration for some music therapists is undoubtedly daunting. However, it is critical that music therapists consider how it may be possible to employ these approaches, for they are fundamental to successful team working. A key purpose of this book is therefore not only to highlight collaborative approaches but also to establish them as valuable and acceptable methods of music therapy intervention. The chapters that follow allow music therapists of all persuasions and experience to gain awareness of and insight into the possibilities of working at different levels with other disciplines, professions and relatives of clients. It is hoped that the book will also serve as a guide for music therapists who are considering joint working but are seeking justification or ideas to commence.

This introductory chapter explores the concept of collaborative working and the importance of team working. It is of particular relevance to understand how music therapists function within multidisciplinary teams as many are employed within them. The history and development of the music therapist's role within the multidisciplinary team is explained, supported by contemporary literature. The purpose of team working is considered both as a professional and personal issue. The chapters that follow examine the rationale, purpose and application of collaborative approaches in different clinical settings, and explore how it has become necessary for some music therapists to adopt these approaches at differing levels in order to survive in a changing working culture. Some of these clinical examples are introduced in this chapter.

COLLABORATIVE WORKING AS PART OF THE TEAM APPROACH

In an ever-changing working culture, workers from a multiplicity of professions are endeavouring to meet the challenges of team working. The type of team that is formed will be reliant on the perceived need or outcome for the client. A significant part of team work is the increasing necessity for professionals to work collaboratively at a variety of levels to promote team success. However, Sines and Barr (1998) state that sound team structure and composition and a clear understanding of what exactly is meant by team work will also be essential if the team is to be successful.

In this part of the chapter, the concept of the team is defined and team working is examined with a review of literature relating to health professionals. The concept of collaborative working is then considered, including a rationale for its necessity and ways in which it can be enabled.

The team

Many authors have written about the concept of the team, and team work (Brill 1976; Øvretveit 1993; Sines and Barr 1998; West and Slater 1996). In 1976 Brill defined a team as: 'A group of people each of whom possess particular expertise; each of whom is responsible for making individual decisions; who together hold a common purpose; who meet together to communicate, collaborate, and consolidate knowledge, from which plans are made, actions determined and future decisions influenced' (p.22). Although Brill's work is now 30 years old her definition is seminal in identifying the characteristics essential to successful team working. A team is a way of coordinating each person's efforts to create a final collective result, and the professional and personal contributions that individual team members make will be influential. Øvretveit considers that the team itself is a configuration of professionals and each person involved will have a different concept of a team. In addition to each team member's work there will be a collective responsibility to achieve shared aims and objectives and a clear structure. In order for this to occur, collaboration and interaction between team members is necessary but requires clearly defined roles.

Characteristics of the team member

It is interesting to consider the type of individual who joins a team. Øvretveit states that 'professionals will join a team only if they perceive it to be in their interest to co-operate or at least in the client's interest for some kind of co-ordination' (1993, p.5). People join teams because they want to contribute to an outcome and achieve a purpose which they could not achieve on their own. Allen and Hecht suggest that it is the social-emotional and competence-related benefits of team working that appeal most to individuals (2004).

Each team member brings a variety of professional knowledge, expertise, skills and personal characteristics to the team. There are also significant key skills which determine how the person functions or integrates within the team. These skills include personal commitment, maturity, self-discipline, flexibility, willingness and ability to learn, an acceptance of others' differences and self-objectivity in relation to others. These key skills have an influence on the person's ability to work effectively within the team and contribute to overall team success.

Personal strengths and insecurities also have an influence on an individual's ability to function as part of a team, and it is important that workers who join teams are aware of these and the way in which they may affect dynamics and productivity (Brill 1976). For most people the team is a source of professional and personal stimulus, providing opportunities for support and friendship. Individuals who seek out social interaction will be more likely to join a team and will ultimately be more fulfilled in doing so (Allen and Hecht 2004). However, some professionals may also perceive team working to be vital in aiding them to succeed in their professional roles.

The effectiveness of team working

The combination of skills and coordination of services which teams can offer provides efficient and enhanced continuity of care for particular client populations (Øvretveit 1993), and the potential of the team model is vast. The synthesis and integration of skills and knowledge within the team can help provide an effective service and can stimulate team members and foster their creativity (Brill 1976). Managers, employees and society alike regard teams as effective, and Allen and Hecht (2004) consider that this belief stems from the psychological benefits of group-based activity. Socially, teams are important for self-esteem, which in turn promotes positive work attitudes. For most professionals the team setting provides employment opportunities for the majority if not the entirety of their working career and for this reason the social-emotional effects of team working are significant.

Since the 1970s the team has been viewed as the answer to providing comprehensive and efficient services to different client populations. The reality, however, is that effective team working is not achieved easily (Galvin and McCarthy 1994). On paper the team can look coordinated and effectual, but due to a number of inherent problems the success of teams often requires great effort. West and Slater suggest that if the team's overall task is motivating and clearly defined there will be a greater possibility of effective team work (1996). Issues relating to team composition and team processes (i.e. cohesiveness, goal setting and conflict issues and, perhaps most fundamentally, time) will be all influential.

Team models

While the structure of a team is usually determined by the need of the client population, the actual team model is influenced by the hierarchical structure and interpretation of the concept of team working. Three main types of team are in existence (Brill 1976; Miller, Freeman and Ross 2001; Øvretveit 1993) and these are distinguished by the level of collaboration that occurs within them (Sines and Barr 1998). It is the classifications of Miller *et al.* (2001) to which we will initially refer. The first is the 'fragmented' team which practises autonomously, using the structure of the team to coordinate work but with no team focus. Professionals within this type of team are employed for a specific purpose: to do the job for which they trained. They are required to complete their responsibilities and access the team for purely functional and logistical purposes, and thus the team benefits them in their achievement of the purpose for which they are employed. In this respect this type of team does not expect its members to work together but just to get their job done.

The second type of team is the 'core and periphery' team. Like the last type, this team is made up of varying degrees of knowledge and skills; however, the difference here is that these team members collaborate together to contribute to the planning and delivery of a service. This team recognises the value of professionals communicating in order to improve their effect-iveness. This team provides an enhanced service, as through liaison professionals gain a greater understanding of their clients and feel that they are contributing to a more holistic provision.

The 'integrated' team is the third model and in this type of team a high degree of collaborative working is evident. This model operates coopera-tively and each member may perform a different role by design (Brill 1976). In this team, workers gain greater awareness and appreciation of other pro-fessionals with whom they work and this is significant in influencing their own work. Professionals in the integrated team seek the experience of others, and realise the potential of the team model. Different levels of collab-orative working exist and this will now be further explored.

The concept of collaborative working

It is the concept of collaborative working between professionals from different theoretical and training backgrounds upon which this book focuses. While many teams may claim to work collaboratively, this collabo-ration can be classified in a variety of ways. Miller *et al.* (2001) note 'multiprofessional', 'multidisciplinary', 'interdisciplinary' and 'inter-professional' as all denoting team work. 'Multi' describes different agencies employed alongside each other who do not interact, as distinguished from 'inter', which implies an interaction between team members, including meetings and information exchange (Miller *et al.* 2001). Increasingly used, however, is the term 'transdisciplinary', which denotes the integration of professionals from different agencies. In this classification joint working exists, and aims, information, tasks and responsibility are shared (Canadian Institutes of Health Research 2003). McCracken advocates that this model is vital if the delivery of services from teams of professionals is to be meaningful (2002).

Lacey defines collaboration as 'a commitment to meet together, plan and work jointly' (1998, p.xii; and see Hattersley 1995). With this in mind, the previous distinctions enable us to assume that professionals in the core and periphery and integrated team models collaborate at different levels to achieve a specific purpose which will ultimately be of benefit to the client.

Richard, the occupational therapist, had been working with Liz, a young woman with traumatic brain injury, for several months before he initiated joint working with the music therapist, Rachel. A primary reason for the joint work was Richard's wish to see whether a different approach, such as using music, would affect Liz's general participation. It was Rachel and Richard's intention that a joint approach would provide an appropriate space for Liz to practise her developing functional skills in a creative way. Their collaborative approach provided both understanding and valuable insights for the professionals involved. (See Part 2: Collaborative Work with Adults.)

Identifying the need for collaboration

Collaboration between professions within health and social care has been an increasingly prominent political issue in recent years (Barrington 2003). The political agenda stresses that collaboration and partnership enables needs to be met, and resources to be used effectively (Macadam and Rodgers 1997). The UK government, in its papers *Valuing People* (DoH 2001) and *Every Child Matters: Change for Children* (DfES 2004), stipulates that team working in both the departments of health and for education is vital to the achievement of positive outcomes and the utilisation of available resources. They state that 'specialist services should be planned and delivered with a focus on the whole person, ensuring a continuity of provision and appropriate partnership between different agencies and professions' (DoH 2001, p.75). Historically, however, this has been difficult to achieve due to separateness in professional development (West and Slater 1996).

Karen, a music therapist, Charlotte, a speech and language therapist, and Jo, a physiotherapist, all undertook separate assessments of young children with complex needs within the special school in which they worked. Through professional discussion they concluded that the process of achieving these sometimes difficult assessments may be made easier if they were undertaken contemporaneously. Specific children were jointly assessed using a dynamic therapy process which proved beneficial and productive for the professionals and children involved and justified the combination of time and resources. (See Part 1: Collaborative and Transdisciplinary Approaches with Children.)

Thus agencies are being encouraged to collaborate because it is considered effective; however, this idealistic notion requires immense effort, and basic tensions and contradictions often prevent it from becoming a reality. Many professionals recognise the value of working collaboratively but question the practicalities of endeavouring to realise this.

The advantages of collaborative and transdisciplinary approaches

There are many potential professional, political and personal benefits to be gained from collaborative working, and those who practise collaboratively advocate its usefulness. Writers suggest that creative and innovative approaches to collaboration can make the best use of existing facilities and opportunities and create new opportunities (Hattersley 1995; Macadam and Rodgers 1997; West and Slater 1996). Clients have easier access to a wider range of therapists, skills and therapeutic approaches, and high quality services and health care can be ensured.

Hattersley states that when embarking on collaborative work the rationale for collaboration and what it will involve should be clearly defined (1995). When undertaken with clear planning and specific purpose, collaborative working can ensure the coordination of appropriate, holistic input and can provide continuity of care, which is imperative for client change and progress. Transdisciplinary assessments can provide greater understanding of clients and can help to determine the need for ongoing therapy. Through collaborative work, a more detailed awareness of the aims of the multidisciplinary team will grow and these can be incorporated into future therapy work.

Collaborative working also provides professional benefit to those involved. Working in this way can promote openness among team members, which will assist in the creation of clear communication channels, support for those in isolated positions and the resolution of issues of conflict with colleagues. Those working collaboratively gain a greater understanding of the professional roles of others and the way in which roles relate to each other. A more cohesive and efficient service can ensue when colleagues from different professions are familiar with what each other can offer. Discussions resulting from collaborative working will be reflective of the clinical work that has taken place and the roles of those involved. Professionals open to questioning their approaches and techniques can feel stimulated from this type of non-threatening discussion. The experiential nature of collaborative work can also provide professional emotional support during difficult phases in clinical work.

On a personal level collaborative and transdisciplinary working can be stimulating, refreshing, complementing and enriching for the professionals involved. It can provide a sense of identity and belonging important to team working and can help professionals cope with the emotional impact of their work.

Adrienne, a music therapist, worked as part of a multidisciplinary team in a residential continuing care ward for older people with severe and enduring functional mental health problems. Within a group music therapy session at the setting the issue of spirituality was raised and discussed by clients. Adrienne felt it was important that she voiced this issue for the clients to ensure the team gained a heightened awareness of this important area. Through a process of ongoing consultation and collaboration with both the multidisciplinary team and spiritual leaders from the wider community a strategy was developed to give clients greater access to their chosen religious or spiritual experiences. (See Part 3: Collaborative Work with the Elderly.)

Enabling collaboration

Why is collaborative working sometimes difficult? First, the construction of a team does not ensure that effective team working and collaboration between team members occurs. Good organisation is crucial for effective team work and for providing a high quality and effective service for clients, and energetic leaders and good management can be powerful in enabling effective collaboration. The creation of a team identity is crucial and complex issues such as self-esteem, self-image and status need to be considered. Agencies need to be highly motivated in order to cooperate, for collaboration will require special skills and additional effort. Writers who explore these issues include Galvin and McCarthy (1994); Hudson (1995); Iles and Auluck (1990); Lacey (1998); Sines and Barr (1998); and Weinstein (1998).

Clear aims and objectives for the team are crucial, as professionals working together towards a common purpose see the value of their work amplified and consolidated by others and feel that they are important to the success of the team. Collaboration amongst team members will be enhanced if the distinctive and indispensable skills and roles related to the identity of professionals are recognised. Individual roles should be meaningful, intrinsically rewarding and clearly defined. In addition, regular interaction between team members is essential and differences should be confronted openly.

Factors that can impede collaboration include personality factors, poor communication skills, individual dominance, status, hierarchy and gender effects. Collaboration may be easier if the knowledge, values and skills required for collaboration are developed in initial professional training before attitudes and stereotypes become established. Ideologies and cultures of different professional groups which are ingrained from training and practice can cause opposition and negative perceptions amongst team members. However, personal contact achieved through joint working has been shown to reduce issues related to professional hostility and attitudes. Collaboration can be enabled when there is mutual support, respect and an understanding of each other's professional skills, roles and relationships within the team.

The issue of time is often identified as a difficulty with many professionals being told that there is not enough time to employ collaborative approaches; the provision of sufficient time to support collaborative team work requires an attitude of flexibility. The work may involve the sharing of records and regular meetings which will assist enhanced and accurate communication; ultimately this can save time and avoid unnecessary overlap of service provision. Some professionals may have particular attitudes relating to confidentiality and sharing information, and it is important to clarify what procedures will be observed in different situations. Writers who discuss these issues are Hattersley (1995); Lacey (1998); Macadam and Rodgers (1997); and Øvretveit (1993).

These challenges are potentially discouraging for the team member who values the concept of team working. Moreover, it is not possible for one individual to impact on the entrenched or historic deficiencies of a team. However, team members who regard collaborative working as important can encourage their teams by investigating team practice and identifying achievable goals for collaboration to enhance overall team performance. Undertaking an audit within a team to measure effectiveness is useful in identifying the professional barriers inhibiting team working; however, this is not often practised (West and Slater 1996).

Tessa, a music therapist, and Alison, a speech and language therapist, were interested in the fact that, despite their different professions, they worked towards the same team aims. They had worked in the same team for a number of years and felt comfortable discussing their different approaches together. Although they had different ways of working, documenting their work and writing reports, they were able to collaborate and run a group together for adults with learning disabilities. They were aware of the amount that they both learnt from each other and this collaborative working further convinced them of the importance of both professions in this clinical area. (See Part 2: Collaborative Work with Adults.)

MUSIC THERAPY AND COLLABORATIVE WORKING: A HISTORY

The next part of this chapter looks at the relevance of team work to both music therapists and the arts therapies professions. It explores the levels of collaboration undertaken by those music therapists working in multidisciplinary teams. Current literature is examined to illustrate the importance of collaborative approaches from the perspective of music therapists and also arts therapists. Lastly consideration is given to the professionals with whom music therapists work collaboratively, and the influence of types of team and client groups on this work.

The significance of the team: to music therapists

In recent years authors have explored the issue of team work in relation to music therapists (Eisler 1993; Hills, Norman and Forster 2000; Moss 1999;

Odell-Miller 2002; Priestley 1993; Sutton 2002). Historically the multi-disciplinary team has been important to music therapists, providing both satisfaction in working with colleagues from different backgrounds and a greater sense of personal accomplishment. Multidisciplinary working has also provided support and sustenance, especially for those music therapists setting up new positions or for those in geographical or professional isolation.

The multidisciplinary team has helped in establishing an identity for music therapists and in assisting in an understanding and acceptance of the discipline by other professionals. However, Eisler and Odell-Miller suggest that this has only been achieved when music therapy has been valued, understood and proven effective. Music therapists have worked to validate and promote their work and this has been positive for the profession, resulting in professional independence and registration with the Health Professions Council (Eisler 1993; Odell-Miller 1993; Wigram interviewed by Loth 2000).

Music therapists consider that their profession has a specific role to play within the multidisciplinary team, offering important insights into clients' difficulties and development. Research into team working relating to music therapists is not common, but one small study found that music therapy was a valued part of the team (Jacobs and Lincoln 2003). It continues to be necessary for music therapists to offer training or information to those with whom they work in order to inform members of the team and potential referrers (Jacobs 2000). Indeed many music therapists consider it vital to work collaboratively in order to be accepted and to function successfully within the team.

Transdisciplinary and collaborative approaches: the music therapist's perspective

Music therapists give many reasons for the use of collaborative approaches at a transdisciplinary level. Central to this is the benefit the client will obtain from a combined intervention (Twyford 2004b). Collaborative approaches can ensure that appropriate input is delivered and continuity of care is achieved, with specialist knowledge from various professions contributing to greater understanding of clients. While this can be difficult to achieve, it ensures that client change and progress is possible (Durham 2002; Watson, Bragg and Jeffcote 2004).

Music therapists who have written about collaborative work with other professions consider that it can enhance the expressive skills of an individual, increasing self-awareness, awareness of others and the ability to integrate with others (Fearn and O'Connor 2004; Zagelbaum and Rubino 1991). Music can provide a stimulus and is effective when used collaboratively with other therapies, bridging the gap between non-verbal and talking therapies. This makes collaboration with music therapists essential for many professionals (Grasso *et al.* 1999).

The profession of music therapy stands to benefit from further integration of music therapists within the multidisciplinary team and from the new and creative applications of music therapy which are created. Collaboration plays a role in the growth and understanding of the profession as it relates to other disciplines (Register 2002). The sharing of different perspectives and skills within the team is a great benefit of this type of work (Watson 2002), assisting other professions in gaining a first-hand experience and greater understanding of music therapy. Collaborative work also has the potential to lead to the creation of new positions and increased referrals as the potential of music therapy is realised.

The significance of the team: to arts therapists

The notion of team working and particularly collaborative working is relevant to all the arts therapies professions (art, dance movement and drama therapy as well as music therapy). Several authors write about the issues to be faced by arts therapists employed in multidisciplinary teams, including the understanding of roles, effective communication and identity (Read Johnson 1985; Smitskamp 2003; Van der Drift 2003). Best suggests that, in collaborating, arts therapists are able to broaden their practice by learning to adapt to and value theoretical, practical and political differences and by taking up opportunities for reflection, definition and growth (2000).

Transdisciplinary and collaborative approaches: the arts therapist's perspective

Literature from the wider arts therapies professions also suggests that collaborative approaches at a transdisciplinary level benefits both the client and the therapist, and that working at this level creates additional opportunities for interaction for the client and promotes parallel reflections and associations between the disciplines involved (Cardone, Marengo and Calisch 1982;

Zagelbaum and Rubino 1991). Cohen considers that therapists will be able to interact with the client in a different kind of creative experience and will be able to observe the correlation between the client's different forms of expression in each modality (1983).

The next part of the chapter considers the different levels of collaborative working within music therapy.

Levels of collaborative working within music therapy

Collaborative work is undertaken by music therapists worldwide and is described as existing at different levels, each level having various classifications. The following paragraphs explore these levels in relation to current international literature.

NEW ZEALAND

O'Hagan *et al.* (2004) describe four levels of collaborative work in existence in music therapy work in New Zealand:

1. Unidisciplinary level: professionals work side by side in a team but work alone in their own discipline.

2. Multidisciplinary level: professionals seek the expertise of other disciplines to assist them in their own treatment process.

3. Interdisciplinary level: professionals focus on the client's needs, put their own therapeutic agendas aside, and work collectively as a team.

4. Transdisciplinary level: this includes practice with other professionals across traditional therapeutic boundaries and, while it requires commitment, team members practising in this way 'support each other in practice: physically, emotionally and intellectually...sharing a common search for meaning in the experience of client care' (p.5).

Working at an interdisciplinary and transdisciplinary level is vital for music therapists in New Zealand, where in comparison with other world music therapy communities a small professional body exists. The reality of professional isolation emphasises the importance of music therapists accessing the multidisciplinary team and working collaboratively within it.

THE UNITED STATES OF AMERICA

Krout (2004) and Wheeler (2003) identify interdisciplinary, multidisciplinary and transdisciplinary models of work in the United States. In addition, Krout proposes a new term for collaborative work – synerdisciplinary. The two authors define the levels as follows:

- Multidisciplinary model: professionals from different disciplines provide separate treatments for the benefit of the client. Professionals may be aware of each other's goals for the client and may or may not liaise regarding needs and progress.

- Interdisciplinary model: music therapists work more closely with other team members to determine goals and implementation plans collectively. Each professional delivers their section of the plan separately and no professional boundaries are crossed.

- Transdisciplinary working: music therapists combine their work with other team members and take an equal responsibility to implement treatment plans and achieve goals. This model requires fluid boundaries between the professional roles of those involved.

Krout offers the term 'synerdisciplinary' to 'capture the creative ways in which music therapy and the different disciplines can come together, play off each other, and interact dynamically' (2004, p.36). He suggests that it is possible in a synerdisciplinary model for the effectiveness of transdisciplinary work to be taken to a new realm, as the use of music holds and connects everyone present in shared space and time.

AUSTRALIA

In Australia, Lee and Baker (1997) describe multidisciplinary and interdisciplinary work within the area of rehabilitation. Similarly to Krout (2004) and Wheeler (2003) they define the multidisciplinary team as a group of health professionals functioning separately, each providing assessment and treatment which focuses on only one particular area of client need. They describe the development and implementation of an interdisciplinary rehabilitation system where treatment goals are established and implemented jointly by the treatment team to achieve a functionally based approach which focuses on a specific area or role which is significant and valued by the patient and family. Kennelly, Hamilton and Cross (2001) discuss the joint use of music therapy and speech pathology in rehabilitation with children with acquired brain injury. They illustrate the benefits of working jointly with other professionals and their level of approach is similar to the transdisciplinary level identified by other authors.

UNITED KINGDOM

Recent research undertaken by Twyford in 2004 suggests that music therapists in the UK work collaboratively at similar levels to those identified by other authors, and provides descriptive levels to describe different types of collaboration (Twyford 2004a). The most central of these is the communicative level, where music therapists liaise with other professionals to share important information regarding clients. This level is vital to music therapists' work as part of a multidisciplinary team, for an ability to function at this level influences the effectiveness of the therapeutic process. While music therapy is offered separately from other services at this level, some team members may share ideas and use a common language to discuss and compare therapeutic changes.

The next level of work in the UK is described as interactive. At this level the music therapist works collaboratively with other team members towards shared aims and objectives, sometimes in addition to the aims of music therapy. Music therapists may work in parallel with other therapists or professionals, with sessions provided separately but planned to include similar themes. This level bears some similarities to O'Hagan et al.'s (2004) and Wheeler's (2003) definitions of interdisciplinary.

The third level identified in the research is a facilitative or observational level. At this level team members from different professional backgrounds are present in sessions together, but one therapist leads the session and the client experiences only one medium at a time. The roles of the therapists change depending on which modality they are working in, as described by Watson and Vickers (2002), and the presence of a professional from a different discipline is influential. This level can also be described as observational because therapists from other disciplines may be invited into music therapy sessions for reasons which may include the interpretation of responses or the education of others (e.g. to demonstrate the potential of music therapy with shared clients).

The final level detailed in the research is a fully integrated level. This exists when music therapists combine their approaches with other professionals and work simultaneously with different disciplines and professions to provide a unique combination of therapeutic intervention for the benefit of clients. Music therapists functioning at this level describe the work as complementary, successful in stimulating fresh and creative approaches and in providing opportunities for communication and shared interaction (Finlay *et al.* 2001; Walsh Stewart 2002). Working at this level also provides the opportunity for music therapists to learn about other approaches, and question, adapt or reinforce their own techniques. The facilitative, observational and fully integrated levels of working relate closely to the transdisciplinary level identified by O'Hagan *et al.* (2004).

Worldwide, different models of music therapy practice exist and, as Maranto suggests, each of these is influenced by differing theoretical orientations (1993). Music therapists may use different models of working depending on the client group with which they work, adapting these accordingly (Ahonen-Eerikainen 2003). Several authors state that if music therapists work clinically from a basis of music itself and consider what music has to offer that is unique, then the types of goals developed and music therapy methods used will be representative of the music therapist's beliefs about music, their role and their relationship to the client and this will give meaning to the therapy experience (Brown 1999; Meadows 1997). With this in mind, we can assume the personality of the therapist involved and the nature and culture of the working environment will partly determine the level of collaborative work undertaken.

The influence of team type and client group on transdisciplinary working

In 2000, 53 per cent of UK music therapists were employed as part of a multidisciplinary team (Hills *et al.* 2000). In work with children this includes educational settings, child and adolescent mental health services (CAMHS), hospitals and music trusts, and the provision of peripatetic services to schools or individuals. In adults and elderly work these types of team include community health teams (mental health and learning disability teams) and those in hospital settings.

Interestingly, recent research (Twyford 2004a) indicates that the majority of collaborative work that music therapists in the UK undertake is with children. This research also showed that the majority of collaborative work was undertaken in the area of learning disability, probably linked to the complexity of need in this clinical area (APMT 2004).

Exploring the professions with which music therapists collaborate

Music therapists work collaboratively with a diversity of professions. Recent research has demonstrated that the clinical area and perceived needs of the client group will influence the professions with whom music therapists work (Twyford 2004a). This will be explored in more detail later in the book.

Music therapy has much in common with the other arts therapies and, because of this, these therapists often work collaboratively (Bonny 1997; Summer 1997). Music therapy literature also highlights work with seemingly unrelated professions such as speech and language therapy and physiotherapy. Kennelly *et al.* (2001) suggest that collaborative work between music therapists and speech and language therapists may be successful due to parallels between musical and speech/language development models. Music therapy combined with physiotherapy or movement therapy is often designed to implement movement experiences in conjunction with music. This type of collaborative approach focuses not only on the physical development of the child but also their emotional well-being.

The case studies in the chapters that follow illustrate the ways in which music therapists work with a multiplicity of professionals using a variety of unique and creative applications which until now have not been documented or celebrated.

BRIEF OUTLINE OF CONTENTS

The chapters that follow describe joint working practices between music therapists and other professionals at a transdisciplinary level. The subject area is comprehensive, and for this reason the book has been divided into three parts to fully explore and present current collaborative practices in existence with children, adults and the elderly. The book includes a number of examples of collaborative clinical work, presented in the form of short case studies. These have been generously contributed from music therapists working in a variety of clinical backgrounds and provide the reader with a creative perspective of music therapy applications, highlighting exciting possibilities for the future development of the profession. The reflections and thoughts from the different professionals involved in these collaborations form an important part of the book. Each chapter concludes with guidelines for good practice.

The first part of the book details collaborative work undertaken with children in both education and health. In Chapter 1, Karen Twyford describes the make-up of multidisciplinary teams in work with children, including the school setting, the child mental health team and the hospital team. Case studies are then used to examine the use of diverse collaborative approaches in both the areas of assessment and treatment. The second part of the book, presented in three chapters, is concerned with collaborative work undertaken with adults. First, in Chapter 2, Tessa Watson explores work with adults with learning disabilities. In Chapter 3, Claire Miller considers the area of adult mental health. In Chapter 4, Wendy Magee establishes the importance of collaborative working in the area of adult neuro-disability. Part 3 of the book (Chapter 5) is authored by Adrienne Freeman, providing a picture of collaborative work undertaken within elderly services.

In the final chapter of the book, Alison Barrington explores the notion of team work in a broader professional context. Her chapter considers historical factors influencing collaboration, including collaboration between clinicians and management and the music therapist's approach to collaboration in the twenty-first century.

For those readers considering collaborative or transdisciplinary work a comprehensive list of guidelines for best practice is included at the end of each chapter. These guidelines provide practical and useful ideas for successful joint practice. The notion of collaborative working is an exciting one and the authors hope that as readers browse through the book they will find new ideas and inspiration in the description of the theory and practice of music therapy that will encourage them to contemplate the potential of these approaches in their own work.

Karen Twyford and Tessa Watson

Part 1

Collaborative and Transdisciplinary Approaches with Children

Chapter 1

Collaborative and Transdisciplinary Approaches with Children

Karen Twyford

INTRODUCTION

Combined practice provides insight into the child's needs and appreciation of each other's professional roles. (Hill 2005, p.88)

Music therapy has long played an important role in the provision of therapeutic services to children in the UK. Progressively its application has extended to include a diversity of applications within the areas of health, education and social services. As the profession expands, music therapists are creating new and innovative positions within a variety of clinical populations. Many are employed as part of a multidisciplinary team where there are varying requirements to work closely and in partnership with other professionals.

As expressed in the opening quote there are many benefits to be gained from working collaboratively with children. The multidisciplinary team is becoming increasingly recognised as an important and extensive resource for music therapists, which should be used to its potential. The ability to collaborate and work jointly at a transdisciplinary level is an acquired skill and if this can be achieved the rewards are significant, not only for the music therapist but also to the profession of music therapy. While essentially this concept is appealing to some therapists, the reality requires an ability to rise to personal, professional and political challenges.

This chapter considers collaborative and transdisciplinary approaches with children and adolescents. It begins by considering the government's viewpoint on collaboration in light of recent policies in which a growing impetus for collaboration between agencies and professionals exists. These thoughts are consolidated by other authors from a wider perspective. A brief overview of team working and the importance of collaborative and transdisciplinary approaches is then given followed by a representational picture of the types of settings and teams in which music therapists working with children are employed. An exploration of the music therapist's role in relation to the multidisciplinary team is also considered.

Following this, models of collaboration in relation to two fundamental areas are examined, that of assessment and treatment. This is supported by a review of worldwide practice. Each area is illustrated with clinical examples which highlight current collaborative UK practice with children in a variety of clinical areas. Within these case studies, all names and details have been changed to maintain confidentiality.

The concluding section reflects on the chapter as a whole and offers music therapists and professionals considering joint working clear guidelines for good collaborative practice.

COLLABORATION IN HEALTH, EDUCATION AND SOCIAL CARE SERVICES FOR CHILDREN

The government perspective

In September 2003, the UK government published the Green Paper *Every Child Matters* (DfES 2003), which led to significant debate about services for children, young people and families. Collaboration became a predominant theme following inquiries into poorly coordinated services which had resulted in unnecessary and unfortunate events involving children. In October 2004, the UK government delivered its White Paper, *The National Service Framework for Children, Young People and Maternity Services* (DoH 2004a). This paper stated that fundamental change in thinking would result in high quality services being designed and delivered.

The National Service Framework (NSF) comprises 11 standards promoting the health and well-being of children and young people. Notably many of these standards state the need for cohesive services in which a high level of collaboration is evident, particularly in hospitals, education and mental health. The seventh standard, for hospital services, *Getting the Right Start*, states that 'children and young people should receive care that is integrated and co-ordinated around their particular needs, and the needs of their family' (DoH, 2003, p.9). It also states that professionals should 'consider the whole child and not simply the illness being treated' (p.9).

The eighth standard, *Disabled Children and Young People and Those with Complex Health Needs*, identifies that an average of ten different professionals will have contact with a disabled child over a year and that the child will make over 20 visits per year to hospitals and clinics. The government states that 'good collaborative arrangements are required between therapists and other professionals to extend current support given to disabled children and also to minimise disruption to their education' (DoH 2004a, p.14). In order to achieve this, however, agencies need to establish a shared vision of intended outcomes, which are developed in collaboration with children and their families. This may be achieved by 'co-ordinated multi-agency assessments leading to prompt, convenient, responsive and high-quality multi-agency interventions that maximise the child's ability to reach his or her full potential' (p.5).

The theme of collaboration is particularly prevalent in the ninth standard, *The Mental Health and Psychological Well-being of Children and Young People* (DoH 2004a). It is here that the government requires multi-agency services to work in partnership, so that all children and young people who have mental health problems and disorders have 'access to timely, integrated, high-quality, multi-disciplinary mental health services to ensure effective assessment, treatment and support, for them and their families' (p.4). In order for these services to function effectively the government intends that specialist multidisciplinary teams will be of adequate size and have the appropriate skill-mix, training and support. It is acknowledged that partnership working across agencies can be a challenging task, due to a lack of understanding regarding respective roles, duties and responsibilities. However, the government believes that effective partnership working can lead to improved outcomes and improved service experience.

Thoughts from a wider perspective

Other authors agree with the government's perspective and highlight the need for children's services to be coordinated, stressing that services should not function disparately but rather be cohesive, as this is vital for children and their families. Wilson and Pirrie state that within education the 'new emphasis is on working together to deliver a co-ordinated and integrated service' to service users (Wilson and Pirrie 2000, p.1). Their study into collaborative multidisciplinary working in education in Scotland high-lighted that there is a shared purpose which has the potential to provide a meta-perspective for the professionals involved.

However, while the government is committed to and acknowledges the need for integrated and coordinated services, it is at the actual service delivery level where the reality of collaboration takes form. The responsibility for professional collaboration really lies with individual professions and the individual team members themselves. A commitment to working in this way is forged from experiences in practice; however, the motivation to collaborate is internal to each agency and this is significant in influencing the level at which professionals will work together (Farmakopoulou 2002; Wilson and Pirrie 2000). Through working together, professionals from differing disciplines can discover that they possess both shared and profession-specific skills and knowledge (Tollerfield 2003).

TEAM WORKING WITH CHILDREN: ONE COMMON PURPOSE
The importance of collaborative and transdisciplinary approaches in children's services

Varying levels of collaboration occur in team working and all of these are relevant and essential to children's services. In light of government directives professionals are being held more accountable for their work and this places increased demands on professionals. Increasingly, professionals working with children are realising the importance of working collaboratively with others. It appears essential that working closely in the planning and provision of children's services requires cooperation, professional interaction, liaison, discussion and an awareness of a child's responses and achievements in each particular discipline present on the team. Collaborative and transdisciplinary approaches promote openness amongst team members and this is an intrinsic value of team working.

These approaches are important because not only does a high degree of integrated thinking occur but also a greater understanding of each profession involved and an appreciation of different working approaches is achieved and this all contributes to a holistic view of the child. When collaborative work comes from client need, has a clear focus and purpose, provides a sense of achievement and is undertaken with an awareness of the roles of all collaborators, then the process has significant potential.

Thus team working in children's services and in particular collaborative and transdisciplinary approaches is gaining increased importance with music therapists as they realise that this work has much to offer the child, their families and the professionals involved. Skewes and Thompson believe that the client may be better served where a transdisciplinary team philosophy is employed and professionals work across the boundaries of specific disciplines (1998). This is due to the fact that while each professional involved can explore new territories and gain inspiration they can also reinforce confidence and strength in their own modality (Brightman and Ridlington-White 2005). When considering collaborative and transdisciplinary approaches it is useful to consider the types of children's teams in which music therapists are most commonly employed.

Types of children's teams

In the UK music therapists work with children in a variety of settings, including schools and special schools, hospitals, community mental health clinics, child and adolescent mental health services, children's hospices, child development centres and family support organisations, to name a few. The breadth of practice is vast and increasingly varied. To consider all facets of team working with children is outside the scope of this chapter. Therefore a representational picture is given of the types of teams in which music therapists are employed and within which they are perhaps most likely to work collaboratively. A description of the different team structures is offered, but this is by no means exact or specific to all organisations.

Music therapists working with children in the UK are employed by the National Health Service, Local Education Authorities, the Department of Social Services and charitable trusts or organisations, or are self-employed. The majority of these music therapists will be employed within multidisciplinary teams and the notion of collaboration and team working may form an integral part of their work.

A brief description of some of the organisations and agencies within these services follows. In reality each team is unique and is determined by the individual service provider and the client population. The role of the music therapist in each of these settings will also differ, reliant on the therapist's individual theoretical orientation and application of music therapy.

- Child and adolescent mental health services, including health, education and social services. The main function is mental health care, and inpatient and outpatient services are provided. The multidisciplinary team most commonly includes child and adolescent psychiatrists, social workers, clinical psychologists, a community psychiatric nurse, child psychotherapists, occupational therapists and art, music and drama therapists.

- School services, where multidisciplinary teams are formed by staff employed by Local Education Authorities (LEAs) and the NHS. Staff may include teaching staff, support staff, music therapists, speech and language therapists, physiotherapists, occupational therapists, educational psychologists, a nursing team and sensory support services. Some music therapists may be employed by the local borough, county music agencies or music trusts.

- The National Health Service – hospitals. This includes specialist healthcare provision, general hospital and community services such as inpatient, outpatient and accident and emergency services and also research, education and training. Employees include medical staff and non-medical staff such as nurses, and scientific, therapeutic (including music therapists) and technical staff.

- Child development centres and services. These are usually established to provide day services to children with a variety of disabilities including autistic spectrum disorder, learning and/or physical disabilities and sensory impairments. These centres usually provide assessment, diagnostic services, family support and information services, and staffing may include a consultant paediatrician, clinical psychologists, social workers, physiotherapists, occupational therapists, speech and language therapists, teachers and music therapists.

- Charity-funded services, typically made up of a variety of professional staff with specialist skills which will ensure the broad-ranging needs of the children and their families accessing them are met.

Playing a part: the music therapist's role in relation to the team

The role of the music therapist within the multidisciplinary team whilst primarily being for therapeutic services will undoubtedly vary depending on the type of team in which they are employed, inherent personal, professional and political factors, and a preparedness to modify their notion of the ideal music therapy position. It is evident in the music therapy literature which relates to children that many of these notions have already been considered. While these concepts are important to all music therapists in multi-disciplinary teams, it appears especially pertinent to those working with children.

Establishing a professional identity is an important part of any new position within a children's team and this can be achieved through various types of collaboration. Initially music therapists may find that it is valuable to play a consultative role in order to define the principles and therapeutic use of music and educate other colleagues about music therapy. This may be achieved in a variety of ways such as through workshops, in-service training, lectures, showing videos, sharing summaries and joint working. This process is invaluable in alerting staff to the specific needs which music therapy can address in children's services and may assist in ensuring that appropriate referrals are received. Education of others is essential for music therapists considering joint working with children for it not only assists others in understanding the therapy process and intended benefits, but also the role that they will play within the joint working. As the music therapist establishes an identity, it becomes easier to emphasise different matters and to work according to the profile of the particular team. These thoughts are shared by many writers (Abad and Williams 2006; Ahonen-Eerikainen 2003; Booth 2004; Edwards 1999; Lee and Baker 1997; Storey 2005; Wigram 2002).

A fundamental part of being employed as part of a multidisciplinary team within children's services is working with the team. To this end music therapists should try to attend meetings to facilitate team knowledge and share practice regarding clients. These may include case conferences and referral meetings in child psychiatry, and individual education programme (IEP) meetings and staff meetings in special education. This sharing of knowledge with others can provide new insight and confirm previous observations made (Carter 2002). In regards to documentation procedures it can be useful initially to follow the procedure of other team members (Edwards

1999). This will demonstrate a willingness to operate as a team member and may be a clearer way for others to gain a greater understanding of music therapy. As the music therapist becomes more established there will be the opportunity to develop documentation accordingly.

Effective communication is an important part of these processes and it is essential that music therapists working in children's services learn the basic terminology of other disciplines. In addition it is important to translate music therapy-specific terms into a language that is easily understood, and to support this with specific observable behaviours. By creating a common language, knowledge and philosophies of related fields can overlap which can have an intrinsic benefit to the child or young person. In the area of education, more effective team development of the child's IEP will be possible when professionals share this type of information.

Warwick states that in the area of special education 'the roles of teacher and therapist should be complementary while acknowledging the differences' (1995, p.224). For many music therapists this is a problematic issue and one that requires a great deal of effort from all concerned. An open and honest attitude assists in dispelling myths and professional jealousies regarding music therapy which can be attributed to not being understood. These types of situations often occur in school settings where the music therapist takes children away from the classroom for individual therapy, an opportunity not frequently afforded to the classroom teacher. Warwick believes that professional envy can occur when therapists isolate themselves rather than 'becoming established as a team member with all the necessary communicative skills that entails' (1995, p.224). For these reasons some music therapists working in special education and in particular mainstream education might also consider more inclusive music therapy services which don't withdraw the child (Jones and Cardinal 1998). This may include the assistance of other staff which has varied potential, including observation and generalisation of approach.

The music therapist working in the school environment must be adaptable and flexible and, as Storey confirms, being accepted as part of the school team is not always an easy task (2005). Some music therapists may be required to work in less than adequate environments and spaces, for example the school hall, a classroom or even the staffroom. While this is difficult and stretches the skills of the therapist, it is important for the purpose of acceptance within the team and it may be necessary initially to make the most of what is available.

Sweeney-Brown (2005) and Schwarting (2005), writing of team working in hospices, discuss the need to be flexible and of having to learn to accommodate the presence of others within sessions due to children's medical needs. Schwarting notes that involving staff and children in an open group session can provide an opportunity for a joint activity where 'there is a sense of identity, of belonging together' (2005, p.123). The incorporation of staff into sessional work can provide important education in music therapy principles and processes and can help to prevent tension between colleagues. It is also important for music therapists to be aware of unconscious attitudes of staff which can occur as a result of the difficulty of their jobs. Understanding this and possessing professional empathy enables good working relations with staff members.

In addition, music therapists employed in all types of children's teams may be required at some point to step outside the traditional therapist role and adopt a more generic role. While there may be concerns about this, it can have advantages (Strange 1987). Those working in child mental health may be required to take the role of a key-worker which may include facilitating meetings with parents, spending lunchtimes with families and undertaking home visits. When working in education these duties may include general education, assisting with lunchtime feeding or transport arrangements or performing playground duty. A therapist's overall effectiveness may be enhanced through undertaking these responsibilities, as opportunities to integrate into the school community provide invaluable knowledge and insight into various aspects of specific children. This involvement can also assist in the generation of team acceptance which in turn will be advantageous to the therapist.

INTEGRATED TEAM WORKING: MODELS OF COLLABORATION

This section of the chapter focuses on collaborative and transdisciplinary work that has taken place between music therapists and other professionals. The areas of assessment and treatment are considered separately to offer a broad example of possible therapeutic combinations.

ASSESSMENT

Assessment forms a key part of any music therapy treatment. The assessment process provides essential information that informs ongoing music therapy intervention and provides in-depth insight for other professionals within the multidisciplinary team including diagnostic information. Many music therapists share information informally with other professionals through discussion and liaison, or formally through regular multidisciplinary team meetings. These meetings provide the opportunity to share practice and concerns, and it is this collaborative problem solving which can generate more innovative joint practice. Describing his role at Harper House Children's Service Wigram wrote that 'all the professionals play a role as a team in trying to unravel the very confused picture many of the children who are referred present' (Wigram 1995, p.181).

A music therapy assessment may also be video recorded and shared with the team afterwards. This allows professionals to observe the child within the context of music therapy and to provide insight on observed behaviour and responses from their own clinical perspective. Some teams may observe an assessment live via a remote video link. In diagnostic assessments, observed evidence of a child's behaviour in other therapeutic assessments, combined with evidence from music therapy, can assist in formulating a clearer diagnosis (Wigram 1995).

The need for joint assessments usually evolves from non-music therapy professionals interested to see their clients' responses within a musical environment. This is especially so where young children are involved. Due to a number of factors, including short attention span and distractibility, it can be difficult to engage children and assess them accurately. Various authors identify varying levels of collaborative assessments in relation to pre-school and school-age children and include those that are:

- multidisciplinary – separate assessments, with individuals reporting to a central body

- interdisciplinary – separate assessments, with individual professionals meeting to discuss findings and form joint goals

- transdisciplinary – assessments where all necessary professionals are present to observe, discuss and evaluate the child simultaneously.

(Vaac and Ritter 1995; Wilson and Smith 2000)

Little has been written on joint assessments involving two or more professionals from differing disciplines working simultaneously. Shaw believes joint involvement in this process can be useful from an observational perspective, providing insight for other professionals into the child's capabilities within a musical context (2006). Music therapy as part of this process provides great possibilities. The music therapist can establish communication and contact through the therapeutic relationship and has the ability to draw out and reveal another side to the child, which other professionals may have not seen (Wigram, Pedersen and Bonde 2002).

Some literature describes the value of co-workers and observers within music therapy assessments. Carter (2002) describes assessments with children which involve a co-worker who is familiar with the children in other situations. She believes that they can provide valuable insight into her work as they can observe specific behaviours that the music is affecting and assist in determining the child's level of engagement in comparison to other interventions. Fearn and O'Connor (2003) describe their co-therapy assessments which also include parental observation and discussion. The two music therapists work jointly, each with specific roles, whilst the parent observes. A discussion takes place before and after the assessment. It is here that the therapists can provide subjective and objective observations and the parents can provide vital feedback relating to the child's observed responses.

Linder's transdisciplinary play-based assessment is discussed by Humpal (2004) in relation to her use of Orff music therapy. All team members including the parents are present; however, only one person facilitates the assessment, following the lead of the child and being guided by the team members. This assessment is referred to by many authors who value its functional approach and the input of the multidisciplinary team (Anthony 2003; Meisels and Atkins-Burnett 1999; Vaac and Ritter 1995).

In the first case study of this chapter, Claire Molyneux describes the value of collaborative assessments with other professionals in the area of child and adolescent mental health. She describes how in her assessment work she is required to take on a dual role and reflects on the impact and significance this has on the assessment procedure.

MUSIC THERAPY AS PART OF A MULTIDISCIPLINARY FAMILY ASSESSMENT PROCESS

Claire Molyneux (Music Therapist)

Introduction

This case study will describe the music therapy input to a multidisciplinary team assessment process for families who have been referred to the child and adolescent mental health services (CAMHS). The assessment process and the contribution made by the music therapist will be described. The experience of co-working as part of the multidisciplinary team is then reflected upon both by the author and colleagues from the unit.

The reflective comments on the music therapy input within this case study are from Dr Ingrid Davidson (Consultant in Child and Adolescent Psychiatry) and Ellisa Fisher (Occupational Therapist), colleagues of the author at CAMHS.

Background

Referrals come from the outpatient teams within CAMHS and are made to the multidisciplinary team at the Children's Unit, a day unit for children aged 12 and under and their families. Families are referred where the outpatient workers have been unable to form a satisfactory understanding of the family dynamics or there are complicated issues between the family dynamics and diagnostic issues. The referral to the unit gives the opportunity to see the whole family over a longer period of time and in a variety of situations. Members of the multidisciplinary team also do a home and school visit which adds to a comprehensive picture of the strengths and difficulties of the family and referred child.

The assessment package has evolved over time from clinical practice. It draws on an eclectic mix of systemic, behavioural and psychodynamic models as well as assessment of parenting and behaviour management strategies to offer a comprehensive multidisciplinary assessment. The assessment seeks to understand the family, their strengths and difficulties and to build a rapport with them to facilitate working collaboratively.

Family assessment programme

Families attend the unit for two days and a programme is devised to meet each family's needs. The programme includes both structured and unstructured sessions. There are also opportunities for the family to discuss their needs and difficulties as individuals and as a group. Staff involved in the assessment typically consist of a psychiatrist, psychologist, psychiatric nurses, occupational therapists and music therapist. Two team members are allocated as key-workers for the family and the whole team contributes to the assessment depending on their areas of training and expertise.

As the approach to family assessment is flexible, adapting to and accommodating each family's needs, the structure of the assessment can vary. Below is a general idea of the process of the assessment:

- team planning meeting
- welcome/introductions
- group/family activities – creative session/music therapy session
- outdoor play
- observed play session
- lunch
- individual assessments for referred child (psychiatric and play assessment)
- sibling group to explore relationships within family
- parental meeting with key-worker
- team discussion.

The music therapy session usually takes place on day two. By this time, the family have become familiar with staff and have engaged in some creative activities and play. As making music is something that can make some parents uncomfortable, it is felt that allowing the family some settling-in time is important. The same two workers (where possible) facilitate the two creative sessions, sharing the role of leading. This allows for consistency of observation and assessment, enabling the family to feel relaxed and at ease with staff with whom they have begun to build a relationship.

By the second day, the team have already met to discuss observations made on day one. These observations and increased understanding of family dynamics inform the planning of subsequent sessions in order to try and answer further questions that have arisen within the team. For example, the team may have noticed a lack of eye contact and attunement between a parent and child and ask for this to be explored more fully in the music therapy session. Alternatively we may be curious about how the parents set boundaries for their children.

Music therapy session

Vignette 1   Mr and Mrs Peters and their three children looked at the instruments with caution and scepticism. Their experience of the assessment so far had been difficult and the staff found them to be hostile and unforthcoming. Over the hour that followed, the mood in the room changed significantly. Mr Peters took a turn to lead the group musically. He seemed to become empowered by the experience of leading both the music therapist and co-worker, sharing a joke with the co-worker as he mimed for the music therapist to play the ocean drum loudly and chaotically. Following the session, other staff commented on the positive shift in attitude in the family, with them becoming more relaxed and open with the team, consequently revealing more of their strengths as a family.

The music therapist already worked collaboratively with the multi-disciplinary team in the individual assessment package at the unit and it seemed natural to extend this to include the family assessments. Whilst the family are observed in a number of different settings with a strong focus on play, the use of music offered something different. In this non-verbal setting, aspects of communication, dynamics and relationships are often strikingly apparent both to the staff and the family themselves. Colleagues at the unit comment that:

> The music therapy session offers a unique and novel way of exploring family dynamics and communication. Many families are experiencing using music together for the first time which can be refreshing and allows them to express themselves and relate to each other in a new way. The novelty of the session allows the therapist to gain valuable insight into how the family approach and manage the situation and how the parents contain feelings of anxiety and excitement in themselves and the children. The session is particularly good for observing non-verbal communication between family members such as eye contact, attending, listening, mirroring and turn-taking.

The model that is used for the session has developed from clinical practice, including individual music therapy assessments (Molyneux 2002). The approach is informed by the work of Amelia Oldfield who has written extensively about her work in child and family psychiatry (Oldfield 1993, 2000, 2006; Oldfield and Bunce 2001).

The session usually lasts for one hour. It is semi-structured, including therapist-directed interactions and improvisation, and has the following points of focus:

- To observe how the family relate to each other in a playful setting using a non-verbal medium.

- To observe how the family relate to, interact and engage with the therapist and co-worker in this setting.

- To assess how the family communicate and respond to each other, to include: eye contact, level of concentration, attention to task and level of ease with which the family engage musically.

- To observe the family dynamics, to include: behaviour, limit setting and relationships.

It is important to stress the flexibility of approach to the session. The overall aim is for the family to have fun, to enjoy being together and interacting in different ways. It is interesting to see families who have very little playful contact experience playfulness in a non-verbal setting. In addition, a family's resourcefulness and capacity to work cooperatively is sometimes surprising given that it may not have been evident in any other part of the assessment.

Building a rapport with the family is especially important over the assessment period. The music session is different to the other creative sessions as the staff are actively involved in making music with the family. We have found that this is often a time when even the most hostile family can begin to relax as illustrated in the first vignette. This second vignette illustrates the benefits of co-working.

Vignette 2   The Johnson family consisted of a solo-mother and her three sons. The boys were aged five, three and two years, respectively. All three children had some developmental delay, but since starting school and receiving significant extra input the oldest boy had begun to make some progress. The mother experienced recurrent depression and found parenting her three boys immensely challenging. She lacked parental control and could not see how things could be any different. In the music therapy session, the boys initially dominated the session, playing the instruments loudly and chaotically. It was only with the support of the co-worker that the mother was able to remain in the room. The music therapist engaged the family in taking turns to lead from the drum, while the co-worker sat next to the mother offering support and encouragement. The boys were lively and boisterous, but all managed to stay within the boundaries of the activity. When it came to the mother's turn to lead, she played quietly and with little eye contact with the children. However, remarkably, the children all followed how she was playing. This was pointed out to her by myself and the co-worker and marked the beginning of this mother being able to see herself as having some potential to take control.

Roles and reflections

Co-working with other members of the team in the music session is important for many reasons, some of which are summarised below and also apply to other aspects of the assessment process:

- Having two staff in each group enables us to discuss our observations and experiences with the family, leading to a more balanced and informed assessment of family dynamics.

- The co-worker can support parents who are struggling to manage children's behaviour enabling the therapist to contain and hold the musical interactions that are taking place.

- The co-worker and music therapist can use reflective questioning or verbalise observations in the session as a way of pointing out to parents what is taking place. In the case of the Johnson family, for example, we were able to comment on how well the children had listened to their mother, thus reinforcing her concept of herself as capable.

- Although an assessment, it has been appropriate at times to model more desirable ways of interacting. Through modelling and encouraging parents to respond differently, it becomes possible for them to experience their potential for change as they engage in more positive parenting and behaviour management strategies with their children.

Music therapist as key-worker

One of the generic responsibilities that all members of the multidisciplinary team share is being key-worker for a family. This role may include facilitating meetings with parents, primarily to gather information, but also to explore the dynamics of family relationships and parental concerns, spending lunchtime with the family, undertaking a home visit and liaising with the referrer. The key-worker is the person whom the family can contact if they have any queries about the process and is also the person who writes the summary once all team members have made their reports. It is recognised that different members of the multidisciplinary team have different strengths and these are taken into account when allocating tasks such as key-worker.

> The team ethos is that of a multidisciplinary, holistic approach to the assessment and treatment of families and within this the music therapist is viewed as an equal member who contributes actively to the overall formulations and treatment plans. The music therapist not only works very well within their own professional expertise but also shares many generic skills with the team such as conducting initial contracting interviews.

I have found the role of key-worker challenging and fascinating. As a music therapist, my primary tool for communication is music, so the need to communicate verbally and often ask difficult questions has brought up many challenges. On a personal and professional level, the experience of co-working with colleagues has been an important learning process for me. I have been able to observe and co-facilitate sessions with experienced clinicians and learn from them. The opportunity to work intensively with a family and be able to place the experience of making music with them into context so completely is unique and has informed my ongoing work as a music therapist in many ways. The discussion and team supervision that takes place during the assessment days is invaluable. Each team member's contribution is valued, staff are encouraged to be enquiring and curious and it is this team approach that enables us all to focus on reaching an objective assessment. It is also recognised that being part of the multidisciplinary team in this way helps to reduce the potential for the music therapist to feel isolated, especially in a service where there are few or even no other arts therapists.

> Music therapy is a rare and valued experience for mental health practitioners. The novelty of the music therapy session allows clinicians to gain new perspectives and insights into families that is refreshing and enriches the assessment and treatment process to benefit both clinicians and clients alike.

Collaborative assessments in special education

Joint assessments within special education are less common than in the NHS. This may be attributed to the demands on school staff to work hard to meet increasing curriculum demands. The music therapist assessing children with special needs may have a variety of aims for the assessment in order to gain specific information and it is usual that many of these are part of the general aims of the multidisciplinary approach (Wigram *et al.* 2002).

Music therapists and other professionals have demanding caseloads and are most likely working in more than one school. Finding time to collaborate is difficult, but can benefit both the children involved and the service providers. In this second case study collaborative assessments with children with complex needs are described. These examples emphasise the value of experiential knowledge acquisition that can be achieved in working in this way, providing immediate opportunities for continuous reflective practice and issue clarification amongst those involved.

TRANSDISCIPLINARY ASSESSMENTS WITH CHILDREN WITH COMPLEX NEEDS

Karen Twyford (Music Therapist), Charlotte Parkhouse (Speech and Language Therapist) and Joanne Murphy (Physiotherapist)

Background

This case study describes a process of transdisciplinary assessment developed by Karen Twyford (Music Therapist), Charlotte Parkhouse (Speech and Language Therapist) and Joanne Murphy (Physiotherapist) whilst working at a special needs school in Kent. The school caters for children and young adults from 4–19 years of age with severe to profound and multiple learning difficulties and also autism. Music therapy, speech and language therapy and physiotherapy were combined to assess young children who had complex needs. Children with complex needs typically have severe to profound learning difficulties associated with physical, sensory and social communication impairments. The complex nature of these impairments makes interpreting the child's current skill level and predicting their future development difficult. Whilst over time these will usually become clearer, they are particularly problematic during an initial clinical assessment as a child with complex needs often finds it difficult to perform to their potential.

The multidisciplinary team working at the school was made up of a variety of health and education professionals. As therapists we had customarily undertaken separate assessments with children within the school. We collaborated frequently through liaison and discussion to interpret observed responses in individual assessments and other forms of intervention. Over a period of time it became apparent that due to the nature of specific children's impairments it might be useful for us to work together. We felt that collaborative assessments may be a way of understanding these children in a more comprehensive and experiential way. This would be of obvious benefit to the child and ourselves, as it avoided having to put the child through unnecessary continuous assessments and professional misinterpretation of responses, and reduced the time we spent on discussion and liaison.

Before the collaborative assessments commenced, we met to discuss how we envisaged working together professionally. We felt it was important to gain an understanding of the purpose of assessment for each discipline and the way that each of us would usually set about undertaking this. We discussed how we would usually work with a child and what type of approach we would employ. It was evident that it would take time for each of us to fully understand and appreciate the ways in which the others worked. Establishing a shared concept of assessment would be fundamental to the process, as would ongoing discussion throughout the period of working together.

The assessment process

Each assessment took place in the music therapy room which was equipped with a variety of instruments, sensory objects and the required physiotherapy equipment. Before each assessment we met briefly to discuss each child, share any previous knowledge and pre-empt situations which may impact on the assessment. We also discussed how we would respond to the child, and what our initial roles in the assessment should be.

The specific role of the music therapist was to provide improvised music. She remained in the same place within the room to reduce the amount of 'active' individuals. With a more active child she usually sat at the piano as it was probable that this type of child would show some interest in the piano and move to it at some point. Alternatively she moved with her guitar or another instrument to work at eye level with a less active child; this included sitting or lying on the floor. The role of the music therapist was flexible, varying in response to the needs of the child and the action of the other therapists. It included leading, supporting, reflecting or enhancing. Music was used to structure the beginning and ending of the assessment session, usually in the form of a hello and a goodbye song. Improvised music and song were used to reflect physical, emotional and communicative responses. An important role for the music therapist was to motivate, support and engage the child musically and also sustain interactions and good positioning.

The role of the physiotherapist was to explore the child's potential in a variety of different positions. This involved handling the child in such a way as to assess the distribution of tone throughout their body and modifying that tone with careful positioning and by handling the child using key points of control (e.g. supporting at the shoulders, the pelvis or the wrist). The physiotherapist sought to stimulate and facilitate good patterns of movement and inhibit abnormal postures. She also observed what structures (joints, muscles or soft tissues) needed stretching, especially those where there was a risk of deformity and contractures forming over time. The physiotherapist selected comfortable positions to make the best use of the child's physical and cognitive abilities. Initially the assessments involved mainly mat work; however, other pieces of equipment were introduced and these included a bench for working on trunk control, a roll for sitting on, a wedge for leaning on and assisted walking devices for mobility around the room.

The role of the speech and language therapist was an active one. She met the child in situational interactions as they explored different stimuli. Of the three therapists she engaged most overtly with the child. This did however depend on the nature of the assessment and the dictating circumstances. Of all of our roles hers was the most changeable from leading, to facilitating and supporting, to being observational.

The process of the assessments was dynamic and child led. The use of music was key in creating and maintaining a secure environment for the child, providing a context for communication, action and self-expression to occur. Each session was generally unstructured, providing opportunities for both the child and therapists to explore a range of activities as situations evolved and presented themselves. More active children would explore their environment independently creating new assessment opportunities constantly. Less active children were more reliant upon situations being created; however, this depended on the positioning, emotional state and motivation of the child at all times.

While the assessments were unstructured all therapists had pre-planned assessment aims. The activities ranged from unstructured to more structured tasks as was felt appropriate, and this was dependent on which one of us was leading at a particular time. Discussion occurred during the assessments which enabled continuous reflective practice and issue clarification. This provided the prospect of extending the assessment process and exploring different options instantly in order to gain a greater awareness of the child's level of functioning.

Vignette   Rebecca suffered low physical tone and found it difficult to maintain positions for any length of time without support of some kind. In the assessment Jo wanted to assess her potential in increasingly demanding positions, for example using a bench for Rebecca to kneel at with support and to bear weight through her arms. She was highly motivated by music and sensory stimuli (in this case a hand-held fan) which resulted in her lifting her head to seek the enjoyable sensory experience. Rebecca could only maintain this position for brief periods of time and Charlotte and Karen both expressed concern that what was occurring was too much for her. Jo judged that, although Rebecca did find this position tiring, she was actually highly motivated and that they should continue their intervention. Clarifying this issue meant that they were able to continue with the activity for a longer period of time with the reassurance that Jo would indicate when Rebecca was no longer responding positively.

Over a number of assessments we were able to develop a specific way of working together, with a continual changing of roles dependent on the child's immediate need and as each situation dictated. Over time we were able to move instinctively in and out of roles in a fluid and effortless way. We considered each of the differing roles as paramount, for each one provided us with the prospect of ascertaining the child's level of functioning from a different perspective and this was important for the purpose of assessment.

Vignette   Four-year-old Amanda had good floor mobility but was not walking. She functioned at a pre-verbal level and had a short attention span. Throughout the assessment Amanda moved freely around the room, exploring the various instruments and sensory stimuli on offer. As she moved around the room to various instruments Jo observed her means of movement and resting postures. Although she supported her physical involvement in various interactions, she also worked directly to assess Amanda's ability to maintain correct postural positions and body alignment. Charlotte moved around the room as much as possible with Amanda, sharing her interest in the stimuli on offer, attempting to maintain joint attention and interact overtly with her, for example by using keywords to reinforce and determine Amanda's ability to turn take. Karen, at the piano, provided musical response and support to these interactions, matching Amanda's mood and manner of engagement. When Amanda showed interest in the piano Charlotte withdrew to an observational role to study her participation while Jo and Karen worked directly with Amanda. The fluid nature of the session enabled all of us to work in a variety of roles and gain a comprehensive assessment from differing perspectives.

Reflections

REFLECTION FROM CHARLOTTE

The opportunity to work collaboratively with a music therapist and a physiotherapist gave me greater holistic insight into the child as a communicator. This is because a three-dimensional view of the child could be achieved in a contemporaneous live context. This meant that I gathered far richer assessment findings. I felt that this occurred because Karen and Jo were able to provide motivation and means of communication – both extremely important to consider during speech and language therapy assessment of complex children and yet so challenging to achieve when working in isolation. Karen's use of rhythmic musical support and responses to communicative attempts gave the children the motivation to remain engaged in the session. Also, Jo's work with the physical skills of the children showed me how issues such as a change of position can affect how they are able to communicate. This may be crucial when considering future means of communication such as high-tech alternative and augmentative communication devices.

REFLECTION FROM JOANNE

I discovered that sharing my knowledge and thoughts in an interactive way with Karen and Charlotte, as we engaged with the child through play, provided a more rounded view of these complex children's abilities. In a physiotherapy assessment it can be difficult to communicate effectively with the child and to engage them in a way that is fun and motivating. These assessment sessions were inspiring as we could see the child begin to open up, react to our prompts and movements and 'come alive' to the music. Music proved a perfect way to facilitate movement with these children. It provided motivation, a context in which the children could explore their environment and a positive reinforcement for movements or physical responses. The use of music and various musical elements enhanced preparation work with the child. Preparation work involves rolling, twisting, stretching and activating the core muscles to 'wake up the body' and prepare it for movement. The use of music also effected change in the child's tone, for example slower and rhythmical music assisted in lowering tone whereas more upbeat music stimulated movement. In working collaboratively I found the child was able to learn functional skills (such as good looking, turning their head or maintaining a head position while looking for the source of stimulation). I was able to direct this activity and adapt handling accordingly whilst the child was engaged.

REFLECTION FROM KAREN

The process of these collaborative assessments was invaluable and essential for informing future music therapy work with these children. Most notably I became aware of the less noticeable changes that music effects. This included physical changes noted by the physiotherapist such as relaxed body tone, which enables the physiotherapist to work more easily with the child. Jo's hands on approach with these children enables her to observe and ascertain that music is supporting a child's motivation to move and sustain positions. For me this is important information as it affects my choice of instrument and use of musical elements. From a music therapy perspective, Jo's knowledge of the child's physical potential is invaluable as this ensures best positioning to access instruments and therefore the facilitation of self-expression. Understanding ways in which children with complex needs communicate and ways of developing this is important in music therapy work and can sometimes be difficult to determine. Charlotte was able to identify each child's communication strategies, such as their way of requesting more of an activity or experience. She also provided developmental knowledge, vital when determining where to go next with these children. Having this combined knowledge base of support and expertise enabled me to work effectively with these children to begin to realise their musical potential and provide an opportunity for creative self-expression.

JOINT REFLECTIONS

In working together we felt that our approaches became inextricably linked. We obtained experiential insight into ways of working with complex children which we believe would have been more difficult had we undertaken the assessments separately. Working collaboratively revealed the potential of each child and informed future planning not only for those of us directly involved but also other professionals involved with the child. Most notably we felt that working collaboratively promoted an openness amongst us which allowed us to learn and appreciate each of our professional roles and techniques. Lastly an understanding developed between us which highlighted a shared responsibility for looking at a child holistically and provided a true sense of team achievement.

TREATMENT

Music therapists working with children are realising the potential of both short- and long-term collaborative work with other professionals. Increasingly new and creative joint partnerships are being realised and these provide the professionals involved with the opportunity to expand their own work and generate a deeper understanding of the children with whom they work (Bertolami and Martino 2002). Walsh Stewart suggests that often the skills learned within the context of joint working can be transferred into other environments (2002). These concepts are essential when working with the child holistically.

With these thoughts in mind the remainder of this chapter explores collaborative treatment intervention undertaken between music therapists and various professionals in a variety of children's settings.

Music therapy and physiotherapy

Music therapy combined with physiotherapy has long been recognised as an effective method of intervention for children and many authors have written on the subject. In this type of collaborative work the music therapist carefully adapts fundamental musical elements such as melody and rhythm with which to provide a supportive and predictive framework to organise movement (Hooper, McManus and McIntyre 2004; Meadows 2002; Wigram 1992). The use of music in a combined approach can assist in addressing movement goals that the physiotherapist may have for the child and in enhancing the child's sensory, perceptual and motor skills (Turnbull and Robinson 1990).

Children with physical disabilities often find movement and handling distressing and stressful, and music therapists have noted that a combined approach is effective in enabling children to relax sufficiently, facilitating their ability to respond by helping to cue movement and providing a context in which to move (Bunt 1994; Elefant and Lotan 1998; Meadows 2002). If the sessions are planned with the emotional and physical state of the child in mind in order to meet the child's therapeutic needs, they have the potential to benefit all involved (Elefant and Lotan 2004). The motivational and attentional aspects of sound and music can also encourage the child to achieve increasingly more difficult stretches and movements.

Meadows identifies different types of collaborative working with children in which music therapists and physiotherapists work jointly to design and implement music and movement programmes (Meadows 2002). In 'physiotherapy with music' the physiotherapist develops specific movement activities and leads the session. The role of the music therapist is to support these movements and provide structure, context and motivation through the composition and implementation of appropriate music. In 'structured music and movement' sessions the programme is developed jointly and both therapists are present in the session. The music therapist leads the session with both physical and musical factors in mind and the physiotherapist is responsible for the child's physical needs. 'Improvised music and movement' sessions are again planned jointly but there is an emphasis for the music therapist to follow the lead of the child and helpers. The movements undertaken result from spontaneous interactions between the helper and child and are always based on both physical and emotional needs. The helper is attuned to the movements of the child, responding accordingly in order to reduce tensions and anxiety, maintain physical well-being and increase awareness of self and others.

Music therapists Fearn and O'Connor have developed an improvised music and movement approach in collaboration with various professionals from the multidisciplinary team. Their use of music and attuned movement therapy aims to hold the child musically, physically and psychologically (2004). The following case study describes the process of developing this approach and draws attention to the importance of working closely with the multidisciplinary team.

COLLABORATIVE WORKING AT THE CHEYNE DAY CENTRE, LONDON

Mary-Clare Fearn and Rebecca O'Connor (Music Therapists)

This case study outlines a method of clinical practice that has developed as a result of collaborative working at the Cheyne Day Centre, London, over a period of 13 years. This therapeutic intervention has evolved into a specific way of working with children who have profound physical and learning difficulties; those who have been unable to develop basic interactive and communication skills due to the severity of their disability. We have called this collaborative approach music and attuned movement therapy.

In the music and attuned movement therapy sessions a music therapist works closely with another consistent professional who acts as a movement facilitator for the child. During the course of therapy, communication is on a pre-verbal level. Patterns of breathing, vocal sounds and movements are acknowledged by reflective improvised music and attuned movements.

A number of different professionals have been involved in the development of music and attuned movement therapy. These have included music therapists, teachers, physiotherapists, occupational therapists, speech and language therapists, nursery nurses and classroom assistants. Over the past 13 years, 40 children have received music and attuned movement therapy for periods of time ranging from six months to five years.

The Cheyne Day Centre

The centre offers a fully integrated service combining education, therapies and health care for children who have profound physical, learning, health and emotional difficulties aged two to seven years. The team embrace a holistic approach and work collaboratively to set aims and plan appropriate activities for each child. The centre's ethos is that all the children are seen as individuals; their contributions are valued, empowering them to develop a positive sense of self. The team provide a rich and stimulating environment, enabling the children to grow, develop and achieve their full potential. Rebecca and Mary-Clare shared a lead music therapy post at the centre for 11 years.

Vignette   Music and attuned movement therapy began in 1993 at the Cheyne Day Centre with a little girl called Claire who had cerebral palsy. Claire was totally dependent on adults for all aspects of her daily living, was blind and had little recognisable voluntary movement. It was hard to assess how much awareness Claire had of her surroundings, she was often distant and at times became upset and tearful. The team were finding it hard to connect with her. Claire's teacher frequently took her out of the classroom and simply sat with her on her knee acknowledging her breathing patterns by matching this rhythm with her own breath and holding her hand on Claire's chest. At the same time, the music therapist was seeing Claire for individual sessions. She too found herself drawn to Claire's breath and used her flute to reflect this and the quality of her cries and vocalisations.

Following team discussions, the teacher and music therapist decided to try working together to combine their similar approaches. Initially sessions occurred three times a week and lasted for 15 minutes. The primary aim at this early stage was for Claire to realise that she was not alone and that she could share something about herself. This was achieved by the combination of reflecting vocal sounds and body movements with flute music and dance patterns.

As the therapist and teacher worked with Claire over a period of time, they realised that their approach was having a significant impact on her emotional state. Claire began to still and calm as she listened to the music. Gradually, she appeared to be developing an understanding that the music and the teacher's movements were reflecting her breathing and sounds. She became aware that she could initiate a response from the adults, often smiling and vocalising as she did so. In the ensuing 18 months, Claire's crying decreased and her conscious ability to communicate with others developed, both in and out of her therapy sessions.

A number of theories have influenced the therapists and co-workers during the development of this approach. Integral to the work has been the writings of Papousek and Papousek (1979, 1981), Schaffer (1977), Stern (1985) and Trevarthen and Hubley (1978). The theoretical stance of dance movement therapist Bannerman-Haig (1999) was also helpful in thinking about the significance of the children's body movements. Stern's writings, in particular his concept of affect attunement (1985), were used as a focus for thinking about the therapy process. Stern discusses how aspects of behaviour can be matched in order to acknowledge and reflect a person's feeling state.

The music therapist mirrors, reflects, attunes and contains the child's input, both musical and physical, with improvised music. The aim is for the child to develop awareness that their movements and sounds are being acknowledged. The music therapist uses the rhythm of the child's breathing as a foundation for her musical reflection: 'breathing itself, a new achieve-ment to the newborn, may be quite interesting until it is taken for granted' (Winnicott 1964, p.59). The child in therapy seems to re-discover an interest in breathing during the early stages of the process. The re-awakening of this interest is usually the start of the realisation that they are able to initiate a response from others. There is often a smile of pleasure as the child realises that a connection has been made. Bannerman-Haig states that 'it is through the body that we can express and get in touch with deep feelings, with conscious and unconscious processes and emotions, in order to facilitate change' (1999, p.157). Dance movement therapy is based upon 'an essential belief that one's movement expression reflects one's psychic state' (ibid.).

The adult facilitator aims to reflect and facilitate the child's breathing and movement patterns, with the overall aim of accessing the emotions that the child could be representing through their body. Stern discusses the concept of mirroring and reflection in relation to affect attunement. He states that 'what is being matched is not the other person's behaviour per se, but rather some aspect of the behaviour that reflects the feeling state' (1985, p.142). In music and attuned movement therapy, the combination of the music therapist's reflective improvised music and the co-worker's attuned movements results in the child experiencing double feedback which appears to hasten the development of the child's awareness of self and self in relation to others.

Post-therapy meetings are essential in order for the professionals involved to discuss the feelings that arise during the session as well as the child's responses and development. Acknowledging and discussing counter-transference within the relationships allows for a deeper understanding of the child's internal world.

Anna

Anna has cerebral palsy affecting all four limbs; she is blind and suffers from epilepsy. She is dependent on adults for all aspects of daily living and has a profound learning disability.

Anna received individual music and attuned movement therapy for a total of five years (aged two to seven). Integral to the development of this approach was the ethos of the Cheyne Day Centre which encouraged and enabled a music therapist and movement facilitator to work consistently with the same child for long periods of time.

Anna began her sessions with much of her lower body in plaster (a hip spica) following a recent hip operation. She was therefore immobilised from the waist down to her knees and set in such a way that she could only be in a seated position. The centre staff felt that she was experiencing a certain amount of pain. Initially, the music therapist played with the rhythm of her breathing, eye movements, any seemingly intentional body movements and vocal sounds. The adult facilitator maintained physical contact with Anna throughout the session – sometimes this involved simply resting her hand on Anna's chest and letting it move up and down with the rhythmic movement of the breath. At other times, she helped Anna to raise her arm following a subtle movement which was taken as an *intention to move*.

This *intention to move* was discussed with the physiotherapist at length. It is obviously difficult in the case of a child with cerebral palsy to decipher intentional movement as so much of their movements are largely uncontrolled due to the condition. It was agreed that, following a period of getting to know a child, there was indeed a *sense* of when a child wanted to move. It was this sense that the facilitator relied upon and developed. Clearly this work is largely dependent upon great sensitivity on the behalf of the facilitator and it is imperative that this person is able to just *be* with a child rather than have any preconceived expectations of what they ought to *do*.

In the early days of working with Anna, there was a great deal of stillness, quiet moments and silence. Consistency and predictability formed an essential part in the growing trust within the trio. Sessions were structured with a welcome song using the guitar where Anna's pitch or mood formed the basis for an improvised song. A concluding song was also used initially which was replaced after time by a talking section, where the therapist and facilitator used words to reflect upon the session.

After six weeks, Anna's plaster was removed. For a time, it felt to both the therapist and facilitator that Anna was unaware of her legs. It was as though she had blocked off this lower part of her body from her physical awareness due to the pain she had endured. Over the proceeding months, the music and facilitated movements helped Anna to regain an awareness of her whole body. This was achieved with a flute accompaniment which reflected movements in Anna's body. Suddenly she appeared to be aware that, if she initiated an upward leg movement which was then facilitated, the music responded with an ascending scale. She stilled, tried again and, when she received the same response repeatedly, she began to smile and vocalise in acknowledgement and delight.

Anna rarely used her voice in the first half of the sessions. The movement duet between Anna and her facilitator enabled her to release tension and reach the necessary relaxed position where she could find her voice. This process was largely dependent on the facilitator's sensitivity to Anna's movement needs. Her vocal sounds became increasingly expressive and she used a wide range of dynamics and pitch. She knew she was in control of the music and enjoyed taking the lead.

Anna's process of developing awareness

As a result of this collaborative working, Anna appeared to develop an awareness of herself; initially this was a physical awareness of her body, then of a subjective self. She grasped the concept of cause and effect; she realised her body movements and vocal sounds could be used to initiate and have an effect on the therapist's music. Anna also learnt that she could make choices. Communication with others moved from being a possibility to a reality, both in and out of Anna's music and attuned movement therapy sessions.

Reflections

REFLECTION FROM CELIA GOODYEAR, TEACHER

It is in the overlap where disciplines meet that practitioners really begin to be creative. The needs of children with complex difficulties deserve to be addressed from every angle. When a child's skills are so fragile and so few, it is vital that every detail is observed and supported. Joint working sheds light and offers solutions from different but complementary perspectives.

REFLECTION FROM TRACY LEDDEN, NURSERY NURSE

When working with children who have such profound and complex difficulties, two things are paramount: professionals working together and the ability to view the child holistically. This work can be at its most powerful in the music and attuned movement therapy situation where two adults surrender to everything that the child brings.

One of the major outcomes from music and attuned movement therapy is that communication skills a child develops in sessions can be transferred into the classroom. These are understood by the facilitator who can aim to interpret them for other classroom staff.

REFLECTION FROM DERYN WATTS, PHYSIOTHERAPIST

I feel very privileged to have had the opportunity to join in music therapy sessions with my colleagues at the Cheyne Day Centre. Sessions gave me a greater appreciation of how each child uses their available movement or postures to express themselves and the importance of allowing enough time without expectations for them to make their responses.

I strongly believe in close team work, sharing our knowledge and skills and respecting each other's roles. I believe that the opportunities I have had to observe and participate in music therapy sessions have not only made me more open to and aware of the needs of the children I see, but have also taken my appreciation of the diversity of skills of other therapists to a new level.

REFLECTION FROM REBECCA O'CONNOR AND MARY-CLARE FEARN, MUSIC THERAPISTS

Working as music therapists within a multi-professional team can at times be difficult and isolating. We have found it crucial and extremely beneficial to embrace input, advice and support from other disciplines. This resulted in a complementary and collaborative approach to clients which greatly enriched our clinical practice.

Music therapy and speech and language therapy

Transdisciplinary approaches involving the combined intervention of speech and language therapy and music therapy with children are increasingly documented within the literature. The validation for these collaborations stems from the empirical evidence which highlights the parallels between both musical and spoken language. Those music therapists who work jointly with speech and language therapists advocate for its effectiveness and emphasise the contributions which each discipline can make to a joint process.

As music works at a non-verbal and pre-verbal level it can assist in establishing the necessary components for language acquisition and this is essential when working with children. At a basic level these components can include motivation, awareness of self and others and listening and attention skills. Music can also assist the stimulation of vocalisation, stressing, phrasing and timing and an ability to produce sounds sequentially (Bunt 1994). In his work with hearing-impaired children Bang developed a programme in conjunction with parents, teachers and speech therapists to aim to improve the voice levels and voice qualities of the pupils. He states that 'both music and speech require the ability to remember and imitate sounds' (1996, p.76). More so, the work may address specific goals including breath control, pitch, volume and coordination of breath and voice.

Therapists may find it useful to work with a specific child independently and jointly during the course of treatment, as did Kennelly, Hamilton and Cross (2001). In these joint ventures music provides the means of expression and the opportunity and motivation to communicate. When working jointly the music therapist and speech and language therapist usually employ a variety of verbal and non-verbal techniques, and the use of live music can provide immediate reinforcement and increase active participation (Farnan 2003). Walsh Stewart consolidates these thoughts further in the findings of her pilot study with children with autistic spectrum disorder (ASD). Music therapy and speech therapy were combined to incorporate psychodynamic music therapy with Division TEACCH, a structured communication programme for use with children with autism. She concluded that this joint intervention 'succeeded in stimulating a fresh and creative approach to complement existing resources available in the treatment of children diagnosed with ASD' (2002, p.184).

Hill researched the use of combined music therapy and speech therapy intervention with children with language and communication difficulties and concluded that this combined practice 'facilitates a union of a unique combination of therapeutic intervention', which promotes communication essential for social and emotional well-being (2005, p.82). She videotaped joint therapy sessions involving a speech and language therapist and music therapist and in her analysis found that the combined practice provided stimulation and learning for the group members. This was achieved through 'clear communication, planning and negotiation of roles and aims' (2005, p.76).

The next case study explores the combination of music therapy and speech and language therapy and details three different types of collaborative approach. Clinical examples illustrate the therapist's ability to be flexible within their approach to meet the specific needs of children involved.

COLLABORATIVE WORKING IN A SPECIAL NEEDS SETTING
Karen Twyford (Music Therapist) with reflections from Charlotte Parkhouse (Speech and Language Therapist)

Background
This case study describes collaborative working developed by Karen Twyford, music therapist, and Charlotte Parkhouse, speech and language therapist, at a special needs school. The staff is made up of a variety of health and education professionals and the school caters for children and young adults from 4 to 19 years of age with severe to profound and multiple learning difficulties and also autism.

Approaches
Within the school each of us was independently responsible for developing, coordinating and implementing the provision of music therapy and speech and language therapy. Pupils and students were referred to each service by staff, parents and other professionals and individual and group intervention was established to meet specific needs. Liaison and discussion between us and with the staff team formed an integral part of our professional practice. In time this led to the establishment of collaborative work which took a

variety of forms and could be categorised into three main types: structured joint sessions, semi-structured sessions and unstructured sessions. Music was central to all these approaches and was one of the main reasons for collaboration to occur.

STRUCTURED JOINT SESSIONS

These group sessions consisted of pre-planned activities based on a theme. Jointly we developed specific activities which aimed to create opportunities for joint attention, anticipation, sustained eye contact and spontaneous communication. Charlotte led the sessions using verbal cues, objects of reference and symbol cards to encourage children to make choices and help to determine the sequence of activities. Her role was vital in linking activities together and maintaining group momentum. Within some activities she actively engaged with the children and in others she played a more supportive role. Karen's role was to use music to reflect, support and enhance the child's participation, pace and level of engagement. Improvised music and original songs were used to incorporate specific aims and interactively engage children. Sometimes she remained static at the piano, at other times she moved freely around the group to interact musically with children.

Vignette   A weekly session called 'Outback Adventure' was initially developed for a class of children with severe to profound multiple learning difficulties. It ran for the period of a school term and was held in the classroom. The children in this group had varying levels of ability and expressive/receptive language and at least half the group was non-ambulant. The specific aim was to use sensory and musical activities to motivate and develop self-awareness, awareness of others, expressive skills, decision-making skills and an understanding of narrative at an affective/sensory level. The role of music was to motivate and reinforce the skills developed and to reflect and enhance interaction and responses. Activities were planned with specific aims, however each allowed for the initiation of individual child responses and spontaneity. The therapists were active and moved accordingly to meet child responses and engage in situational interactions.

The group began each week with the same piece of recorded Aboriginal didgeridoo music. This aimed to promote group awareness, early conversation skills, listening and response skills and self-expression. The activities used in the group included music and sensory experiences introducing the ideas of a snake, the hot sun and a cultural story: 'How the birds got their colours'. Sensory and musical stimuli were used to engage the children and encourage their responses.

The children were particularly responsive to this joint approach, which classroom staff also noted. Collaborating further Karen, Charlotte and the classroom teacher adapted and combined the activities to develop a class scene in the school's end of year production. This provided the opportunity for the children to share their experiences, responses and acquired skills in an appropriate and meaningful way with parents and the wider school community.

SEMI-STRUCTURED SESSIONS

This type of collaborative work was mainly used with small groups. An underlying theme was chosen to shape the session, and a few activities were used, loosely structured to allow for spontaneity. The use of improvisational activities promoted creativity amongst the group members. The use of language was kept to a minimum in these sessions. Its function was to reflect, encourage and embellish child-initiated responses. Our roles as therapists in these sessions were more interchangeable. We shared the responsibility of leading and facilitating the session, and moved in and out of roles as need and situation dictated.

Vignette   A 'Tree Narrative' group was established, involving four children from the junior school: three with autistic spectrum disorder, and all with severe learning difficulties. As children with autistic spectrum disorder typically find the areas of social interaction, communication and symbolic and imaginative play difficult it was intended that the group would aim to meet these needs.

The session aimed for the participants to take part in a motivating event and then reflect on and express their experiences linguistically and musically. We were also hopeful that the children would show an awareness of others and listen and respond to their contributions. A theme of 'trees' was chosen to provide a group identity and as a focal point for the group. One of the group members was particularly interested in trees and we felt that this would appeal to him and also be something he could share with other group members.

The weekly group took place in the music therapy room. During the first week the group went outside to an area of trees within the school grounds. Together we explored the area with the children, encouraging them to notice different aspects of the trees, sounds that could be heard or made when moving amongst the trees and bushes and how they could affect this, for example by shaking or tapping branches. They were also encouraged to explore the feel of the tree and its leaves. This experience was videoed by another staff member and was used each week to stimulate discussion, interest and creativity.

Each week the group began with the same piece of pre-recorded listening music and a body awareness activity to emphasise the participants' sense of self and orientate them to the session. A drum round incorporating children's names was used to focus attention, encourage awareness of others and provide all participants with the opportunity to sound in the group. An excerpt from the tree video was played on a television screen. During and after the video Charlotte described and highlighted the event using simple subject, verb and object (SVO) sentences and symbols. Following this a group improvisation took place, led by Karen (on piano or percussion). Group members chose from tuned and untuned percussion instruments and were encouraged to play in response to the event. The group concluded with quiet listening and a holding of hands to a set piece of music, providing the opportunity for reflection of self and the experiences that had been shared together.

A definite sense of group cohesion was established between group members who were able to begin to develop an awareness of and an ability to interact with each other through shared sensory, musical and narrative experiences.

UNSTRUCTURED SESSIONS

These sessions usually involved one child and two therapists. They were dynamic in nature and guided by the child's emotional and communicative state. The sessions were wholly unstructured to enable opportunities for interaction to evolve, although a greeting and a goodbye song were sung to indicate the beginning and ending of the session. Specifically these sessions aimed to develop a relationship of trust in which the child felt secure and could express themselves freely. Any action, vocalisation or interaction that the child made was reflected and supported by the therapists to promote further participation. Charlotte responded vocally and physically (using gestures), while Karen responded musically. This immediate combined reflection of responses assisted children in developing increased self-awareness and interactive potential. During the session the therapists used eye contact, gesture and discussion to determine which direction to take. Discussion before and after the session was also vital for ascertaining how to progress the sessions. While close examination would possibly identify our specific role at any one time we felt that our partnership, which moved fluidly in and out of roles, was paramount to the success of this joint intervention.

Vignette   Alice was 11 years old and suffered global developmental delay resulting in severe learning difficulties. She was a large girl both in height and weight with a vibrant character and great physical presence. Alice was determined, and was prone to violent outbursts and tantrums if she did not get what she wanted (usually triggered by her obsession with food). Her expressive language consisted of vocalisations, one or two words (e.g. bye), pointing to desired symbols/objects and taking what she wanted. Alice was particularly musical, singing to herself when happy and also when upset.

Initially Alice received individual music therapy sessions and developed a close relationship with Karen in which they shared many positive spontaneous musical interactions using improvised music. One year into these sessions it became apparent that Alice needed something more, as it had become increasingly difficult to provide music that could match and contain her expression and emotion and maintain her engagement. It is worth noting that at this time her behaviour had become extremely difficult in the classroom.

Charlotte was about to begin working with Alice and liaised with Karen about her responses in music therapy. After discussing the current situation they decided that working jointly with her may be appropriate. They explored a couple of different options before deciding that Alice's needs would best be met with both therapists working jointly with her in an individual capacity. General aims for the session were established and included: for Alice to engage and interact through spontaneous music making and for her to sustain her own attention and remain engaged in the session for as long as possible.

During sessions, Karen sat mainly at the piano providing improvised harmonic and rhythmical support to match moods and expression of feelings and engage Alice in meaningful and extended musical interactions. Charlotte moved within the room to join Alice at her choice of instrument, attempting to share, interact and engage with her. Over the next seven months (with a break for summer holidays) Alice's participation, interactions, attention and mood improved notably within the sessions and a secure relationship of trust developed between all three present. During the course of the sessions Alice moved to the senior part of the school and this proved a difficult time for her. The joint sessions however became her 'sanctuary', a place where she could go and be listened to, express and share her inner self, with no expectations.

Reflections

REFLECTION FROM KAREN

Working jointly with Charlotte in such a variety of ways provided great insight and inspiration. Working in a structured way gave me knowledge of specific speech and language therapy techniques which are highly effective with children with severe and profound multiple learning difficulties and can be used in my independent music therapy work. Working in an unstructured way allowed me the opportunity to share the potential of working in a non-verbal and spontaneous way through music with Charlotte. Our partnership became a natural one where we could work in synchronicity with each other and move in and out of leading and facilitating roles with ease. The opportunity to share responses, interactions and achievements with these children provided me with an appreciation of Charlotte's professional role and enhanced my therapeutic skills.

REFLECTION FROM CHARLOTTE

The therapeutic partnership that Karen and I developed during these sessions enabled me to support and improve students' communication in a greatly enriched manner. Karen's ability to use music to provide a powerful communicative conduit as well as giving emotional support was extremely effective when making connections with young people at the pre-verbal and early developmental levels. The opportunity to work with Karen helped me to understand and appreciate the process of music therapy in an experiential way. This, in turn, gave me the courage to take a more process-oriented approach in my general work.

Work within hospitals

Seriously ill children within the hospital setting will often be visited at the bedside by the multidisciplinary team (Edwards 1999). As part of multidisciplinary treatment programmes music therapy can be offered in conjunction with other therapies or can incorporate goals from other disciplines. While it supports the shared goals of the team, the aims of music therapy are also to provide emotional support and self-expression. It is not unusual that a number of professionals and/or family members will be present during music therapy sessions and the music therapist will be required to work closely with all of them. In the area of rehabilitation, joint working aims to encourage the development and maintenance of a child's optimal skill level (Edwards and Kennelly 2004). In order to provide effective support professionals need to develop complementary and different knowledge and this can be achieved through working jointly.

While collaborative work is important for the child and their family, there is also great value for other professionals involved in the approach. Indirectly, music therapy can provide emotional support and optimism for team members, helping to maintain a healthy balance in a difficult environment and humanising clinical relationships (Aasgard 2000; Petersen 2005).

The following case study by Nicky O'Neill highlights some of the issues of working with children within the hospital environment. She emphasises the importance of working collaboratively with the team in this setting.

COLLABORATIVE WORKING IN AN ACUTE PAEDIATRIC HOSPITAL
Nicky O'Neill (Music Therapist)

Context and setting

The setting for this case study is a well-established acute paediatric hospital in the UK. This position, which I have held for 13 years, working one day a week, is fully funded by Nordoff-Robbins Music Therapy. The children with whom I work have acute life-threatening physical health conditions, including cancer. My current role, which has developed over the years, is to provide clinical sessions, liaise with the multidisciplinary team and deliver training to fellow multidisciplinary professionals and students both within and outside the hospital. Both my clinical work and my role are organic in the sense that they have evolved together within this context from a position of 'not knowing'. When I commenced working in the hospital I had no UK role models or colleagues in this speciality and very little music therapy literature existed in the field.

The psychosocial team

Within the hospital there is a clinical multidisciplinary team for haematology and oncology which includes clinical professions such as nurses, doctors, physiotherapists, occupational therapists, psychologists and dieticians. Within this large multidisciplinary team is a smaller psychosocial team. Core psychosocial team members include the social worker, psychologist, play specialist, music therapist and nurse. In addition, an occupational therapist, physiotherapist and a teacher from the hospital school attend when needed.

As a member of the psychosocial team, I attend the weekly meetings and have always taken a leading role in the organisation of them to ensure that they occur on a day on which I am working. This role is indicative of my philosophy and belief in multidisciplinary team liaison and communication. Within a highly medicalised environment, the psychosocial team provides a forum for this through regular, non-medical and intimate meetings. The purpose of the psychosocial team meeting is to share information and discussion regarding children and families, focusing on those who are experiencing psychosocial difficulties. Each member of the team may refer to each other's speciality.

Essentially, the role of the psychosocial team is to support the children and their families who come to this hospital. These children have acute and often complex illnesses. Their lives are frequently in the balance and they are severely life-threatened. A less explicit role of the psychosocial team is to provide support to colleagues within the team.

Reasons for joint work

The reason for joint working in its many guises is to capitalise on all our varied professional skills in order to help the child and family cope with their period of hospitalisation. By sharing knowledge we can optimally understand the child and their responses from all our different perspectives, which is essential in the provision of care. The demands, pressure and effects of treatment and being in the hospital environment can have a dramatic impact on the child in the immediate and long term, both medically and psychologically.

Collaborative work is an integral part of my work as a music therapist in the hospital. Referral, discussion and negotiation are central to my work and occur continually with other staff members. Working with the children was a huge emotional shock for me when I first started. I needed support and for these reasons it has always been essential that I work within a team. Seeing the same people, at the same time each week, gives stability, especially given that this is a setting where nurses are on a shift system and the lives and presence of the children are so unstable. Unsurprisingly, perhaps, in my clinical work I find myself using a lot of musical structure, a lot of repeated music and forms, including ground bass and motifs.

There are two key factors which have influenced my reasons for joint working: one is potential professional/personal isolation which led me toward needing contact with other professionals in order to continue providing therapy; the other is the relentless pace of change at the hospital which challenged the notion of regular, in-depth or reflective team thinking and practice. These factors were exacerbated by the fact that the music therapy post has always been part-time. Within an acute hospital there are many complex layers of organisational, social, professional and cultural structures, all interacting. As a music therapist it can take much time to negotiate these, and I have had to create structures and order to my day which can enable me to work effectively and communicatively and feel part of a team.

How does joint working happen?
Joint working happens in four main areas:
1.   referrals
2.   case discussions in psychosocial team meetings
3.   teaching sessions
4.   shared consultation, including nurses or play specialists supporting a child during music therapy sessions.

Due to the unpredictable nature of the children's illnesses and its influence on hospital life, these can all happen informally as well as during structured meetings. Often I have to act quickly and see a child, due to the precariousness of their condition. I do not use referral forms. Some of these ways of working are now described.

REFERRALS
Referrals usually take place within the medical hand-over meetings at the start of the day. Ideally this occurs with the nurse in charge, who has an overview of all of the children. Depending on the particular nurse's working knowledge of music therapy and her subjective assessment of the children's psychological needs, either she will suggest suitable candidates or I will probe for further information, pointing out some key reasons for referral (for example, if a child is withdrawn, very sick, unable or unwilling to communicate).

   Once a list of children is established, I liaise with the nurses to find a time which can be relatively free of treatment. While this is not always possible, the discussion leads the nurses to appreciate the need for the child to have some space uninterrupted by medical procedures.

CASE DISCUSSIONS
In addition to these referrals are those which come from collaborative case discussions in the psychosocial team meetings. During these, either I will

focus on one child's appropriateness for individual or group music therapy, or the suggestion could come from any other team member. Due to the perspectives from a wider range of professionals it is possible to gain a broader and more in-depth understanding of each child within their family/social context and more accurately identify the children and families in need of music therapy input.

TEACHING SESSIONS

Another form of collaborative working and an integral part of my job are the teaching sessions I provide on advanced nurse training courses. In these sessions I demonstrate how I work with audio and video case examples and the feedback is generally positive.

SHARED CONSULTATIONS

Another aspect of my collaborative work includes shared consultations with other psychosocial team members, such as the physiotherapist and psychologist. Sometimes a child will not engage readily with a physiotherapist, which severely compromises their health. Here, I can complement the physiotherapy work using activities with improvised music which might contribute to their recovery; for example, standing to play a drum, reaching up to crash a cymbal or blowing a horn. At other times, a child or family might be adverse to intervention by the psychologist, whereas they will readily engage musically. Professional titles such as psychologist and physiotherapist can sometimes preclude an open mind from the child and family, whereas music therapy is generally seen as non-threatening. Before and after the session I can confer with these professionals using a shared consultancy model, so that the resulting collaboration means that the child gets the best possible support for their needs.

Vignettes

The following vignettes aim to illustrate the importance of flexibility, communication between professionals, families and children and the need to be constantly alert to opportunities and make quick assessments about how to use one's role.

Vignette 1   Late in the morning and again after lunch I will stroll down the haematology and oncology wards in order to assess who's up to joining the music therapy open group at 3 pm. I have in mind the sessions from the previous week and the discussions within the psychosocial team meeting which helped to add context. There are ten individual cubicles on each ward. Some doors are open so I can pop in to say hello, quickly assess the child's emotional/medical state, remind the child and parent of the time of the group – or they may comment, 'Ahh, it's Wednesday, it's music day!' Some children are in the corridor, some doors tightly shut. I spy a woman who I suppose is the mother of a two-year-old who attended the open group last week. The child suffered a relapsed brain tumour ten weeks ago. She is a strong, silent child who has sustained a degree of developmental delay as a result of the relapse. Her five-year-old brother is often present on the ward and I wish to encourage him to join the group as concerns were raised about his behaviour in the psychosocial team meeting. I introduce myself to the mother and comment how well Sophie did last week and emphasise how Josiah (the older child) is welcome to join this week. Their mother jumps at the opportunity to go out, asking how long the session is and could she leave them with me. I ask how long she needs and say I will liaise with the play specialist, who is then able to support them during the session, along with a volunteer and after the session until their mother returns. In the psychosocial meeting before the open group, the social worker comments how important this is as their mother never leaves the children.

In a second and final vignette the importance of emotional support and trust between colleagues and with the parent of a critically ill child is conveyed.

Vignette 2   The play specialist and I have worked independently with a 19-month-old boy for the last three months during his bone marrow transplant treatment for relapsed leukaemia. Unfortunately the treatment has not been successful and Davey is nearing the end of his life. His stomach is severely distended and he needs to be held all the time. The person holding him has to be someone he knows and trusts, so this tends to be his mother or the play specialist. He is very uncomfortable and we are cautioned that too much movement from him could bring on a 'bleed'; however, he still wants to 'do music'. His mother is torn between desperately needing a break and frightened about leaving him in case he dies. The play specialist and I want to provide for both of them, but we're also rather apprehensive. So, after discussion with the nurse about safety, she puts the speaker phone on and says she'll keep looking in. We all feel confidence in one another and the session begins, with Davey draped across the play specialist's legs. Davey grunts at each instrument offered, before eye-pointing to the end of the keyboard. We manage to angle the keyboard so that he can lean/lunge toward it. He plays with strength, smiling with satisfaction before relaxing back into an exhausted, brief sleep. He's done it! We've enabled this with our combined effort.

Reflections

REFLECTION FROM THE WARD SISTER

Music therapy is so important for the children who need the opportunity to vent their feelings, for those who have developmental delay and for those with a language barrier. As nurses we don't have the skills or the time to do this therapeutic work. Nicky's feedback is vital at the psychosocial team meetings.

REFLECTION FROM NICKY

Within my work my aim is to make my practice more open and transparent, in order to communicate what I do. My hope is that other team members can understand the relevance of my work and that this will enable more joint working. Joint working has provided me with the emotional support needed in order to work with children and families who are coping with the challenges of life-threatening conditions. It has also opened my mind and thinking to consider the whole child and their needs in regard to their medical, physical and psychosocial states. Joint working has also expanded my knowledge of other disciplines and has highlighted the importance of developing a broader knowledge outside of one's own speciality, and an openness to consult others, in order to provide the therapy that is appropriate for the child and family.

Through working at the hospital, I have developed a new model of working, different from the one I had been taught on the training course and used in other settings, such as a music therapy clinic or school. Over the years, rather than 'going it alone', I have developed my role with a great deal of joint working. This is as a result of adapting to the environment and working with and learning from all those involved in the child's care.

Work within the field of mental health

It is well documented that music therapy can offer something unique to the field of mental health work. Joint interventions can help address some of the critical issues associated with emotional and social problems (Bunt 1994). Linking with other therapists such as psychologists may assist in the immediate processing of experiences and personal insight gained from musical improvisations. It may also serve as a primary mode of therapy for treatment in resistive and emotionally disturbed children (Figlure Alder and Fisher 1984; Wells and Stevens 1984).

The next case-study author, Claire Molyneux, has written elsewhere of short-term joint work with an occupational therapist and psychiatrist within a child and adolescent mental health service. She believes that collaborating with another professional develops close working relationships; these professionals are usually the referrers to music therapy and 'involving the referrer as closely as possible in the process and handing over at the end of the therapy ensures continuity for the individual and family' (Molyneux 2005, p.65). Molyneux maintains that continuity for the child and their family achieved through close working relationships also assists in integrating the therapy into the wider-support network that is offered by the service (2005).

The case study that follows describes work between a music therapist and clinical psychologist to develop a healthy attachment within a sibling group. It illustrates the central roles each professional played and how importantly the collaboration also extended to include the children's foster mother.

THE STONE FAMILY

Claire Molyneux (Music Therapist)

The following case study took place in a unit for children aged 12 years and under and their families, where Claire Molyneux worked as music therapist within the multidisciplinary team. The unit is part of the child and adolescent mental health service (CAMHS). It offers a day service for children and families and takes referrals from the out-patient teams of the CAMHS. Dr Jeanette Allen, a clinical psychologist, works for the Looked After Children team, taking referrals for children who are in care. Both teams include a mix of clinical staff, and collaboration between the multidisciplinary team at the children's unit and the outpatient teams is common. Co-working can help to ensure a more collaborative and 'joined up' approach to working with families, particularly when the families have complex needs.

Background

In her role as clinical psychologist, Jeanette had been working with the Stone family for some time. Behaviour management strategies such as setting clear and consistent boundaries and addressing problems around sleep and bedtime had been implemented and the foster mother had attended a group programme facilitated by Jeanette for foster carers examining the impact of children's early traumatic experiences from an attachment perspective. The family then attended a group at the children's unit that focused on strengthening relationships and supporting parents in their behaviour management. Following this the oldest child, Philip, had a series of individual music therapy sessions. It was during this time that it was decided to work with the whole family using music therapy and it seemed natural to involve Jeanette in this work as she knew the family well and had a good understanding of the difficulties they experienced.

Family history
Philip (10), Milly (6) and William (3) were the birth children of Rebecca and David. Rebecca and David had three children together prior to Philip, Milly and William, all of whom had been removed, due to child protection concerns, and placed for adoption. As a result of this, Philip, Milly and William were placed on the Child Protection Register at birth under the category of 'at risk of neglect' and 'at risk of physical abuse'. Despite careful monitoring and a high level of support by Social Services there were several incidents of unexplained injuries to the children and increasing concerns about the standard of care the children were receiving. Philip's relationship with his mother was particularly difficult and all three children were removed into Local Authority care and placed together in a long-term foster placement when William was about two months old.

At the time of the referral to the CAMHS the children had been living with their foster carer, Carol, for three years. Both Philip and Milly were identified as having mild learning difficulties and significant behavioural difficulties. Philip was described as oppositional and defiant. He reacted with extreme anger to any boundaries or limits placed on him by Carol and would have frequent violent outbursts. He would often seek revenge following such an incident, which usually took the form of verbal or physical aggression directed towards Milly. Carol described Philip as vindictive and spoke with great sadness about how she felt that she had a good relationship with Milly and William but found Philip a difficult boy to like.

Milly had severe temper tantrums which could last for several hours. These typically occurred at bedtime. Milly's sleep was severely disturbed which was having a detrimental impact on her day-to-day functioning. She suffered with nightmares and was very difficult to settle afterwards. At the time of the referral to music therapy, Milly's sleep pattern had improved significantly following both group and individual intervention with Jeanette.

Carol was feeling more positive about managing the children on an individual basis but continued to find it difficult to manage them as a sibling group. Philip's aggression towards Milly remained an area of significant concern and there were few positive interactions between Philip and Carol.

Setting and roles

The music therapy sessions took place in a large room with a good supply of instruments. The goals of the sessions were to address the issues of communication and relationships within the family and provide a place where they could have fun and enjoy spending time together. We also hoped that we could model ways for Carol to interact in a playful and positive way with the children. We used mostly therapist-directed musical experiences and also some solution-focused techniques such as asking the family to identify positives and exceptions. Art materials were sometimes made available and offered another way to explore family relationships. We also made time for one of us (usually Jeanette) to meet separately with Carol. This time was used to discuss current concerns and feedback about progress within the home and to reinforce the positive interactions that were observed in the music therapy sessions.

As well as being a positive therapeutic experience for the family, the sessions gave us a chance to further assess the children's strengths and needs. Using music gave the children a chance to engage and interact on an equal level, without the need to understand complex verbal constructs. Using music also meant the family were engaged in activity together and it was hoped that this experience would have an effect on how the family interacted and shared time together generally.

My role in the sessions was to facilitate the music making and hold the creative experience for the family. Jeanette was in the role of reflector, observing what was taking place, commenting and reflecting on it as appropriate to provide opportunities for the family to learn and try new things and gain a positive experience of spending time together. With two of us in the sessions, we could comment on what we saw taking place and both model and suggest ways in which things could be different. We were also in a good position to re-frame some of the children's behaviour. For example, loud boisterous play on the instruments was re-framed as a positive expression of fun rather than disruptive and chaotic behaviour. We both took on the role of modelling appropriate patterns of behaviour. This took the form of modelling attentiveness, playfulness, using eye contact appropriately, taking turns and respecting other people's place in the family. We also modelled acceptance and empathy, within a structure that was safe and contained. A significant experience for Carol was being able to facilitate forceful expression for Philip without him losing control or her feeling overwhelmed by his emotional expression.

Music therapy sessions

The music therapy intervention was brief (four sessions over five weeks followed by a further four sessions after a break) with the understanding that we could offer the family a positive experience of being together and empower them to continue to make changes themselves. Jeanette would continue to support the family following the end of the intervention.

Jeanette and I met prior to each session to plan and at the end of the session to review and reflect. It became clear in the first session that Philip and Milly were able to enjoy being together and did have a positive regard for each other. It was hoped that we could bring this to Carol's awareness and foster the growth of a positive relationship between the siblings.

The sessions usually started with checking in to find out how things had been going. We felt it was important to maintain a positive approach and so encouraged each family member to think about something they had enjoyed doing together. There was then a time of sharing a hand-held drum and greeting each other individually. It was interesting to watch how each family member used the drum, who they offered the drum to and how they shared it with other family members and staff.

One of the structured activities that we used frequently involved taking turns to lead the music. This was a valuable and important activity within which the children could explore what it was like to lead and follow in a playful and contained environment. Jeanette and I worked together with Carol to help the children co-regulate their responses. By placing one of us in the role of leader of an improvisation we could enable the children to follow the adult's lead. They could be encouraged to explore the potential for expression of emotions within the music, whilst being contained by the adult who was leading and looking after the boundaries of the interaction.

Another activity was used where each person had an instrument and had to interrupt the person playing before them. This was a useful way to explore the children's sense of self and regard for others in the session. It was interesting that the first time we used this activity (in session 1) it was Carol who initiated playing out of turn and also encouraged Philip to do the same. There were other examples in the first session where Carol initiated 'rule-breaking' such as tapping people's hands as we shared the drum to say goodbye. We were unsure as to why she did this and co-working meant that we were able to model more appropriate behaviour and interactions. As the sessions continued, she was able to be more consistent in her responses such as setting boundaries and also having realistic expectations.

On an emotional level, the use of music afforded opportunities for difficult emotions to be expressed. There were many times where it was noted that family members used the instruments to express tension or other feelings that were present in the room. There was also a marked difference in the way that Carol played instruments with Philip and Milly and we were able to point out her sensitivity in recognising the children's different needs. Carol commented at the end of the four sessions that she felt Philip could express his feelings safely in the music and then move on to the next thing. This was in contrast to the home environment where he often held on to his difficult feelings and expressed them at other times as 'payback' which Carol found difficult to manage and empathise with. The opportunity to create music together gave her time to listen and accept each child's contribution and to attune to them.

It became clear that the focus of the work was the need for Philip to address the relationship with his siblings and come to terms with the events that had led to him being in care. This coupled with his ambivalence towards Carol and his idealisation of his birth mother needed to be addressed as a whole and it was not reasonable to expect Philip to be able to make changes without involving the whole family.

Reflection
REFLECTIONS FROM CLAIRE

The experience of co-working with Jeanette was a very positive one for me. My frustration at the individual work not effecting positive change was met and shared by Jeanette and together we were able to find a creative way of trying to support this family. It felt natural to work together as we could share our resources, skills and knowledge.

Part of the collaborative approach was working closely with Carol and being open and honest about what we hoped to achieve in the sessions. Her task was not an easy one, parenting three children with histories of significant neglect and trauma. Through working together, I found that Jeanette could hold some of the theoretical framework and comment objectively on what she saw taking place which in turn left me free to offer the family different musical and non-verbal experiences. A therapeutic alliance already existed and, although Carol was initially rather wary of using music, she seemed to find Jeanette's presence reassuring as Jeanette expressed similar feelings of discomfort at using a different medium to that with which she was familiar.

Jeanette had a good deal of expertise in working with this client group from her position in the Looked After Children team and brought with her a solid understanding of working with children in care. Together, we were able to provide a creative environment through which we could nurture a positive and healthy attachment for this sibling group. Through the foundation of a healthy attachment it became possible to see change taking place in the children's physical, emotional and cognitive development.

A different perspective – work with families and carers

Increasingly authors working with children describe collaboration with family members and care givers within music therapy sessions. Allgood stresses that: 'promoting a strong parent/professional relationship is vital because the parents are a source of knowledge about the child, parents are affected by the disability and parents can promote generalization of skills' (2005, p.93). Other authors assert that it not only helps to empower the parent or care giver but also gives them a part in being accountable for the growth of their child by providing balance, direction and an opportunity to interact (O'Gorman 2006; Oldfield 2001; Shoemark 1996). All of these experiences help the parent to focus on a child's strengths rather than their weaknesses and provide confidence that this progress might help their child in other settings (Woodward 2004).

Molyneux (2005) believes that in working jointly with parents and their children the music therapist can address attachment issues by providing opportunities to re-create early interactions. Music provides a common aesthetic level which helps to form a basis for understanding. Being present in music therapy sessions can therefore be a positive experience for parents, especially those experiencing bonding issues, as it can provide a supportive opportunity to play and share enjoyment with their child and experience equal and positive interactions (Abad and Edwards 2004; Oldfield 2001; Oldfield and Bunce 2001; Voight 2001).

Abad and Williams (2006) used music therapy to encourage closeness and bonding with adolescent mothers and their children. Their programme empowered mothers to learn new ways of interacting with their children. Working jointly with parents has also been found to be effective in helping parents experiencing parenting difficulties by instilling a competency in addressing behavioural issues (Oldfield, Adams and Bunce 2003; Voight 2001).

From the child's perspective Seytter (1998) suggests that using a triadic approach with children, whereby children experience positive relations to more than one person at the same time (triangulation), can be helpful in addressing separation–individuation issues which children may experience with their parents.

For the music therapist, working jointly with the parent in an observatory, assisting or participatory role can also offer valuable insights (Voight 2001). Parents are familiar with their child's physical needs and are often willing to assist; parents provide information to therapists and also provide insight into the parent–child relationship; and they gain confidence and learn transferable skills and enjoy the positive abilities of their child. Woodward states that 'working with parents is very rewarding for the therapist, as it puts the work in a wider context' (2004, p.13). Proctor gathered expert opinion to justify reasons for having parents as co-therapists in his collaborative research project investigating parental involvement in children's music therapy. He states that 'we know that there are good reasons for involving parents; their commitment can make a difference to the therapy itself' (2005, p.53).

The final case study in this chapter, by Ann Woodward, describes collaboration between music therapist and mother. It highlights the importance of collaborating with parents and illustrates the affording of new insight, understanding and opportunities that this type of partnership can provide.

MARTHA AND RIO: COLLABORATIVE WORKING WITH A PARENT AND CHILD

Ann Woodward (Music Therapist)

This case study describes collaborative working between me and Martha, the mother of Rio, an eight-year-old boy with autism. In preparation for writing this, one year after the work ended, Martha and I met to reflect on the work again.

The work took place at Resources for Autism, a London-based charity. Most referrals to music therapy come from children's parents, and as it is usually the parent who brings the child to sessions, the therapist can establish a close working relationship with them. Sometimes it is appropriate for the parent to attend the sessions themselves, either as an observer, or taking part actively. This can be particularly useful with very young children, or where there are specific reasons for working with parent and child together.

The latter was the case with Rio. When Martha referred him, her prime concerns were his behaviour (aggression and throwing objects), lack of social interaction and limited communication. Although Rio had good verbal comprehension, he would not speak to anyone other than his mother and presented as selectively mute. As a single mother, Martha often found herself dealing with these difficult issues alone.

Rather than offering one-to-one sessions for Rio, I felt that there were several clinical reasons for working together with Martha:

- Given Rio's difficulty in relating to anyone other than his mother, I felt that Martha's involvement would help Rio to begin to form a relationship with me.

- This would provide an opportunity to observe and think about their interactions and how this impacted on Rio.

- Martha would have an opportunity to think with another adult, and to be supported through the process of making changes.

Rio attended weekly music therapy for 18 months. Each session lasted around 30 minutes, and Martha and I had a few moments' discussion after each session. We also met for fuller discussions periodically to reflect on the process, Rio's progress in other settings, and what direction future work should take.

The sessions contained both free improvisation and semi-structured activities to explore the recurrent themes that emerged during the course of therapy, including boundary setting, finding the positive, expressing feelings and separation. I will now explore these themes, illustrating how the collaborative process enabled positive change to occur.

Boundary setting

Rio tested the boundaries of acceptable behaviour in the sessions in a variety of ways. Sometimes he played so loudly, almost aggressively, on the drum and cymbal that I worried that he might damage an instrument or our ears. Sometimes Rio did things that he knew were not allowed, such as throwing objects, like he did in other settings. Martha responded like she did at home: becoming cross with Rio, shouting at him to stop, telling him how to play, or making threats that she could not follow through. As at home, this tended to inflame the situation.

Music therapy, however, provided the opportunity for joint thinking. This enabled Martha's understandable anxiety to be contained, and for new solutions to old problems to be explored. Martha and I discussed what behaviour we could reasonably ignore, what we definitely needed to respond to, and how. We agreed that if he was treating an instrument roughly we would calmly ask him to stop. If he persisted we would remove the instrument from the room for five minutes.

This strategy was helpful for Martha (and me), by providing a calm and consistent way of responding which seemed to work. Martha's comment, a year later, was: 'Music therapy helped me stop shouting at Rio, and to keep control. Shouting doesn't help; it just gives out negative vibes.' It was important that this was not *my* strategy, but a *joint* one. When working with parents, the way that the therapist positions themselves is crucial. A therapist's training and experience can be a valuable resource for parents in helping them to find new ways of interacting with their child and building their confidence in parenting. However, if the therapist positions themselves as 'expert' they risk undermining an already vulnerable parent. Martha had struggled with Rio's behaviour, largely alone, for years. She came to music therapy with little confidence in her own parenting skills and it was important that our work should support her and increase her confidence.

Finding the positive
In Rio's initial sessions, there was much anxiety that he would do something destructive, and a lot of negative interaction between Rio and his mother. Martha confirmed that this was the same at home. A negative spiral had developed (see Figure 1.1).

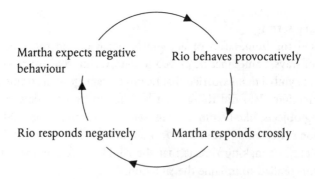

Figure 1.1 The negative spiral of Martha and Rio's relationship

Martha was very honest about how hard it was to be positive with Rio. Since there was so much negative behaviour it felt impossible to see anything positive. Finding ways to praise Rio or to be enthusiastic with him was a real challenge for her, which she rose to courageously. With support, she engaged in playful games with Rio, such as kazoo duets or musical imitation, and gave praise whenever she could. These games, reminiscent of mother–baby interactions, helped to establish positive interaction, playfulness and trust, even though this was initially very hard for Martha.

Martha was very honest about just how hard it had been to see anything positive:

> I had to train myself to think of more positive things to praise. At first it felt wrong to praise the few positive things that happened. This was difficult at first – it was hurting inside at first to say positive things, but when you say negative things, you can see that he feeds on it.

Given how challenging this process was for Martha, it is all the more remarkable that she was able to engage so fully. Our collaboration enabled her to try out new things, even taking emotional risks. Her efforts certainly bore fruits, and Rio responded with more positive behaviour. This is a change that Martha has maintained, and which other family members are now following.

Expressing feelings

Often Rio played loudly to provoke a reaction from Martha, but sometimes his intense drumming felt expressive. At these times, I provided a piano accompaniment, supporting and containing his playing. I wondered if Rio would be able to verbalise any of his thoughts, and I asked him: 'If that music had a name, what would it be?' Rio quickly responded (though speaking to Martha rather than me) 'Jamal' – the name of a boy who used to attend his school. Martha was able to explore this further, discovering that Jamal had bullied Rio. Although this had now stopped, the memory still frightened Rio. The musical improvisation enabled Rio to express feelings that he might not have been able to verbalise at that stage, and the supportive setting gave Martha an opportunity to begin to understand Rio's feelings. Martha herself said: 'In the drumming, he was able to let out what he had been bottling up. He was able to communicate and express himself in different ways through music.'

In my view, the collaboration between Martha and me was central here. Martha was able to see a new, vulnerable, side to her son. From my perspective, working with Martha was invaluable. Without her presence I doubt that Rio would have mentioned Jamal, or that I would have understood the significance of what he said.

Separation

Ironically, separation was one of the central issues in this collaborative work. I was aware at the outset that Rio and Martha were highly focused on each other and that this was reinforced through negative patterns. For example, by speaking only to his mother Rio guaranteed her exclusive attention, and by being the sole 'translator' for Rio, Martha maintained her exclusive role, mediating between Rio and the outside world. Their intense relationship excluded others (literally so, in respect of Rio's speaking), with little space between them to allow for change or growth. Our musical activities allowed Martha and Rio to explore new ways of interacting with each other and to begin to enable them to separate from each other. This would help Rio to interact with other people, but it would also be a challenge for both of them.

A musical activity gave Martha control of the process. I suggested that we all play together, on whatever instruments we liked, with no rules about how we should play, except that we would try to listen to each other so that our music could fit together. I asked Martha to observe Rio closely and when she felt that he was settled and ready to play more independently she should withdraw. Afterwards, we would discuss how it had felt for her and what she had thought. The first time we did this, Martha and Rio immediately started playing the piano together and I played a tambourine in a matching rhythm. At first, Martha showed no signs of stepping back, and I wondered whether she would feel comfortable to do it, but after a few minutes, sensing that Rio was ready, she gently withdrew so that Rio was playing the piano alone and I was accompanying him on the tambourine. Both Rio and Martha made attempts to re-engage the other – Rio by calling to his mother, and Martha by giving Rio instructions – but they managed to sustain the separation for a time. Afterwards, Martha said that she thought that Rio would start being 'naughty' when she withdrew. She had found it hard to create this brief separation, and had been surprised and pleased that he had been able to keep playing.

Over the following weeks, this individuation increased, and Rio began interacting with me more easily. Initially, this was purely musical, but gradually Rio began to speak to me, at first whispering without looking at me, then gradually giving eye contact. Martha and I both now felt, after one year of therapy, that Rio was ready to attend part of the session without his mother. Again, it was important that Martha felt in control of this process, since it would signal a major change in their relationship. I suggested that Martha should come in to the start of the session, and then choose a moment to leave the room after 15 to 20 minutes. Rio was told in advance what would happen. He coped so well with this that Martha left the subsequent sessions earlier each time. After seven weeks, Martha decided that Rio would be able to come in by himself, which he did.

Rio had eight further sessions without his mother, during which his confidence in communicating and interacting continued to grow, until finally he could talk to me in a natural voice and give appropriate eye contact.

Conclusions

Rio showed much progress during his music therapy, which was reflected in positive change at school and at home. Martha's collaboration in the process was central to this:

- It created opportunities for joint thinking, and for both of us to see things from a different perspective.
- It provided a containing environment where Martha could explore new ways of interacting with Rio.
- It enabled Rio to develop a new relationship.

It might have been possible to work with Rio by himself from the outset, but I doubt that the therapy would have been as helpful. Working with Martha allowed Rio's 'challenging behaviour' to be thought about more broadly, in the context of other relationships.

There are undoubtedly situations where working with a parent is more successful than others. There are also situations where even though it would be preferable to work with the parent it is simply not possible for practical reasons. Working collaboratively with parents is exciting, and can challenge therapist and parent alike. I very much hope that more therapists will be encouraged to explore it.

Woodward identifies two important considerations for the practitioner when working with parents. First, that it is important that there is respect for the parent–child relationship. The therapist can support and guide the parent, but must not see themselves as an expert with all the answers, rather solutions should be explored together. Second, she also stresses that supervision of this work is essential, as working with parents and children together can resonate with our own experiences of being parented, or of being a parent, and this needs to be considered.

CONCLUDING THOUGHTS

Coordinated care is high on the agenda for the majority of service providers. It is clear from these case studies that music therapists believe that a sharing of knowledge provides a greater appreciation of the child and their abilities from differing perspectives, which in turn ensures an increased awareness and identification of needs. The value of working closely with other professionals from differing theoretical and practical backgrounds is recognised by all contributing authors in this chapter, who believe that co-working provides an experiential appreciation of the diversity of skills of other therapists. This not only serves to broaden therapists' knowledge outside of their speciality, but in addition enriches practice and offers professional support. It also strengthens existing collaborative bonds and promotes openness and shared responsibility amongst professionals.

GUIDELINES FOR GOOD PRACTICE

These concluding guidelines encapsulate the guiding principles on which the co-workers in this chapter have founded their work. These will be useful to professionals from all disciplines who may be considering undertaking joint work with children.

- Be open to sharing your skills, abilities and knowledge. Work with and learn from others.

- Be clear, open and honest about the purpose and objective of working together and what you hope to achieve.

- Acknowledge anxieties about working collaboratively and discuss these with each other. Pre-empt potential difficulties and plan how you will address these.

- Be prepared to adapt to your working environment. Acknowledge different theoretical approaches and other ways of working which may be more or less structured and consider combining the two.

- Make time for continual review and reflection. This can include ongoing discussion and clarification of professional methods and observations.

- Find a common language – think carefully about the terminology you use and how and when you use it.

- Plan and problem solve jointly, taking into account the objectives of others. Clarify aims and identify that you are working towards the same goals. This may be partly achieved by attending case meetings and Individual Education Plan (IEP) meetings.

- Be prepared for differences of opinion, and acknowledge and discuss these.

- Be flexible of thought and prepared to accept the limitations of music therapy.

- Receive supervision on collaborative work, to ensure that arising issues are identified and worked through.

Part 2

Collaborative Work with Adults

Chapter 2

Collaboration in Music Therapy with Adults with Learning Disabilities

Tessa Watson

INTRODUCTION

> *'It has enriched my working career, my way of thinking about the clients and my way of working...gives me a lot more skills and techniques up my sleeve, if I choose to use these... Yes, it's very energising, keeps you on your toes and keeps you vibrant and listening in a different sort of way. And it's a great opportunity to share the work.' (Tyas, in Twyford 2004a, pp.115 and 116)*

This quotation describes the benefits of collaborative work in the clinical area of adult learning disability. Tyas summarises the positive aspects of working together. Pressures of time and money might create barriers to collaborative work, but the possibilities of providing a richer, more facilitative clinical environment and of developing skills through combining approaches are compelling reasons for music therapists working with adults with learning disabilities to join with their colleagues in collaborative work.

This chapter introduces the idea of collaborative working in adult learning disability services. The chapter begins with an outline of the client group, and the services that are provided for these clients. Then literature describing collaborative work is presented. The benefits and challenges of collaborative work are discussed. At the heart of the chapter are case studies by four music therapists and their colleagues that describe collaborative work in this clinical area. These case studies include reflection from the clinicians involved, helping to explain the motivations behind collaborative work and the benefits gained for clients and clinicians.

ADULTS WITH LEARNING DISABILITIES

The accepted definition of a learning disability includes the presence of a significant intellectual impairment and deficits in social functioning or adaptive behaviour (basic everyday skills) which are present from childhood (Emerson *et al.* 2001). The cause of a learning disability may not be clear, but often biological, environmental or social factors play a part. People with learning disabilities may experience additional communication and sensory difficulties, emotional and behavioural problems and health problems such as epilepsy (Emerson *et al.* 2001).

The level of intellectual impairment the person experiences can vary widely and therefore the impact upon quality of life may be equally diverse. Some people with mild learning disabilities may live independently, and have a job, fulfilling relationships and an active social life. Others may struggle with the impact of their disabilities and need significant support to maintain a satisfying life. People with more profound disabilities will need more support in all areas of their lives; perhaps living with family or carers and often requiring 24-hour care in order to manage everyday events. There is thus a need for the provision of a wide breadth of health and social services.

The concept of collaboration in work with people with learning disabilities has a strange resonance, as for many years this group was segregated and isolated from the rest of society, in hospitals or institutions. Recent thinking and guidelines for work with people with learning disabilities stresses the importance of integration and valued roles in the community for clients, and of collaboration between agencies and between the able and disabled populations. In the UK, the Department of Health stated that staff working with people with learning disabilities should be 'confident in working in multi-professional teams, and across agency boundaries' (Emerson *et al.* 2001, p.98).

COLLABORATIVE WORK IN THIS CLINICAL AREA

Macadam and Rodgers (1997) remind us that,

> bearing in mind the range of people who have a role to play in improving the health of people with learning disabilities, a creative approach to collaboration can make best use of existing facilities and

opportunities and create them where they previously did not exist.
(p.191)

The health and social care of adults with learning disabilities is most frequently provided by statutory governmental organisations (national health
services or social services). Music therapists are often employed as part of a
community team, though some may be employed by small, privately run
organisations or charitable bodies. Some specialist units also exist, for
example for people with learning disabilities who also have behaviour that
challenges services, or a forensic history. NHS teams often include the disciplines of speech and language therapy, psychology, nursing, physiotherapy,
psychiatry, care managers, occupational therapists and arts therapists. These
disciplines provide services as diverse as individual and group therapy, the
prescribing of medication and advice on appropriate seating and equipment.
In the UK these community teams are frequently now joint health and social
services teams; two traditionally separate cultures in collaboration. These
teams have developed greatly in the past few years, particularly in response
to the government white paper *Valuing People* (DoH 2001). This recent
guidance stressed the importance of communication and collaboration
between agencies and disciplines in order to provide a comprehensive,
coherent service.

Partly because of these developments in guidance and theory, services
now often use collaborative working as a matter of course. This collaborative
working might cover the multidisciplinary, interdisciplinary and transdisciplinary methods of collaboration discussed in the introduction of this
book: from music therapists discussing work with other staff, attending case
conferences, or working in the therapy room with other disciplines. The colleagues with whom music therapists might work are varied, including other
arts therapists, care managers, nurses, occupational therapists, physiotherapists, speech and language therapists and psychologists. Most often, work
seems to have been undertaken with speech and language therapy, psychology and physiotherapy colleagues, perhaps because of areas of shared
interest within the clinical work.

LITERATURE

In the early days of music therapy, lone working in large institutions was
common, and collaborative working could allow greater links to be forged

with colleagues, thus communicating more widely the nature and benefits of music therapy. Some of this work is described in the music therapy literature. In 1979, a report in the *British Journal of Music Therapy* described Odell working 'closely with doctors, occupational therapists, and the speech therapist, physiotherapists, nurses and psychologists' (Odell 1979, p.12). This illustrates the long history of music therapists working collaboratively in this clinical area; indeed nearly 30 years later many music therapists working with adults with learning disabilities will find themselves working closely with the same disciplines.

Ritchie describes both difficult and positive liaisons with her colleagues (1991, 1993a and 1993b), and in later writing advocates for colleagues to work together 'in a cohesive fashion, to break down barriers and to learn from other people's experiences' (1993b, p.26). Wigram describes joint work with physiotherapists and an innovative and collaborative multi-disciplinary assessment (1988). Karen Sayers writes as a music therapist with only one year's experience of working with adults with learning disabilities. She writes about her work with arts therapies colleagues, where they are

> experimenting with various ideas: people listening to live music as they paint; playing how they felt when painting a group picture; using an individual instrument as inspiration for a piece of art work; and doing individual art but coming together for a group musical improvisation. (1993, p.24)

Sayers also questions whether music therapists might feel able to 'borrow techniques and ideas from other media... Should we be more flexible?' This therapist, at the start of her career, speaks of her lack of security in relation to joint working, and questions whether music therapists 'have a tendency to set ourselves apart, to be seen as "special" and "different" (ibid.).

Often, collaborative working enables music therapists to explore areas of practice between the discipline of music therapy and another discipline. Hooper and Lindsay, a music therapist and a psychologist, write about their research project studying the effect of music on anxiety (1990). Hooper also writes about collaborative work in sensory integration with physiotherapists and occupational therapists (Hooper *et al.* 2004). He describes the excitement in working with these colleagues, and the way in which it enabled both greater gains for clients and greater understanding of each discipline for the professionals involved. Indeed, he states that, 'as music therapists working with clients who have a developmental disability, we need to broaden our conception of music therapy and acknowledge the significant role that it can play when joined in therapeutic work with other modalities' (Hooper *et al.* 2004, p.21).

Skille, Wigram and Weekes describe joint work between physiotherapists and music therapists in their explanation of vibroacoustic therapy, which uses the physiological effect of sound (1989). Later, Wigram reflects on this experience and describes in detail the way in which music and movement can help clients with profound and multiple handicaps:

> [T]he combined approach of both music therapist and physiotherapist to achieve a protocol that met the treatment aims of both disciplines results in a form of 'co-training' – involving a shared education. Music therapists had to learn a lot about physical handling, and physiotherapists had to learn a lot about musical structure and tempi, as well as metres and part-metres. (Grocke and Wigram 2007, p.241)

Toolan and Coleman describe a joint research project concerned with the level of engagement in therapy and the therapeutic relationship (1995). Usher (1998) describes her collaboration with a psychiatrist and the influence of neuronal assembly formation on her clinical practice. Other writing, such as that by Richards and Hind, describes music therapy work undertaken jointly by two music therapists, in this case a group (2002).

The literature described above focuses on the outcomes of music therapy collaborative work, and the reader is left wondering exactly how the music therapists planned and carried out sessions with their colleagues, and what the experience of collaboration was like for the music therapist.

Gale and Matthews describe the process of a collaborative assessment project between an art therapist, dramatherapist and music therapist (consisting of six sessions, two in each modality). They give importance to the expectations and knowledge that each professional had about their colleagues and the roles that each would take, and describe how these issues were explored in supervision, experiential sessions and in a discussion day about the work. In this honest account, the authors tell how the collaborative venture 'inspired some anxiety... [W]e felt wary about it in practice' (1998, p.174). In the conclusion to this chapter, the authors reflect on the use of the media, the structure and the objects available to the clients:

> Team members had often wondered whether one of the other media would be more useful. The assessment group offered an opportunity to make some quite direct comparisons and contrasts. Sometimes it did

seem that the nature of the medium made engagement more possible for certain clients… Relationships in the group were at the heart of the work; it was in concentrating on these that the contributions of the different arts therapies media were seen in a clearer light. (pp.182 and 183)

More recently, Twyford's research into collaborative working within music therapy in the UK allows for a fuller description of collaborative working approaches. Two of her respondents are working with adults with learning disabilities and they reflect on work with disciplines as varied as speech and language therapy, nursing, occupational therapy, dramatherapy and education, and consider their learning in the process of the work (Twyford 2004a).

The current author has explored collaborative working in previous writing, both in this clinical area and in mental health work (Jeffcote and Watson 2004; Watson 2007; Watson and Vickers 2002). Watson and Vickers describe music and art therapy projects that included group experiences in the community at Tate Britain. They reflect on the way they planned their work together, stating that 'we found that in our own modality we naturally took a dynamic therapeutic role whilst the other therapist had a more continuous containing presence' and note that 'clients identified strongly with our experience of "not knowing" about the other arts medium' (2002, p.134).

Watson (2007) includes a chapter describing a case study of a group of people with profound and multiple learning disabilities run by two music therapists, and a chapter on collaborative working. This chapter includes a team dialogue on the way in which the music therapist works within an adult learning disability team. Within this chapter two case studies describe joint working with art therapy and speech and language therapy. These short vignettes reflect on some of the professional and clinical issues that were considered in the conceptualisation of this work with adults with learning disabilities and for this reason are useful to quote in some detail. For example, when planning the art and music therapy group the author states that,

whilst the therapists found that they had much in common in their training backgrounds and in the way that they might think about the work or run a session, it was useful to discuss theoretical and practical approaches and to find out more about the similarities and differences between the two professions. This process of discussion enabled both therapists to feel more confident working together, and also meant that they learnt more about the other profession. (p.130)

Watson (2007) also states:

[W]orking together in this way provided clients with a rich therapeutic experience of two mediums, with the benefit of two therapists thinking together about the process of therapy. Additionally, it provided the therapists with a supportive and rewarding learning experience which deepened their understanding of the similarities and differences between the two disciplines, and of how each might help clients. (p.130)

Collaborative working in this clinical area also allows music therapists to assist other workers in the development of additional skills in relating with clients. This is illustrated first by Agrotou (1999), in her video portraying music therapy work with adults with learning disabilities and their carers. More recently, Leaning and Watson have written about a collaborative project where a psychologist and a music therapist develop their own skills, and the skills of care workers, as they run an intensive interaction group (2006).

WHY DO MUSIC THERAPISTS WORK COLLABORATIVELY IN WORK WITH ADULTS WITH LEARNING DISABILITIES?

The literature just reviewed shows us that music therapists collaborate to produce a richer clinical environment for clients, to develop their relationships with colleagues, and to develop their own clinical practice. Hattersley (1995) confirms these benefits of collaboration, stating that it:

- enhances communication between professionals, clients and carers
- provides opportunities for learning
- enhances team work and gives support to team members
- provides 'easier access to a wider range of therapists, skills and therapeutic approaches' (p.264).

Greater benefits to clients

One advantage of collaborative work in this clinical area is the possibility of bringing new perspectives and wider expertise and thinking to work with clients who have significant disabilities. Macadam and Rodgers state that, 'if professionals and agencies are faced with an individual whose particular needs are beyond their capacity to meet unaided, collaboration may take place on a "needs must" basis, with immediate and clear benefits' (1997, p.195).

Because people with learning disabilities often have additional health problems associated with their learning disability, it is likely that several different disciplines will be involved in their care. For example, a client with a profound learning disability may also have physical disabilities that mean they have regular contact with a physiotherapist, or communication difficulties that require support from a speech and language therapist. Collaborative working may, therefore, be particularly relevant when working with clients with multiple disabilities. As Lacey states, 'the complexity of needs presented by people with profound and multiple learning disabilities makes it impossible for one person or discipline to meet them all' (1998, p.xi). Where clients are unable to speak or use complex communication systems, it is particularly important that professionals communicate effectively.

Learning from fellow professionals and improving services

Sines and Barr, writing about collaborative working in learning disability services, suggest that committed collaboration involves 'explicitly shared team goals; an accurate understanding of one's own role and the role of other team members; and the presence of mutual trust and respect for other team members' (1998, p.349). Thus, collaborative working encourages professionals to learn in detail about other disciplines and their role within the clinical area, and to respect the differences between the disciplines. It also encourages the building of support networks across disciplines.

When therapists are working with a very disabled and little changing client group, collaborative work can help to bring new insights, knowledge and perspectives to the work. It can help the music therapist to reflect critically on their practice and consider issues such as difficult counter-transference and institutionalisation. New knowledge in practical areas is also gained; as Tyas comments:

'I certainly learnt a lot from the speech therapy techniques and from occupational therapists in terms of positioning, and physiotherapists, and I learnt a lot from dramatherapists as well. So I think all those disciplines and joint working have informed and formed the way I work now.' (in Twyford 2004a, p.108)

As well as this learning, hearing about the client from different perspectives can help workers to stay aware of the potential for development and progress.

Additionally, many disciplines working in this clinical area have a long history of working in collaboration with families and carers as well as fellow professionals (for example, speech and language therapy, psychology and physiotherapy). Part of their engagement with the client may be in their support, advice and training to carers, enabling standards and service to be improved. In the same way, music therapists may collaborate with carers, providing workshops and training, to equip carers with greater skills in being with and supporting people with learning disabilities.

Difficulties in collaborative work in this clinical area

A quotation from Owens, Carrier and Horder (1995) summarises the difficulties in collaborative work:

> Dramatic changes in the 1980s in the NHS and other public welfare service systems have highlighted the increasing need for close co-operation between professional groups. But differences in educational backgrounds, financial structures, expectations, roles and systems create barriers to mutual understanding. (p.1)

Other writers suggest specific challenges are different work cultures, professional power differences and tensions, lack of time and issues around confidentiality (Hattersley 1995, p.2665; Macadam and Rodgers 1997, pp.193–19). In particular, the differences in health and social services cultures may mean that workers approach client contact from different theoretical perspectives (Weinstein 1998). It can be challenging for workers to examine their valued beliefs and to accept new values and theories in order to engage in a meaningful way with colleagues in collaborative work. An important part of planning collaborative work can be for colleagues to talk together about their training, beliefs and approaches in order to allow greater understanding of their different perspectives. Differences in policy or practice, such as note or report writing, may also need to be discussed and negotiated in order to find a strategy which is acceptable to both professions.

Collaboration can mean that our perceptions of our colleagues' roles are put under scrutiny. This can be uncomfortable and can provoke conflict if our perceptions do not match with our colleagues. For music therapists it may be that their work becomes thought of as an activity, described as a 'music session' that can cheer a client up, rather than a therapy that can help to contain and process difficult and distressing feelings. This may happen if a colleague or family member finds it difficult to consider the fact that a client may be distressed or unhappy and need some therapeutic help. Therapists may also become aware that their work is envied by colleagues who may feel that the creative approach of a music therapist, who spends 30 or 45 minutes with clients, is an enjoyable and perhaps easier role than theirs. Sensitive discussion and training for new staff can help to address both these difficulties. If colleagues are to work in the therapy room together, it is essential that perceptions or feelings such as these are resolved in order to ensure that the clients, and not tensions between colleagues, are at the centre of the work.

Even if planning has been thorough, tensions can arise once collaborative work has begun. Difficult events that take place in the therapy can give rise to anxiety about the value of the work. Transferences and projections from clients (particularly within group work) can give rise to difficult feelings in workers, and it is important that experiences in the sessions and feelings that arise from these experiences can be freely and productively discussed in order to reflect usefully on the client's use of the sessions. An interviewee of Twyford's talks about the way in which 'tensions and difficulties can so easily spiral and build and I just don't think that's very helpful for anybody and not helpful for the client as it won't be as effective' (2004a, p.111). This therapist suggests that focusing on the client's needs can help to work through tensions. Supervision is also essential in helping collaborating professionals to address and work through challenges. This may be provided by senior colleagues within the organisation, or by an external supervisor, of the same or a separate discipline. Supervision gives a useful outside perspective, allowing a positive learning environment within which concerns and worries can be aired and solutions generated.

Despite the challenges described above, those writers who describe challenges suggest that a user-focused model can still allow different professionals to contribute jointly to care, and indeed this model of working has been strongly developed in recent years in learning disability services.

THE PROCESS OF COLLABORATIVE WORKING

Whilst a review of the literature and an examination of the benefits and challenges of this work has presented a thorough picture of the history and diversity of collaborative working, we have not yet heard the voices of practitioners reflecting on their experiences. The four case studies that follow allow these voices to be heard. The authors describe work with colleagues in a wide range of professions: dance movement therapy, drama therapy, physiotherapy, psychology and speech and language therapy. Music therapists join with their colleagues to describe these collaborations in detail, describing the impact of the experience for clients, and workers, and reflecting on the way in which collaborative work has allowed deeper learning about the discipline of music therapy, and about partnership with other professions.

The first case study describes innovative transdisciplinary music therapy and physiotherapy groups: the powerful combination of two sensory experiences used to benefit clients with profound and multiple learning disabilities (PMLD).

A MUSIC THERAPY AND PHYSIOTHERAPY GROUP
Sally Watson (Music Therapist)

Introduction
This case study describes the evolution of a music therapy and physiotherapy group which has been effective in achieving therapeutic aims for people with PMLD accessing specialist health services in Nottingham. It shows why the initial group was formed and how it changed over time, influenced by rigorous evaluation of the group and the needs of the members. It also includes description of the group and reflection from the different members of staff involved.

Background
The group began in November 1999 with an evaluated block of 20 sessions for two clients. The group aimed to offer a space where joint therapeutic aims and objectives could be met, through the combined use of music and movement, offering a stimulating, sensory and holistic environment. The group was structured to include purposeful movement activities with music (e.g. songs), free improvisation and time for reflection. Detailed evaluation took place using an action research model, and it was felt that physical

movement combined with music was a positive experience for clients, and that staff had gained valuable experience and a better understanding of the role of another colleague.

The group evolves

In 2001 I joined with another physiotherapist, two physiotherapy assistants and day centre support workers to run three consecutive blocks of sessions, each with different clients. These groups were based on ideas and learning from the previous evaluated joint work, adapted to respond to the individual needs of the clients and staff involved.

Group 1 consisted of Jack, Daphne and Sarah who are all pre-verbal, have significant mobility/physical health issues and were at risk of being socially isolated. All were in the process of moving to supported living placements in the community from long-stay hospital care. The focus of this group was therefore to look for ways of developing and supporting communication and links with each other, and to share, as appropriate, observations with those who would be caring for them.

Thirty-minute feedback sessions after each group, and separate evaluation sessions, created a space for feedback and reflection on staff development, as well as the progress of therapy. After the final evaluation session, staff members visited each client in their new homes to feed back observations and share helpful approaches with care staff.

Group 2 involved John, Daniel and Louise, all from the same day centre area, and ran for ten weeks. All three clients use wheelchairs, communicate non-verbally and have significant physical needs. It was felt that they wished to communicate with each other, but often found the environment of the day centre a barrier to this. This short-term therapy work aimed to evaluate further therapeutic input of future longer-term benefit to each client and to ascertain if their experiences and development in the group could be generalised to the day centre. The aims for each client were similar and focused on development of communication and interaction, offering a means for emotional expression. Again, the staff group met after each session and at the end of the group to evaluate what was happening.

Group 3 ran for 20 weeks and again involved John and Daniel, joined by Peter, who had similar needs. In addition to the aims for Group 2, staff wished to further integrate the use of touch, movement and sound, and to lessen the structure of the session to allow the clients to better control interaction. This group was somewhat disrupted by client illness, and our staff feedback meetings were important in enabling us to consider the impact of this, and to hold a sense of cohesiveness. Again, the staff deliberately looked for ways of supporting clients to extend developments within sessions to other areas of their lives, the day centre worker acting as a 'link' person to other professionals, carers and families.

The sessions

The same basic structure was used in each of the three groups, being adapted to the differing needs of the clients. The use of structure, in addition to consistent boundaries of time, duration (one hour) and venue, enabled each group to develop a sense of safety and stability. We observed that the structure relaxed as the groups progressed, probably due to the staff team becoming more competent in their understanding and use of each other's techniques, and gaining greater confidence to improvise musically.

The basic structure was as follows: verbal introduction, hello song (accompanied by guitar), rocking activity (one-to-one work on movement in wheelchairs accompanied by piano/singing), parachute activity (stimulating and encouraging clients to move into active choosing), choosing, leading to client-led improvisation, reflection from staff and clients, and goodbye (sung to each client in turn using the tambourine).

Roles

It was interesting to reflect on how the roles of staff in the groups changed and developed over the three blocks of sessions. Initially the physiotherapist took the role of general 'leader' of the group, overseeing the structure and transition between activities, and I led the musically focused parts of the session. During activities or improvising I took a supporting role, using my own music to provide a sense of cohesiveness, and observing the whole group. The physiotherapist complemented this by supporting and overseeing the movement of the group. The other three staff each directly supported one client, the same each week whenever possible, in order to develop rapport and closer knowledge of them. They played or moved with the clients and closely supported their expression (e.g. by holding instruments or vocalising with them). All staff talked during sessions, commenting as it felt appropriate to do so. Over time the role of leader became more fluid, with the physiotherapist and I swapping the role of overseer/observer, possibly due to gaining confidence in using each other's techniques.

Outcomes

The experience of the first music therapy and physiotherapy group showed that evaluation was crucial in order to observe changes and benefits for clients and to justify the high level of staff input and resource needed for this approach. We used three forms of evaluation:

1.   Weekly recording. Group case notes and process notes were completed and an entry made in nursing notes. These provided information for written reports at the end of the group and allowed observations to be shared with parents, carers and the multidisciplinary team.

2.   Weekly independent monitoring. A carer/parent for each client completed a simple monitoring sheet at a similar time after each session, involving circling words which best described the client's state, mood or behaviour before and after the group. Those that were completed regularly yielded simple scoring that could show change.

3.   Video recording. Video was taken at different points during each group, and discussed by the team. This enabled objective and closer observation of clients and constructive feedback concerning staff approaches and skills.

Many and varied benefits were observed and recorded for the clients involved. Examples are:

- increased use of voices in meaningful interaction

- increased emotional expression and contact with each other and the environment

- increase in physical closeness and working with touch (client to client)

- increase in communication on different levels (social, emotional)

- development in areas of social interaction, choice-making and sense of control

- generalisation into wider life, e.g. greater motivation to explore, choose, walk or interact

- increased involvement of others in the multidisciplinary team with evaluation/feedback, therefore positively impacting on clients' ability to achieve elsewhere

- increased ability to initiate contacts and lead interactions or music-making.

It was felt that these and other benefits would not have been observed to such an extent if these clients had been engaged in separate music therapy or physiotherapy sessions. The combined use of sound, touch and movement, plus the thought and effort put into creating the group environment, yielded significant results. This collaborative approach has been greatly valued by respective team managers and the Learning Disability Service, and it is intended to offer it again whenever the needs of clients on the music therapy or physiotherapy caseload indicate it would be useful.

Reflections

It was clear throughout the three groups that all staff involved wanted to focus on the clients' needs, putting them in control of their experience, and there was genuine openness to trying new approaches or learning new skills in order to support this. In feedback sessions and evaluations there was great honesty from staff about their feelings in the groups. This was vital in maintaining healthy dynamics, and in monitoring or observing clients' progress. There was a feeling throughout of excitement, at first due to the sense of 'pioneering' a new way of working with this client group in this service, and later due to the benefits which were observed. We also identified several benefits for the staff, including:

- increased confidence in utilising different therapy techniques (which had an impact on practice in each discipline)

- increased ability to share skills and ask for help from each other

- increased awareness in using silence, touch and music-making and being wholly person-centred

- increased knowledge of and empathy with clients.

This case study concludes with thoughts from some of the staff members involved.

REFLECTION FROM THE MUSIC THERAPIST

Although a steep learning curve for me, it was a joy to work in such an intense and focused way with clients who are often very isolated due to their disabilities. I felt these groups were true examples of joint working in that we moved from combining music therapy and physiotherapy ideas to developing a new way of delivering therapeutic input which has become a really valuable tool. I have greater awareness of physical, environmental and movement issues for people with profound and multiple learning disabilities who attend music therapy sessions and therefore the quality of their experience in music therapy has been improved.

REFLECTION FROM THE PHYSIOTHERAPY ASSISTANT

It was a pleasure to learn and work in a new way for me. I learnt so much about conversation with our clients, and using music with them. I thoroughly enjoyed the experience.

REFLECTION FROM THE PHYSIOTHERAPIST

In my career as a physiotherapist working with adults with learning disabilities I have always been aware of the power of music in motivating people to move. I was therefore delighted to be given the opportunity and time to work alongside my music therapy colleagues to develop this exciting area of work. I felt we facilitated, through jointly agreed objectives, a safe space for each client to feel empowered to move, explore and interact in the way of their own individual choosing. We were all, staff and clients, able to experience the sheer pleasure of having a conversation without the need for words.

REFLECTION FROM THE CARE SUPPORT WORKER

The power of music in the group was plain to see; the clients attending the sessions had a great response to it. Their movement and facial expressions were a delight to see. To touch an instrument and savour the sound they created brought pure pleasure, not just for the clients but also for me.

In conclusion, the opportunity for music therapists and physiotherapists to collaborate in working out a new therapeutic approach led to significant benefits for people with PMLD and for the staff supporting them.

The second case study in this chapter describes transdisciplinary work between music therapy and psychology. The work shows how careful planning and conceptualisation of a joint approach allowed a client with significant problems to progress.

MUSIC THERAPY AND PSYCHOLOGY: A JOINT APPROACH

Maria Radoje (Music Therapist) with Sara Betteridge and Michael Zivor (Clinical Psychologists)

This case study describes work undertaken between music therapy and psychology within a multidisciplinary community team for adults with learning disabilities.

Maria

Within this team, I usually received referrals for clients whose verbal abilities were severely limited, and because of their level of need I worked with them on a one-to-one basis. In this instance, I received an urgent referral for Jim, a 46-year-old man with Down's syndrome and a long history of self-harm. It was suspected that he was sexually abused by his father (now dead). He had a turbulent relationship with his mother who was seriously ill, and a history of mental illness. I noticed that a separate referral had been made to the psychology team, and after reading his case notes I saw that Jim had previously received separate input from both art therapy and psychology. I decided to put forward the idea of joint working and discussed this with Linda, lead psychologist, who allocated Sara to work with me, and later, when Sara moved to a different team, Michael.

We met several times to discuss possible approaches to the work, and Sara visited my clinical space. I felt strongly that we should try and integrate words and music for this client, and that both therapists should play, as well as make verbal interpretations. My main anxiety was related to the adequacy of my verbal skills, but as the work progressed and we had time to discuss our theoretical approaches I discovered that we seemed to share similar theoretical backgrounds which made me feel more confident verbally. It was essential to impart some musical skills to both co-therapists to enable them to participate as fully as possible within the music. Role play proved useful in this respect as a way of thinking about what the client was trying to say musically, and how we might respond.

During the sessions, I usually played the piano or sang, taking a leading and more containing musical role, whilst Sara or Michael used the percussion instruments to respond to other aspects of Jim's music. We made sure there was time for reflection after each session, and we were jointly supervised by Linda, which enabled us to think together about the splitting that occurred during the sessions. We also received regular individual supervision.

Initially Jim used sound as a defence – Sara and I were unable to speak, and often unable to make music, as he filled the space with his words and music in a kind of monologue which we were unable to penetrate. Any attempts to do so were usually ignored. This proved very difficult and we had to work hard in the reflection period and in supervision to think about why this may be. Jim seemed to ignore Sara most often, spending much of the session facing me and directing his music and words at me. When Jim did acknowledge Sara, she felt special; when he was ignoring her, I felt guilty. We thought about this as a possible recreation of an abusive relationship.

At times it felt as if Jim was attempting to obliterate us with his sounds – even with the piano lid up, I sometimes could not hear myself play, especially when he used the gong. I needed Sara to be confident enough to produce sound to match his; and eventually after much discussion in supervision and with more musical role play (where I demonstrated some techniques to produce different qualities of sound on the instruments), she was able to do this by using a large Chinese drum. When we discussed this music we often felt that it seemed a fine line between matching and containing his sounds, and perpetuating something unhealthy.

We aimed to help Jim express himself in an appropriate way, without resorting to self-harm. This was very difficult as his habit was so deeply ingrained. It seemed as if those around Jim had become de-sensitised to the painful way he expressed himself – seeing him as mischievous, or attention seeking. It felt important that we were able to convey, in case reviews for instance, the severity of the problem (here Sara's experience proved invaluable). The psychology team regularly gave advice to the home, and I was also able to contribute to this.

Sara

This was my first experience of working collaboratively with music therapy and my initial thoughts focused on expectations: those of music as a therapeutic medium, of the client's responses, of the development of a co-therapy relationship between me and Maria, and those expectations that I had placed upon myself.

Looking back, I remember the anxiety around working with musical instruments. As a non-musician I wondered how I would participate with any meaning in the musical aspect of the therapy, and how it would be interpreted. Would I understand the nuances of the music therapeutically?

Through many discussions reflecting on the work with Maria, these anxieties were addressed. I was able to support other sounds in the room, and by developing our co-working relationship our non-verbal communication was enhanced. However, more practical sessions would perhaps have been beneficial for me and decreased anxieties around creating appropriate sound. There were sessions where I became 'lost' in the music and followed Jim's music rather than providing my own interpretation of what I felt was happening in the room. Through discussions with Maria I came to the realisation that it was not always helpful to simply follow what Jim was playing. I struggled with this concept and felt my lack of understanding of music as a therapeutic intervention. These difficulties meant that it was of paramount importance that Maria and I met following each session to discuss what we both felt had happened in terms of what Jim brought to the session, our interpretations and subsequent interventions.

Despite the difficulties, it can be noted that the integrated approach seemed to produce a more positive therapeutic effect than previous psychotherapeutic interventions with Jim, who had not responded to talking therapy, usually remaining silent. Interestingly, we initially found that we were unable to speak or interject through the continuous monologue that Jim presented in our sessions, but eventually the music *was* able to break through this and allowed Jim the space to explore his emotions without having to use words. It took time before any meaningful verbal communication could be incorporated and initial sessions relied heavily on interpretation of his music and issues he spoke about in sessions.

I saw my role primarily as a musical extension of Maria, with the aim of intervening more in terms of therapeutic process, adding my interpretation of what I felt was happening in the room. However, Jim directed most of his speech toward Maria, which I felt reflected her central role at the piano. This observation was discussed towards the end of the therapy and we moved the layout of the room so that the piano was not so central. This seemed to have a positive effect on my integration into the room.

These types of issues were helped immensely by two factors. First, our regular discussions, peer supervision, individual clinical supervisions and joint supervision with a consultant clinical psychologist, and second, the positive therapeutic co-working relationship that Maria and I developed. This relationship became increasingly important for mutual support and the development of the therapeutic approach.

Jim responded well to this integrated approach: the music did seem to reflect his mood and therefore it can be argued that Jim was able to use the music as an emotional outlet. Additionally, it was observed that Jim was able to express himself verbally in a more meaningful manner than in previous psychotherapy, giving the psychologist more detailed information with emotional content with which to work.

Maria

Despite our concern about how Jim might react to Sara leaving and Michael arriving, he welcomed Michael warmly to the first session. Michael hoped to help Jim to fully integrate his thoughts and feelings, and worked more directively. New material emerged – Jim was able to tell us about running away from home, his mum calling the police to have him removed, and finally acknowledged that he was capable of damaging other people's property, thus integrating the 'good and bad' aspects of himself. I noticed that his voice seemed to become more expressive and melodic, and he had also begun to listen, imitating Michael's rhythms.

Michael

Working jointly with Maria in the music therapy sessions was a unique intellectual and emotional experience. There were a number of difficulties in arriving at a comprehensive psychological formulation for Jim mainly due to his avoidance of communicating clearly and verbally his internal world. These difficulties were viewed as rooted in both his cognitive diffi-culties, and in his personality. It was thought that Jim chose to avoid affect, and to suppress his significant psychological needs. For me, this joint work was an attempt to explore Jim's reasons for inhibiting communication as well as to experience the unique nature of music therapy.

Maria provided a secure base for Jim (and for me) in these non-directive sessions and enabled us to feel Jim's experience. I saw my role as an explorer, trying to get into Jim's world, without hurting or damaging his fragile aspects. Jim's limited vocabulary made my work interesting. Throughout the sessions I asked him to explain, repeat and explore a variety of messages that he communicated with us. I thought that being slightly directive, and communicating with him my own, and possibly others', difficulties in understanding him, may increase his insight into why people perceive him as avoidant.

The meaning of several of Jim's repeated narratives, such as being chased by the police, flying in an aeroplane and going to college, was explored and this enabled us to differentiate emotionally significant narra-tives from those that were less important. This understanding brought us closer to a clearer psychological formulation and to a better future prediction of possible self-harm behaviour. Being concrete with Jim and staying with his cognitive abilities made this intervention easier for us. We found that Jim could only identify two types of emotions: happy and sad. Understanding this enabled us to use his language, and to avoid suggesting that he feel and think that which he is unable to express.

Unfortunately, due to NHS changes, we were required to terminate this work prematurely. During the work with Jim I developed an objective tool to assess the effectiveness of music therapy. Asking Jim to respond positively or negatively to emotions before and after sessions enabled us to assess whether there was an improvement in his mood. The results suggested that Jim benefited from music therapy, and often left the sessions with an increase in mood.

Reflections

REFLECTION FROM MARIA

I feel that a joint approach to working with this client was especially useful, although challenging. It enhanced and enriched my practice, and I believe that it had benefits for Jim, as I witnessed him change over the 12 months that we worked with him.

REFLECTION FROM SARA

Our experiences have led to the conclusions that perhaps future transdisciplinary working should be more structured in terms of responsibilities and expectations, aims of therapy and clearly defined roles, employ standardised baseline measures for both the psycho-emotional state of the client and the effectiveness of professional collaboration, and incorporate more practice for the non-music therapist on musical instruments.

REFLECTION FROM MICHAEL

Through this experience I discovered that non-verbal therapy has a significant value and effectiveness in working with people with learning disabilities. To be with others in a compassionate, accepting and reinforcing environment was an eye-opener for a psychologist trying too hard sometimes to change a client's experience, and believing that words should be sufficient for a psychological change.

The next case study describes a group run jointly by a music therapist and a speech and language therapist; two communication approaches joined together to provide a rich environment for adults with learning disabilities.

A MUSIC AND COMMUNICATION GROUP

Tessa Watson (Music Therapist) and Alison Germany (Speech and Language Therapist)

This case study describes work that was undertaken within a community team for adults with learning disabilities in London. The team is a joint health and social services team and includes the therapy professions of art therapy, music therapy, speech and language therapy and physiotherapy.

Collaborative work within this team

TESSA

I have worked within the team for many years and see collaborative working as essential to my role. Open discussion about the role of music therapy, its similarities and differences to other professions and the ways in which professionals can learn from each other are all of great interest to me. Collaborative working can mean discussion with colleagues and carers (multi- or interdisciplinary work), joint working within a therapy session or jointly running training sessions for carers and other professionals (trans-disciplinary work). In this team I have run therapy groups jointly with the professions of art therapy, speech and language therapy, physiotherapy and psychology. Maybe collaboration is particularly important in a learning disability team, where most clients have significant barriers to communication and may not be able to share information easily with carers and professionals. An effective communicative and collaborative network needs to be established with and around clients to allow for the most appropriate input at the right time. With this in mind, I am also aware that collaboration means the concepts of privacy and confidentiality should be considered carefully.

ALISON

Multidisciplinary inter-agency teams for adults with learning disabilities have been in existence for several decades; this model is now being followed by other services, as seen in the current integration of services for children. Within a multidisciplinary team the specialist skills of the speech and language therapist lie in the assessment and management of difficulties with communication and/or eating, drinking and swallowing (dysphagia). An adult with a learning disability may be referred because of difficulties in either or both of these areas. For each individual we need to know which other professionals are already supporting them, or could be doing so, and to consider whether to combine our skills and expertise in the ways outlined above. As dysphagia is usually a physical problem, physiotherapy, occupational therapy and speech and language therapy often need to work together for joint assessment and problem solving. With communication, a significant role of the speech and language therapist working for people with a learning disability is often to facilitate the work of other professionals by advising on communication strategies (signs, symbols and other techniques) which will enable the individual or group of clients to benefit from the service offered. Alternatively the person's communication per se may be the focus of the speech and language therapy intervention: making sure the person has a symbol chart if they need it, teaching carers signs for a new activity the person is participating in, and helping carers to encourage simple choices rather than anticipating needs. But sometimes this type of intervention just does not work; at an emotional level the person is not ready to learn new skills or benefit from new opportunities. Here we can and should consult with colleagues from psychology, art and music therapy and see whether there are different ways to help the person to develop.

The group

In this case study we will describe and reflect on a group that we ran together. The group was one of several run by Tessa and various speech and language therapists within the team. Two frequent areas of overlap in referrals to speech and language therapy and music therapy are communication and interaction. It seemed natural to bring together the two disciplines in order to address these common reasons for referral.

The group was run to address issues of communication and interaction for clients with severe learning disabilities. It ran for ten weeks and aimed to provide opportunities for clients to develop skills in the following areas:

- find different ways to greet, be with and say goodbye to each other
- interact freely with others
- gain attention and initiate contact
- make choices (say 'yes' and 'no', choose instruments)
- share experiences with others, and develop greater awareness of others
- express individual personalities and feelings.

These aims were met through the use of music, talk and Makaton sign language.

We discussed how we might structure the group, and devised a clear plan which we considered each week in light of each client's use of the group. For both the communication and musical parts of the session we used a mixture of structured and unstructured activities, including a spoken or signed greeting, a greeting song accompanied by guitar, a chance to choose instruments, to say or sign something about the music and time for free improvisation. Each therapist led the session when the emphasis was on their modality. Alison led the communication structures such as the opening greetings, the use of Makaton and the introduction of new words or ideas. Tessa introduced and led the musical parts of the session such as the hello song and the improvisation. We found that this allowed us each to take the lead in the medium in which we felt most comfortable and skilled. Although we both participated in all activities, we naturally fell into supportive roles when the other therapist was leading their part of the group. This meant that we could move around the group assisting and supporting individual clients, and this also allowed opportunities for close observation of the group.

As the group developed, it felt as though it was an arena where personalities and skills could emerge, and we could get to know each client in a new way. Whilst communication and expression was encouraged, it was not imposed, and this meant that each person could work at their own level and be in control of the amount of input they gave. After each session we discussed what had happened, made notes and made decisions about what to do the next week. As we considered the material (musical or otherwise) that clients had brought to the group we tailored our interventions and interactions to suit each client. Our discussions also helped us to feel more relaxed working together and we became more confident in our roles in this joint group as the weeks progressed.

Reflections

REFLECTION ON THE OUTCOMES OF THE GROUP FROM ALISON

Most of the clients in the group had been known to speech and language therapy for many years. Many had had individual signing or symbols programmes or worked on signs and symbols in a speech and language therapy group. Many of them were seen as passive communicators. Within the music and communication group, however, non-verbal communication through music was paramount. I found it fascinating to see how under Tessa's skilled guidance the music gave opportunities for communication. People had the chance to lead, to follow, to perform centre stage, to take turns, to stop and listen, to protest, to annoy, as well as to share enjoyment.

In addition, at certain points within the time structure of the group, people had the opportunity to interact with each other outside of the music. Examples were shaking hands in greeting, signing to request more of some playing that had stopped and waving goodbye at the end of the group.

Communication also arose spontaneously from unplanned events such as instruments being dropped, favourite instruments being chosen, or extremely loud playing. For the majority of clients their confidence within the music increased their confidence in communicating, both about the music and socially. The group allowed free and creative expression in music, talk and non-verbal communication. One of the main outcomes was the way in which clients had an experience of being in control of interactions within a group. Each client's individual and unique communication was recognised and developed within the group setting.

Can one think of such a group in terms of measurable outcomes? One might attempt to measure transferable skills or the effect on individuals' emotional well-being; to quantify this would be time-consuming and probably of little benefit to the individuals themselves; what we did do was to report in detail to carers and other professionals on how we thought people had benefited from the group and give ideas for how they might build on what they had achieved.

There is a model of speech and language therapy intervention that stresses the need for 'opportunities' for communication, along with a means of communication and reasons to communicate (Money and Thurman 1994). One can see this group as offering a very specific opportunity: for each person to access music therapy in a group setting specifically structured to provide opportunities for communication, and where the individual's use of those opportunities is fostered by having both therapists working with the group for its duration.

REFLECTION ON THE EXPERIENCE FROM TESSA

In each case, when planning a joint group, I hoped that combining the disciplines would allow a richness of therapeutic input that isn't found when working alone. This was always the case. I should stress that I don't think this means music therapy or speech and language therapy is less valuable on its own; rather that when addressing specific aims like these, combining the two professions really seemed to allow a rich communication environment which often felt more than the sum of its parts. Interestingly all the speech and language therapists I have worked with have been interested and active in music in some kind of way, and this meant openness to the value of music from the start, which was a great bonus. I really valued Alison's expert and detailed knowledge about communication and I felt very clear that she was the expert in that area, so I could relax and allow my music to reach people, knowing that Alison would be able to spot any communication possibilities and develop them. I experienced this as a real luxury: the chance to completely focus on the music and know that someone else was thinking about practicalities at that moment. I felt as though we quickly found a way to work together; this seemed to be partly because we were very respectful of each other's knowledge and experience, and we listened carefully to the reasons why we might each do something in a particular way, rather than being defensive about our own ways of working. I remember the challenge of needing to explain clearly my rationale for practice; this really helped me to clarify my thoughts! I remember the group with great enjoyment, and would definitely repeat this kind of work in the future.

REFLECTION ON THE EXPERIENCE FROM ALISON

Before we started to plan the group I did wonder what my role would be: Tessa had more experience of group work, was trained in intensive interaction, and had many years of experience in communicating with people with a learning disability. Where I found my skills could enhance the group were first in the planning stage: planning a time structure that would make sense to people; offering people choice but not overwhelming them; and anticipating what people might offer in terms of communication. Because of this planning, clients were able to make use more quickly of the time available. Second, during the sessions themselves I learned to rein in my speech and language therapy tendencies to model, prompt and impose what I thought should be happening. I was surprised what intense concentration was required to wait and respond. After each session it was then really interesting to share observations from our different perspectives and to use this shared information to plan for the next session.

We hope and believe the clients benefited from the fact that we ran the group together; we know that we worked hard to combine our different areas of expertise. This was an opportunity for interdisciplinary communication not to be missed.

The last case study in this chapter is a description of transdisciplinary work between three disciplines. Elements from all three therapies are brought together to provide a rich and supportive therapeutic setting.

BUILDING BRIDGES: JOINT WORKING WITH DRAMA, MUSIC AND DANCE MOVEMENT THERAPY

Rosanne Tyas (Music Therapist) with reflections from Justine Souster (Dramatherapist) and Cloe de Sousa (Dance Movement Therapist)

The music therapy department and Bridge Project are part of the therapies service of the learning disabilities directorate of Sutton and Merton Primary Care Trust. Other therapies on site include occupational therapy, physiotherapy, dietetics, art, drama and aromatherapy. The team meets regularly to allocate clients to the appropriate therapy programme.

I have always sought out transdisciplinary working, initially due to working in isolation and increasingly as I have seen its value to clients and to mutual understanding amongst professionals. The process of merging skills, ways of working, insight and experience has sometimes felt like a journey from separate parts into one entity and has been well worth the effort.

Joint sessions with physiotherapy, occupational therapy, speech and language therapy, dramatherapy and further education departments have had different rewards and challenges. I have learnt a lot from these disciplines and have incorporated this knowledge into my music therapy work. Clarity of communication, use of symbols, giving clear informed choices, use of cue in phrases from speech and language therapy, the importance of positioning and ways limbs can be helped to relax from occupational therapy and physiotherapy are all points of learning from joint work. Clear focus on achievable aims and objectives and a consistent approach were gains from joint work with further education, and the use of story telling and observation of changes in the body from dramatherapy.

Although each of these pieces of collaborative work has been different, there have been common elements. The need for respect for each other's training backgrounds, real listening, openness to challenge and questioning and at times the need for compromise are some of the factors that have contributed to effective programmes. It has been really important to build in time for feedback and note writing together after the sessions as well as allocating longer periods of time for discussing and reflecting on the work. I have noticed that the ride has been rockier if for practical reasons these could not occur on a regular basis. The journey has been smoother if there has been proper consultation at the beginning of the programme of therapy, and an acknowledgement that this was joint working rather than one person or discipline being an adjunct to the other.

The piece of work I am going to describe is a recent joint arts therapies initiative termed the Bridge Project. The Bridge Project was initially set up to therapeutically support adults with a learning disability who were moving from an established hospital setting into the community. It developed a wider brief of assisting clients in processing their feelings around loss of mobility, fragile health and bereavement. The team consists of a dance movement therapist, dramatherapist, speech and language therapist and music therapist. This project was different from other joint ways of working I had experienced as it was set up as a joint initiative from the outset.

The particular group in question included three clients, a dance movement therapist, a dramatherapist and a music therapist. The clients were referred to the project because of their perceived need for emotional support if changes of accommodation were to take place. We discussed how we would work together but left this process quite free to develop organically. We agreed that there would be a keyboard and that we would use words, movement, props and instruments as appropriate. In the early stages of the group there seemed to be uncertainty both from clients and therapists – maybe about what was expected and exactly how we could work together. In reflection after the sessions we decided to use a storyline to structure the sessions and give a focus. The story was entitled *Four Friends* (Gersie 1992). It describes the friendship that grows between four animals who support each other in difficult circumstances. It acknowledges difference in character, behaviour and personality. Different animals were chosen to suit the clients' personalities. This story became a useful tool: the distance of characterisation helped the clients to express deep, complex emotional states and the wider concept of a journey not only reflected the clients' possible move into the community but their journey towards one another in the sessions. It also reflected the journey of the therapists working together.

Various responses were communicated including strong, wide-ranging vocalisations, expressive play on percussion instruments, use of inflatable balls and engagement with material and movement and massage. Each of the clients responded differently, identifying with their 'character' in the story.

Key parts of the story had different intensities of response. There was the theme of a storm which two clients particularly responded openly to whereas the third member chose to hide. This theme did seem to relate to the emotional experience of the clients. Another theme was a fountain which seemed to become a symbol of a refreshing meeting place where strength was drawn from the fountain and being together. Another part of a story was also used with a character from under the water called the Nicky Nicky Nye (from Ryan 2001). This symbolised feelings of chaos and disruption which it was helpful to surface and explore.

From a music therapist's point of view the focus on characters and storyline was an exciting challenge as the characters and their responses could be directly reflected through musical themes. The keyboard provided a containing sound world for the story to develop and characters to emerge. We all felt that there needed to be a section with drumming, which was sometimes led by the music therapist and sometimes by the dance or dramatherapist. We also passed around the ocean drum as a way of connecting the group members. Materials were used to engage the clients such as a piece of bubble wrap which one client enjoyed rolling over with his wheelchair. The resulting sound seemed to meet the chaotic force which he often exhibited. Another technique was the dance therapist's use of pressure and release and approach and avoidance which was also reflected musically. The drama and dance therapist also worked with the mirror in the room and after the sessions we discussed the importance of self-image and searching for the self.

There was openness between therapists to take on one another's roles. This is not to say that we became another arts therapist or even felt skilled in those areas, but that openness allowed for experimentation and exploration of the different media in the sessions.

Reflections
REFLECTION FROM JUSTINE, DRAMATHERAPIST

If one of the therapists was absent the other therapists would provide the clients with the level of interaction that the absent therapist would usually provide in the form of props, body or music. As a dramatherapist I was used to using music in groups but did not have the skills to play the keyboard in the same way as the music therapist. Initially in the group my use of the keyboard allowed for playfulness with sounds, but as the group developed and the group's story unfolded with its own unique soundtrack I found it difficult to use the keyboard in a way that was appropriate in the group. The keyboard became a symbol of the music therapist's absence. Sometimes a client would initiate play on the keyboard which felt like an appropriate acknowledgement of the missing therapist and the loss the client felt. This became an important part of the group's process which was to explore loss and change.

REFLECTION FROM ROSANNE, MUSIC THERAPIST

Flexibility in the use of each other's media also meant that if an emotion or way of being was picked up by one therapist they felt able to express it to the group in a number of ways which felt appropriate at the time. For instance the dance or dramatherapist might start a rhythm on the drum, chant or use a musical instrument with a client, as well as using movement, materials and storyline. I felt increasingly able to comment on an emotion in the story or use a prop with which I was previously unfamiliar. Initially there was anxiety both regarding confidence in trying these new approaches and in terms of my contribution as a music therapist (for example, is it valid and appropriate, am I swamping or not doing enough?). We discussed our roles, which was very helpful, and on reflection could have been explored more. We talked about the flexibility of using different media and how different clients brought up different emotions in each of us which were expressed to the group where appropriate.

Longer periods of reflection were built into the programme. One particularly helpful way of discussing the group together was to each write several words or phrases which encapsulated each client's response; for instance, sensitivity, humour, identity, constancy and search for intimacy. From this discussion, themes emerged. One theme was journeying; what we meet on the way and encountering obstacles. Another theme was 'we've all got something to say' which became a chant in the sessions. We also discussed how we felt in the group and how this may reflect the clients' experience. We also fed back to the care staff together. A useful learning tool was sharing relevant articles and books on loss and bereavement from each of our disciplines. This was professionally enriching.

REFLECTION FROM CHLOE, DANCE MOVEMENT THERAPIST

My experience of working within the multidisciplinary team was very rich. I had been lone working and had sought a team in which to share skills and reduce the stress of reflecting on the client/group process continually on my own. I was greatly attracted by the premise that each therapist and therapy could contribute to the analysis of the work. The Bridge Project team at Orchard Hill fulfilled this aspiration.

Once established in the team, I was more than happy to see the benefits to both clients and therapists, due to the multidisciplinary way of working. One of the greatest benefits was our ability to serve our clients more proficiently. For example, one therapist's medium suited one client, while another therapist's medium suited another. As the client's preferences and needs changed, they could be served by each therapist in turn. This took place within single sessions or over the lifetime of the group. Providing all these specialist mediums within one session created a container of strength and variation from which the clients seemed to benefit. This container seemed to get stronger and stronger the longer that we worked together.

Having a shared reflective time also seemed to enable us to hold more of what was taking place in the sessions, further serving the clients. In terms of 'parallel process' each therapist was able to work through their own responses to the sessions. As this was brought to light the awareness around our interventions in the sessions also strengthened the container in which the clients were held.

ROSANNE

The group was difficult to end. This was partly because it was an enjoyable experience for the therapists to work together, as well as there being reluctance to end the therapy when there was still potential value for the clients. However, we did feel that initial aims for the individuals and group had been met. Each client had made progress in terms of expressing some deep and complex emotional material. They had also travelled together and come together as a group.

JUSTINE

This was my first opportunity to work as part of a multidisciplinary team and I found it deeply fulfilling on a professional and personal level. Being an arts therapist often entails a lot of lone working. The professional and personal relationships I formed during this work will remain with me always and the skills we shared I shall add to my dramatherapy toolbox until I need to source them once more.

ROSANNE

As a music therapist, I found this programme of joint working exciting, challenging and rewarding. I feel its success was largely due to regular feedback and periods of reflection between the therapists being built into the programme, but most importantly, as a result of the openness, respect and honesty in working together which directly benefited the clients and contributed to the effectiveness of the joint therapy programme.

CONCLUDING THOUGHTS

These case studies richly illustrate the benefits and challenges described at the beginning of the chapter. It is clear that these practitioners are convinced of the value of collaborative working. Their case examples show that their collaborative work has been challenging, but also enriching and enjoyable for the therapists involved. As the discipline of music therapy becomes more professionalised the requirement to make links with varied partners for the benefit of clients will continue, and in this chapter the message from writers and practitioners is clear: collaboration is an important part of the work that music therapists undertake with adults with learning disabilities.

GUIDELINES FOR GOOD PRACTICE

This chapter concludes with good practice guidelines for collaborative work in this clinical area.

- Find common ground and start from there, building in less familiar ideas or practices as you develop your plan.
- Discuss your expectations (related to your roles, the content of the work, the outcomes of the work).
- Be adaptable and flexible.
- Be open and honest about your worries/anxieties, which will be different for each discipline.
- Allow time to plan your collaborative project.
- Discuss the input of the different disciplines, drafting and then clarifying specific roles and responsibilities.
- Consider amalgamating approaches (for example structured communication routines and free improvisation).
- Think about the differences in boundaries, and why this is, and agree the boundaries for the collaborative work together.
- Consider practical details such as how long the project will be, the focus or aims of the work and what happens if one of you is absent.

- Consider undertaking some role play to help non-music therapists to feel comfortable when working with music. Rehearse some of the content of the sessions prior to starting to dispel anxiety.

- If the therapist with whom you are working is not used to working with emotions, share ways of processing difficult or challenging experiences and feelings.

Chapter 3

Music Therapy and Collaborative Working in Adult Mental Health
Creative Connections and Destructive Splits

Claire Miller

INTRODUCTION

This chapter considers music therapy and collaborative working within the context of adult mental health services. The first section gives a short outline of the field: the different settings and the complex health and social care needs that may bring people to these services. It briefly reviews current policy and initiatives which place interprofessional and interagency collaboration at the centre of service provision. It then examines more closely the relationships that take place, with a focus on underlying dynamics and defences that are an inherent part of interprofessional working in this setting. The author's approach is influenced by psychoanalytic theory which informs the discussion of the nature of working relationships and multi-disciplinary endeavours.

The rest of the chapter explores these issues in relation to the music therapist's role and includes an examination of the advantages and difficulties of collaborative working via a review of the music therapy literature and discussion of emergent themes. The final section presents three case studies by different contributors, illustrating music therapists' experiences of collaboration on three different levels (team working, co-working music therapy with another discipline and developing an integrated approach with another discipline). The examples aim to highlight ways of working creatively with the challenges identified and to describe the resulting benefits to service users and practitioners. The chapter concludes with a summary of themes relating to good practice.

THE ADULT MENTAL HEALTH FIELD AND INTERPROFESSIONAL COLLABORATION
The modern mental health service

Developing and modernising mental health services has been high on the political agenda over recent years. *The National Service Framework for Mental Health* (NSFMH) states that:

> Mental ill health is so common that at any one time around one in six people of working age have a mental health problem, most often anxiety or depression. One person in 250 will have a psychotic illness such as schizophrenia or bipolar affective disorder (manic depression). (Department of Health (DoH) 1999, p.3)

Other commonly diagnosed mental health problems include eating disorders, obsessive-compulsive disorder, personality disorders, panic attacks, phobias and trauma.

It lies beyond the scope of this chapter to detail the many different diagnoses and forms of mental distress (see *The ICD-10 Classification of Mental and Behavioural Disorders* (World Health Organization 1992) and the *Diagnostic and Statistical Manual of Mental Disorders: DSM IV* (American Psychiatric Association 1994)). However, fundamental to individuals' experiences are 'problems in the way they think, feel or behave' (Stewart 2006, p.2). Disturbances in relationships and in the capacity to relate to others are often central. Family and working life (including cognitive capacities) can be severely affected and difficulties with self-care or managing daily life independently can become overwhelming. People with a severe mental illness (e.g. psychosis) can experience profound emotional, perceptual and psychological distress.

A comprehensive range of treatments and settings are needed to respond to the diversity of mental health problems. Community-based care is considered a priority and, within this, the importance of primary care is strongly emphasised. Also:

> Specialist services…should ensure effective and timely interventions for individuals whose mental health problems cannot be managed in primary care alone, for example, patients with severe depression or

psychotic disorders. Specialist services are essential when these problems co-exist with substance misuse – co-morbidity or dual diagnosis. (DoH 1999, p.4)

Specialist mental health services include:

- community-based care coordination (CMHTs)
- crisis resolution and early intervention
- acute inpatient care
- assertive outreach
- continuing care, day services, rehabilitation and residential care, vocational and work programmes
- services for people with complex and special needs: forensic, dual diagnosis and people with personality disorders.

(Sainsbury Centre for Mental Health (SCMH) 2001, p.8)

Policy and initiatives for multiprofessional and team working

Due to the complex range of social, emotional, psychological and medical needs that may be associated with severe mental illness, the involvement of and collaboration between different specialities is essential. Inter-professional collaboration and team working are now widely considered to be central to the effective provision of mental health care. Policy and guide-lines emphasise the need for partnerships between service users and service providers, between disciplines and across different agencies with an emphasis on providing more seamless health and social care (e.g. DoH 1997, 2000, 2005a; SCMH 2001). The NSFMH states that service users can expect care to 'be well coordinated between all staff and agencies' (DoH 1999, p.4). This includes partnerships with the independent sector and 'agencies which provide housing, training, employment and leisure services', where necessary, for people with severe and enduring mental health needs (DoH 1999, p.4).

The central tenet is that workers involved in a patient's care should be part of a multiprofessional, person-centred process. Accordingly, team working skills and abilities are seen as core for mental health practitioners. *The Capable Practitioner* document (SCMH 2001), commissioned by the National Service Framework Workforce Action Team, outlines the set of skills, knowledge and attitudes required for implementing effective modern mental health care and emphasises capabilities for integrated working and partnerships. (See also *The Ten Essential Shared Capabilities*, DoH 2004b.)

Who is involved?

Traditionally, the core disciplines involved in providing care for adults with mental health problems have been: psychiatrists, mental health nurses, social workers, psychologists and occupational therapists. Now, depending on the setting and locality, a wide range of other professions and treatment options also exist within services, including: arts therapists, psychotherapists, specialist drug and alcohol support services, education staff, dieticians, work rehabilitation services, physiotherapists, speech and language therapists and physical activities staff. The role of pharmacists, who have important expertise and ability to advise patients and medics, is becoming progressively more visible. Increasingly, teams are also involving 'non-professionally aligned staff such as community support workers, and service users as survivor workers' (Newbigging 2004, p.146). Forums and channels for facilitating service user and carer involvement in the development of services are becoming more prominent, in line with national policy. Different settings will of course require different configurations of services and ways of working.

This multiprofessional and multi-agency picture can become further complicated, as in the case of forensic psychiatric services. Here, due to the impact of the offender patient's behaviour on society, the criminal justice system becomes involved. In many cases the Ministry of Justice (previously the Home Office), in consultation with other agencies, makes decisions which have a central impact on treatment (Glyn 2002; Loth 1994), for example concerning the restrictions that are placed on the patient and the way that specific therapies, such as work on recidivism, are prioritised.

Collaboration and team working: ideals and realities

Multidisciplinary teams are widely considered to be the best vehicle for effecting collaborative working. 'A multidisciplinary team is typically conceived of as a mixed group of professionals working together in the same place to achieve the same end; that is, improved health and social care status of an individual' (Newbigging 2004, p.146).

The policy and initiatives detailed above, alongside the comprehensive list of experts and professionals involved, could be seen to imply an ideal in which all needs can be met in a joined-up, mutual and comprehensive way. However, it is widely acknowledged that the reality often falls short of this ideal: the mental health literature highlights that the nature of collaborative and team working is a concern across the different disciplines.

In a chapter exploring good practice within multidisciplinary team working, Newbigging (of the Health and Social Care Advisory Service) reviews different perspectives on the variety of barriers to achieving effective team working. These include the inherent complexities of organising mental health services and a 'lack of attention to the clarity and detail that is needed in the development of multidisciplinary teams' (2004, p.145).

There are difficulties with identifying and defining the core elements of good collaborative practice which has led to a call for more research. It has been suggested by healthcare researchers that, although multidisciplinary teams are ubiquitous and supported by expert opinion and clinical experience, 'little research has evaluated what components of team work (e.g. team meetings) are more effective' (Burns and Lloyd 2004, p.311). Further, the effects on service users and staff are still under-researched and there is a lack of clarity and conclusive evidence relating to how to train staff to do it (e.g. Zwarenstein et al. 2000).

What seems to be central to a consideration of the functioning of teams and collaborative efforts are the underlying dynamics, which are of interest here. This is an area that may be ignored or defended against within this idealised and implicit view of a consensus or 'democratic' model of collaboration (e.g. Onyett 1999).

Tensions and conflicts and the often unconscious denial of these are inevitably inherent aspects of cross-professional collaborative endeavours. Psychoanalyst Cordess points out that, far from effecting smooth collaboration, multidisciplinary work can raise issues that are 'painful and potentially divisive, involving as they do our place within an ensemble or group' (1998, p.97). Issues may include difficulties around professional identity, lack of clarity about responsibility and accountability, divergent views on treatment goals and care (Hills et al. 2000), status and professional envy and rivalry.

Additionally, team functioning is often affected by dynamics introduced by the client group. These can powerfully reflect something of the presenting health problem. Emotional or psychological difficulties are communicated unconsciously from client group to staff group where they may get played out in interactions between professionals. Halton, in his chapter on unconscious aspects of organisational life, states:

> In an institution, the client group can be regarded as the originator of projections with the staff group as the recipients. The staff members may come to represent different, and possibly conflicting, emotional aspects of the psychological state of the client group. (1994, p.14)

Recipients of such projections may unknowingly identify with these states and act them out. Whilst such communications and projective processes take place in all relationships, these can be particularly primitive and powerful for people experiencing severe psychological distress. Cycles of projection of unacknowledged, unwanted feelings from clients and countertransference responses in staff teams, including splitting, can take place. If unrecognised, these may significantly obstruct effective care-giving and collaborative working.

It can be important, therefore, for those engaging in collaborative working in mental health services, to have resources for identifying, understanding and working with dynamics and unconscious processes originating in the team or in the client group.

The rest of this chapter will explore these issues as they relate to the music therapist's role within mental health services. It will first look at relevant music therapy literature regarding the benefits and difficulties of collaborative working. Emergent themes, specifically related to challenges and underlying dynamics, will then be discussed further.

MUSIC THERAPY AND INTERPROFESSIONAL COLLABORATION IN MENTAL HEALTH
Literature review

Despite being a crucial and complex aspect of the music therapist's work, there is limited writing focusing in detail on music therapy and interprofessional collaboration in adult mental health settings. This is an important area of our work as we continue to establish our place both within the allied health professions and as a psychological/psychotherapeutic profession.

The simultaneous advantages and struggles of collaborative working receive some attention within the general music therapy literature. Hills *et al.*

(2000) investigated these issues with a survey of the members of the Association of Professional Music Therapists across all settings. They looked specifically at 'burnout and job satisfaction in relation to multidisciplinary team membership' (p.32). They found that, in comparison to therapists who worked independently, those who were team members experienced higher levels of 'personal accomplishment' but similar levels of 'emotional exhaustion' and 'depersonalisation' (p.32).

The concept of collaborative working and good links with other professionals as sources of support is evident (e.g. Davies and Richards 1998; Eisler 1993; Stewart 2000). Importantly, the increased safety of shared responsibility of care within a multidisciplinary team helps contain the anxieties of working within mental health settings (Hills *et al.* 2000). The potential for fostering shared learning and understanding is also clear, for example in multidisciplinary supervision, case discussion forums or co-working with other disciplines (e.g. Loth 1994; Priestley 1993).

Also apparent is the benefit to clients of effective collaborative communication between disciplines in terms of relapse prevention (Odell-Miller 1995a), timely 'tip-offs' about patients' admissions or transfers (Priestley 1993, p.26), holistic care-planning or making the difference between a service user's successful engagement in therapy or perhaps being overlooked.

Many of the challenges of integrating into a multidisciplinary setting are highlighted within the literature about setting up music therapy services in adult mental health. Eisler (1993) and Odell-Miller (1993) focus on the hard work involved in showing the multidisciplinary team what the profession has to offer mental health services. In our current climate of evidence-based practice, this continues to be a pressing issue. Moss (1999) reports on a collaborative approach to an 'evidence-based research project' (p.49), which piloted a music therapy service. This involved input to the research design – a quantitative study – from other disciplines and management. Within the design, evaluation of the service by team members and service users was central. Moss' study could be seen to reflect a concern with developing a language to communicate the effectiveness of the work to a wider audience. This is echoed in other research literature, as is a perceived emphasis on quantitative approaches to evaluation, with which the medical setting has historically been more familiar (e.g. Edwards 2002).

In describing the process of setting up a service, Odell-Miller asserts the need for the visibility of music therapists in multidisciplinary team settings and the promotion of understanding about their work. She underlines interdisciplinary tensions that can make developing a collaborative and integrated approach difficult. These include tensions around issues of confidentiality and ways in which the therapy can be unconsciously sabotaged by institutional pressures such as conflicting models of treatment and unrecognised interprofessional envy (1993, p.25).

Sloboda and Bolton's chapter (2002) notes that the tasks of establishing a role and identity vary according to the service. It compares the different roles and treatment aims music therapists may have in general psychiatric settings with forensic services and shows how the contact and collaboration with other team members may vary greatly. For example, the music therapist may be the main therapeutic input for a service user in the community or one of many staff involved in an intensive multidisciplinary in-patient therapy programme.

The need for close, integrated team working to mitigate against potential splits between disciplines and within the therapy is highlighted by several authors. In the same chapter, Sloboda shows how, in forensic work, the therapeutic purpose of music therapy can be denied by patients and located solely in other psychological interventions in which they are involved. Music therapy becomes 'just music' (Slobada and Bolton 2002, p.139). In her example, the psychologist recognises and acknowledges such a split, helping the team to contain the work and maintain its effectiveness.

In his exploration of the importance of music therapy supervision in the forensic mental health setting, Glyn (in press) examines the music therapist's position in relation to the rest of the multidisciplinary team. He describes complex projective processes within the therapy situation unconsciously aimed at denying the reality of the therapist's professional role and relationships with others (e.g. with the multidisciplinary team). Instead an exclusive, 'fused' state with the therapist is sought. He shows how the therapist can then experience pressure to enact unhelpful splits with the team.

Glyn talks of therapists encountering the forensic setting for the first time and how a 'healthy questioning of the system' can become

> susceptible to a more extreme and destructive type of splitting in which all the bad qualities [are] thought to reside in the institution and the benign ones in the patient...the pattern is a familiar one...and when it persists can be highly damaging to team working. (Glyn, in press)

The chapter emphasises the role of supervision in understanding such processes so that effective team links can be maintained.

Glyn also describes how different and opposed parts of patients may get projected into the therapist and the team respectively, leaving both parties rather isolated and mutually uncomprehending. For example, one party might get caught up in a manic defence (e.g. where recent progress is the over-riding focus) and the other party may be primarily in touch with a patient's unwanted feelings (e.g. of powerlessness) raising concerns about potential risk or vulnerability. Again an understanding of the workings of the patient's unconscious processes and an ability to unravel the counter-transference is essential to enable all members of the team to see the whole picture and respond effectively. The first case study, below, expands on this.

Odell-Miller (2001) confirms the importance of understanding such countertransference issues and talks of the 'disturbance in the institution' (p.146). She gives an example of work with people who need long-term residential care and discusses the experiences of staff who spend long periods looking after people who are confused. She shows how these interactions may lead to forgetfulness or confusion in staff which she links to incidents such as forgetting to bring patients to their music therapy sessions. Again, the need for an awareness of the unconscious life of institutions is emphasised if the therapist is to establish and develop effective collaborative links when responding to such events.

Watson et al.'s chapter (2004) is a collaboration between music therapist, occupational therapist and clinical psychologist and explores issues of how multidisciplinary practice may be integrated. Their work is with women with severe mental illness and disturbance in secure settings. They state that the team's joint task is 'to maximise each woman's therapeutic opportunities and demands whilst also keeping her safe' (p.93). They draw upon attachment theory, stating the need for the environment to provide concrete physical, medical and emotional containment. This can then become a 'secure base' from which patients feel able to move towards taking more risks within the context of therapy and personal change. They outline a process of multidisciplinary needs assessments and care plan meetings tied in with the Care Programme Approach (CPA). Case examples provide illustrations of how the different disciplines may integrate their input to achieve shared treatment aims, whilst also highlighting the difficulties and tensions within the team arising from the work. The examples make evident the need for close communication and support between team members as well as regular supervision to counter the impact of unconscious processes such as pressure to respond unthinkingly, punitively or dismissively.

Recent music therapy literature has put the spotlight on the concept of 'community' and service users' roles within collaborative projects. Maratos (2004) writes about an experimental collaboration in which an operetta, composed by a psychiatrist, is rehearsed and performed by a multi-disciplinary group of staff and patients. The project aimed to integrate the whole community, addressing both staff and service user issues. It provided an opportunity to explore existent relationships and some of the projections often at work within and between these two groups. The work involved a 're-negotiation of traditional boundaries on many levels, and a rethinking of some of the basic tenets of music therapy practice' (p.132). Maratos goes on to discuss the benefits and challenges of such a departure.

Challenges in multidisciplinary working

In an environment where the consultant psychiatrist (or responsible medical officer) has had ultimate responsibility for the patient, there has often been a clear medical dominance.[1] The initial need for medication can make it hard for a team to embrace a holistic approach where all interventions are valued equally. The inevitable hierarchies within teams can lead to different disciplines feeling concerned about how they are valued. As Cordess states, 'matters of hierarchy, status, leadership and power...and the necessary demarcation and maintenance of personal and professional boundaries are not easy' (1998, p.98).

As mentioned earlier, envy and rivalry can play a part in professional relationships, and are often related to fantasies and misunderstandings about each other's role and function. The full range of skills and abilities of each discipline are infrequently recognised by the whole team. Disciplines can be seen in a one-dimensional way which can lead to professionals devaluing those aspects of their own work (Wrench 1998). For example, music therapy may be seen by other disciplines as a way of engaging patients in activity. This can be related to the very real concern that many patients are not managing to participate in *any* activity. However, music therapists may diminish the team's primary interest in attendance in the pursuit of recognition as psychological therapists and experience envy towards those professions that are more clearly identified with that role.

Developing an understanding of different disciplines' roles could be seen as central to the task of achieving effective collaborative working. Opportunities for team members to communicate about their work and finding effective ways of doing this are vitally important. There are many potential forums including team meetings, ward rounds, therapies meetings, case conferences, away days, presentations, staff reflective practice groups, clinical governance activities, etc. However, depending on the setting, there is not always ready access to such forums and, when there is, there may be defences at work that form barriers to effective communication. Halton points out that, like individuals, institutions develop defences against threatening or unwelcome emotions, which can 'obstruct contact with reality…and hinder the organisation in fulfilling its task' (1994, p.12). For example, team members may find it hard to fully 'take in' or use feedback from colleagues working in experience-, and emotion-oriented ways (such as music therapy). These ways of working may allow the patient to communicate their great mental distress and disturbance, an awareness of which is difficult for staff who must work for long hours with large groups of patients (Menzies-Lyth 1988).

Teams may unconsciously employ defences which serve to distance staff from the emotional experience of patients such as viewing the complexity of individuals' difficulties within the narrow constructs of medical diagnoses or, conversely, minimising a patient's disturbance. Further, integrating material from therapies such as music therapy into the team's thinking and planning may be challenging as it deals with 'not knowing' but exploring and formulating hypotheses about someone's internal world. The lack of easily quantifiable, measurable outcomes may be difficult for a team that becomes anxious about straying from the pragmatic and concrete, partly due to institutional pressures of *having* to quantify aspects of risk, need and care. There may be an unacknowledged wish for this 'not knowing' to be eradicated and, in the minds of team members and patients, the music therapist may become a music teacher or occupational therapist, which may feel more 'knowable' or accessible to them.

Intense working conditions such as in-patient mental health settings can also activate splits within teams whereby those who work with patients within time-boundaried sessions, such as therapy staff, may be viewed as not having to manage ongoing difficult situations on the ward whilst being able to offer something 'special' to patients, for which they may be envied.

In her seminal studies, Menzies-Lyth discussed the systems of defences unavoidably built up in institutions as a way of managing the anxieties of working with severe illness (1988). Clearly, therapists are not immune to such processes. Supervision and personal reflective work are essential to recognise, contain and understand anxieties and minimise any negative impact.

Within team settings and collaborative working professional identity is very important and concerns about role-blurring are a real and current issue, as highlighted in the following clinical examples. However, difficulties can arise when team members develop their allegiance strongly and rather exclusively with their own professions where they may more readily find a shared language and understanding. For our profession, this can happen particularly when music therapists are physically located in discipline-specific (or arts therapies) departments where they may spend the majority of their non-clinical time. Although there are important benefits to these departmental structures, there is a risk of professional 'protectionism' (Jeffcote and Travers 2004, p.21) which needs to be counter-balanced by developing the links with other multidisciplinary team members. Conversely, difficult dynamics (e.g. competitiveness) inevitably exist *within* such departments too.

The previous section has outlined some of the issues and defences that are part of the complex task of developing collaborative working. It has further highlighted themes relating to team dynamics and to the unconscious life of multidisciplinary teams arising from the difficulties experienced by the client group. These issues include developing the role, being understood and valued, finding a language to communicate within a setting of divergent models, managing unconscious envy/rivalry and powerful projections and splitting. We can see that there are a number of ways in which collaborative efforts may be undermined if there is insufficient opportunity for acknowledging and working with difficulties.

The following section offers examples of different approaches to working with these challenges to integrate the work of distinct disciplines. These examples cover a range of settings and represent different levels of integration:

1.   working to shared aims within team work

2.   co-working music therapy with other disciplines

3.   integrating two different disciplines.

Perhaps one of the most effective ways of fostering mutual understanding and successful team working is through co-working or close collaboration. The following examples explore this process.

CASE STUDIES

All names and identifying details have been changed within clinical vignettes in order to maintain confidentiality.

In this first case study, Paula Hedderly discusses the potential for a defensive cohesion or fragmentation within a team, mirroring clients' difficulties with separating out and managing difference. For the music therapist, this brings with it a need for, and attempts to define, a clear identity and role. At the same time, the example shows how vital it is for staff teams to work together to manage and understand powerful emotional material arising from the work and to prevent team relationships from enacting destructive splits. This attention to team functioning is a key part of the task and enables staff to work towards offering a coherent, interdependent and ultimately helpful service.

A TEAM APPROACH: THE REWARDS AND CHALLENGES OF COLLABORATIVE WORKING WITHIN A PERSONALITY DISORDER TREATMENT SERVICE

Paula Hedderly (Music Therapist)

It has been recognised that in groups 'the forces of cohesion can act as resistances to differentiation and development' (Pines 2000, p.54). Pines juxtaposes this view with the dictionary definition of coherence as connoting 'an integrity which makes the whole and the relationship of its parts clear and manifest' (p.54). His assertion that this concept is key in the evolution of effective group development will underpin the following discussion of a multidisciplinary team approach.

Introduction

THE SETTING

I work as a music therapist at an NHS day hospital three days a week, which as a main part of its service provides an intensive psychoanalytically informed group treatment programme (lasting approximately 18 months) predominantly for people with a diagnosis of borderline personality disorder. Patients frequently have secondary diagnoses, such as an eating disorder or obsessive-compulsive disorder. Commonly, people who attend the outpatient programme have a history of abuse, trauma and emotional disturbance, usually as a result of early and severe attachment difficulties, which have had an enduring impact in later development. Much of this distress is communicated through self-harm and suicidal behaviour, substance misuse and in their unstable relationships with others. Clients can experience extreme emotions and shifts in mood, which at times feel impossible to regulate, leading to an expelling of feelings through impulsive and destructive acts.

CLINICAL THINKING ON BORDERLINE PERSONALITY DISORDER

People with borderline personality disorder experience significant deficits in their ego development, which severely impact on their sense of self and other, subsequently impinging on their relationships with others. Bateman and Holmes summarise Kernberg's definition of borderline personality disorder as: 'ego weakness'; a diminished 'capacity for reality testing'; and 'the use of "primitive" defence mechanisms' – especially 'splitting and projective identification' – as a way of separating off and 'coping' with unbearable feeling states (1995, p.224). There exists a 'mental environment where ideas are too terrifying to think about and feelings too intense to experience' (Fonagy *et al.* 2004, p.373), which Bateman and Fonagy describe as a failure to mentalise, or 'think about oneself in relation to others and to understand others' state of mind' (1999, p.1565).

GROUP WORK

The group as a catalyst for change as well as regressive functioning is well documented. Pines (2000) compares defensive ways of functioning in groups which create a false sense of unity or cohesiveness, with group processes which involve individuals coming together to develop an authentic voice where similarities and differences can be shared, contributing to the group's 'coherent' identity. The multi-relational aspect of group work is a particular difficulty to this client group and yet offers the potential for exploring often fixed and destructive ways of relating.

I wish to illustrate the ways in which collaborative working within the multidisciplinary team serves to retain the staff's psychic space, so necessary and beneficial to working with processes of splitting which frequently emerge when engaging therapeutically with these clients, and how this specific team approach has impacted on me as a music therapist.

The therapeutic framework

At the day hospital special emphasis is given to the programme's therapeutic framework, influenced by Bateman and Fonagy's research (1999) on their work with people with personality disorders. They asserted that an effective treatment programme for this client group should involve an intense combination of group and individual psychotherapy approaches, which foremost adopts a 'theoretically coherent treatment approach' (p.1568).

Part of this coherent approach is the collaboration between members of the multidisciplinary team at every stage of an individual's care. As a music therapist I regularly feed back to the team the ongoing music therapy work with patients. The diversity of the staff team (music therapists, art psychotherapists, occupational therapists, psychiatrists, mental health nurses/practitioners, technical instructors) allows for a varied group programme, so as to meet individuals' complex needs, and a major part of the joint working involves bringing together the different clinical disciplines that each of us holds.

To facilitate this there exists an intense series of supervision and feedback meetings, and a weekly staff support group, which daily requires an exchanging of clinical ideas, experiences and feelings in a shared space. Zulueta (1997) cautions against acting out in the face of powerful provocations from the patient, so as not to reflect back disturbing experiences in an undigested and harmful form. At the day hospital there is an understanding of the team's alpha-function (Bion 1962), whereby clients' communications can be thought about reflectively and contained. An emphasis on the whole team sharing material and holding each patient in mind is vital as the potential for individual clinicians to feel overwhelmed is very real.

Within the team, individual workers may hold different, even contrasting, experiences of a patient. At times a patient's suicidal thoughts may create a sense of alarm within staff, resulting in an urgent wish to rescue the patient through hospital admission. Other staff may connect to the more resilient part of the client, understanding the urgency as a need to manage the unbearable distress through a sense of doing rather than thinking. In these situations much processing within the team may need to happen so that these differences do not lead individual staff to feel split in their thinking. Rather these alternate responses in the team are vital to understanding the vulnerabilities and capabilities of the client, both of which get powerfully projected into the team. Care coordination duties take place on-site to further draw the patient's treatment under one roof so as to minimise the conflicting approaches that can develop when numerous services are engaged.

Clinical vignette: an illustration

This example is not a specific case study, rather it is based on real themes which have emerged in the clinical work.

In my work with a patient, music therapy offered her the valuable experience of being able to express emotions in a physical and creative way, through musical improvisation. She herself acknowledged finding meaning in the way she could picture her feelings by observing the contact she made with an instrument, and consequently by being able to play around with the shape and intensity of her feelings through her changing musical sounds. In the talking groups this patient could be experienced as paralysing, as she spoke in long, confusing sentences, leaving little or no space for others to respond. Staff and patients struggled to challenge and engage with her, especially as she rapidly shifted into states of high emotional arousal and had a history of impulsive behaviour. There was often a sense of hopelessness and resignation in the clinical work.

Through the team meetings it was possible to communicate how the weekly group music making allowed myself and other group members not to be silenced and provided opportunities with which to tolerably interrupt her and join in with her musically. In my music I was able to imitate small passages of the client's playing, which I then explored, for example, by repeating the phrases at various pitches, supported with changing harmonic accompaniment. This development of the client's musical ideas allowed me to emphasise and differentiate particular aspects of her playing, helping to structure the frequently continuous and meandering music. In response, shape and organisation in the client's own music emerged as she began to include pauses and space in her playing. Brief moments occurred when we could share a silence or play along together at the same pulse.

By connecting up these good and bad experiences within the whole team we were able to hold in mind the paralysis and intimidation aroused when working with this patient's difficulties, as well as the potential for safely interacting in a meaningful and creative dialogue. Gradually this patient became more known and understandable, as staff and patients felt more confident to clarify what she was saying and to alert her to her role in the groups.

Dependency and autonomy in team working

As is characteristic of therapeutic communities (McGauley 1997), the collaborative owning by the team of patients' care extends to a joint responsibility for the whole programme, with each member of the team also holding generic responsibilities. Currently my clinical responsibilities are more diverse than is common in music therapy practice, which has implications for my identity as a music therapist. In addition to providing a music therapy service, I co-facilitate a large verbal psychodynamic group and undertake generic assessments and care coordination duties. These other tasks have afforded me added insight into patients' treatment, while renewing my awareness of the qualities unique to music therapy. Sometimes patients unfamiliar with music therapy might begin the treatment alliance in the verbal psychodynamic group before feeling able to engage in music therapy and vice versa. Within groups and assessments there is an emphasis on joint working so that feelings of countertransference can be experienced and thought about from various positions to prevent ideas and feelings becoming rigid or polarised, as is often the internal map of the borderline patient.

But what are some of the inherent difficulties in collaborative working, particularly with this client group? Does such close working intensify fears of merging identity and a dependence on the structure? Nitsun writes that 'the demands of group existence themselves arouse considerable anxiety and potential for regression' (2003, p.106). He links this, in particular, to fears about the loss of identity. While these anxieties are pronounced in patients for whom difference and a sense of other feels disorientating and frightening, there must exist related fears in staff, particularly within a team which emphasises partnered over lone working and where there is a frequent overlapping of generic duties.

As a music therapist I have needed to reflect on my own feelings of loss associated, paradoxically, with my broadening role. Historically, there has been a need for music therapists and other arts therapists to maintain clear boundaries around our practice in order to establish and preserve the value and authenticity of our clinical work. There were concerns for me as to whether generic responsibilities would blur, or even diminish, my identity as a music therapist. Brown (2000) states that it is the 'capacity for empathic sensitivity that increases our relatedness to others, through both identification and differentiation' (p.83). On reflection these concerns were in part an attempt to highlight and differentiate the particular skills and training I brought to my position, whilst I engaged in the opportunity to develop new skills within other areas of patients' treatment.

Group processes – conclusion

According to the phases of group development (Agazarian and Peters 1995), groups operate several modes of functioning – flight, fight, authority struggle, symbiosis and separation – before true interdependent working is reached. A maturity towards interdependency is a challenge to a team working with people with personality disorder, for whom a sense of 'self and other' is exceedingly fragile. Within collaborative working there is the potential for a rich and creative dialogue to exist between staff, which can sensitively inform and integrate the therapeutic work with clients. Supervision and staff support forums are central to assisting the team with this playing of ideas, where alternative perspectives can be exchanged and processes such as splitting and merging can be observed and reflected upon, in order that a coherent approach can be developed.

In the next case study, Ann Sloboda highlights the benefits of an integrated team in which a range of therapeutic input is wanted and valued. This facilitates a fruitful collaboration with ward staff whose distinct role and skills add much to the co-working.

CO-WORKING MUSIC THERAPY WITH OTHER DISCIPLINES: CO-WORKING A MUSIC THERAPY GROUP WITH NURSING STAFF

Ann Sloboda (Music Therapist)

Introduction

As mentioned earlier in this chapter, it is important for music therapists to establish and maintain a clear professional identity and role, but a delicate balance needs to be maintained between this activity and that of forging links with other professionals. As a relatively new profession, music therapists are vulnerable to anxieties (described by Obholzer and Zagier Roberts 1994) about both actual survival in the external environment and psychological survival.

This case study describes a part-time music therapist setting up a new service in a small psychiatric unit. The clinical material is in fact my own work from the early 1990s, but I have used the third person as some of 'Alison's' experiences also reflect those of several music therapists I have supervised in more recent years. I worked with two male co-therapists during my time there and 'Steven' is a composite of both.

It is probably significant that in the following clinical example the music therapist had a very small post within the service. The only possible base for therapists there was the ward itself, maximising the possible contact with other staff, particularly nurses.

Setting up the group

Alison began working as a music therapist in a newly established post for one day a week in a small 16-bedded psychiatric unit. A dramatherapist and an art therapist were also employed for a day each, on different days of the week. The job description for each discipline included co-working a group with a member of nursing staff. The nursing team had discussed the introduction and integration of the arts therapies to their service and several people volunteered to be involved. Steven, a qualified and experienced nurse, was particularly interested in co-leading the music therapy group. He was introduced to Alison shortly after she started working there and they planned the group together.

This joint involvement in the planning was a critical factor in the sense of shared ownership and successful co-working. In many larger establishments such a commitment to involving nursing staff in therapy work is often stated as an aim but proves difficult in reality. In this case it was possible due to a ward manager who held this activity in mind as a priority and arranged staff shifts so that the co-leaders could be consistently available on the day of their group. In a larger unit with more conflicting priorities this would be likely to be more difficult.

Alison's previous experience of co-working with other disciplines had been difficult. She had felt anxious, under scrutiny and criticised by nursing colleagues. The freely improvised basis for the music played in the group had been criticised by her previous co-worker, who had wanted the music therapy group to be more performance-based. Although in this setting there appeared to be a strong belief that arts therapies would be helpful, she approached the initial sessions of the group with trepidation. However, she found that Steven was able to offer thoughtful and reflective support.

The unit was too small to have a separate therapy room, so the music therapy group took place in the lounge. Steven participated in all the practical aspects of running the group, including carrying instruments from the cupboard where they were kept to the lounge, and writing up notes afterwards.

Most importantly, Steven supported the process of the music therapy group in:

- identifying patients who might benefit from the music therapy group
- encouraging patients to attend regularly
- providing feedback in ward rounds (which Alison was unable to attend) on how patients used the group.

This communicative link was vital in ensuring that the patients' experience in the music therapy group was spoken about to the wider team and its presence highlighted.

The patients suffered from a range of affective disorders, many suffering from severe depressive illness (including post-natal depression as the unit had some mother-and-baby beds), and others with bipolar disorder. Many had led successfully functioning professional and personal lives. There was a sense that their illness had struck them down, leaving them crippled and defenceless. In the personal account of his depressive illness, *Darkness Visible* (1991), the writer William Styron actually cites the experience of being moved by music as the catalyst that turned him towards recovery. The question of why arts therapists were wanted in a unit staffed by experienced nurses, psychiatrists and psychologists was never fully articulated, beyond the belief that creative activity was important, but the value of it seemed to be understood at an implicit level by the staff.

Much of the psychological work done in the unit was on a cognitive level, but there was concern that some people participated in this, whilst avoiding emotional engagement. This linked with Winnicott's idea that, when work is done through intellectualised material, 'this work needs to be repeated in another form with feeling in it' (Winnicott 1988, p.89). Although this was written in the context of psychoanalytic work, it nevertheless rings true in this context. It seems to capture something of the wish to employ the arts therapies in the hope that they could provide a medium in which patients could make some link with their emotions.

Sessions took place weekly. In principle, anyone on the ward was eligible to attend. In practice a regular core developed, but new patients on the ward often tried it out – some didn't return, others returned and attended regularly. The group therefore had both old and new members. Alison and Steven could never be sure who would be present at any one session. This reflected the structure of the unit where in-patients often became day patients prior to discharge. Some patients were discharged and then re-admitted due to a relapse.

It was agreed that Alison would lead the musical activity and take responsibility for devising musical structures, whilst Steven could be more free to respond and participate in the improvisation. The group did not have a plan as it was important to allow whatever patients brought to the group to influence what happened. Alison began to develop an approach in response to the fluctuating population of the unit and the paralysing anxiety felt by many members. She encouraged patients to make use of the musical medium by employing structures designed to minimise anxiety. These helped to ease people into the process of improvisation. Clear structures where one instrument was passed around or where everyone chose an instrument and played with their eyes closed (thus feeling less exposed) were successful in getting people started. It was important that Alison shared her ideas for potential musical structures prior to the group, so that Steven had some idea of what might happen and could support the group by taking part. He could also give feedback to Alison as to what he felt had worked well and whether the patients had been able to understand and respond. His particular relationship with patients as a primary nurse was an acknowledged element in the group dynamic. Steven made the comment that the non-verbal medium, coupled with the fact that he was free of the responsibility of leading the session, allowed him to interact with some patients in a refreshingly creative way.

Clinical vignette 1   In a session in which members took turns to drum in pairs, Steven was paired with Dennis, a man in his early 60s suffering from severe depression. Dennis' drumming was rigid and regular, with a persistent crotchet beat and a low, heavy quality. Steven found himself responding instinctively with quaver, dotted rhythmic syncopations. Dennis' volume and tempo increased in response to this. In the discussion afterwards, Dennis said, 'You were pushing me!' Steven spoke of his wish to encourage Dennis to be more positive and, in discussion with Alison after the group, was able to talk about his countertransference of enormous frustration and anger in his one-to-one nursing sessions with Dennis, and of his wish to shake him. He felt that in some ways he had been doing this in the improvisation and that Dennis had been able to recognise it but respond positively.

A prominent theme in all the sessions was that of the inability to function: feelings of uselessness and a lack of confidence. Many patients' sense of identity and potency was severely shaken by their need to be in hospital at that time. This co-existed with a sense of relief that they were being looked after and were safe.

Clinical vignette 2   Six patients attended the first session: four women and two men. All sat anxiously in a circle as instructed. Pat, Dennis and Beth all stated that they couldn't play anything. The other three were silent. No one responded to the suggestion that they might like to try any of the instruments. Alison picked up a wooden slit drum and played a short rhythmic pattern, introducing herself, then passed it around the circle. Everyone played it briefly, Pat commenting that she had never seen this instrument before, and asked what it was called. Alison then suggested that members should try out some instruments and choose one they liked. An improvisation ensued in which half the group played rhythmic instruments, and the other half played pitched or melodic instruments. The rhythmic group provided a constant basis for the others to move on top of, whilst the melodic group served to give the rhythmic group an accompanying role. Alison joined the melodic group on a xylophone, whilst Steven provided a steady rhythm on a bongo drum.

Dennis put down his own drum and said, 'It's a shame none of us can play music: perhaps we'd better all shut up and listen to Alison – she's the only one here with training. The rest of us might as well give up.'

Steven responded by saying, 'The way I see it is that playing music is just what we have been doing.'

Beth said that actually she had been pleasantly surprised that it sounded OK.

Reflection on the collaboration

Jeremy Holmes (2002) describes how depression severs the connection between the sufferer and others, or to life itself, 'depression is dark, lonely and disconnected' (p.9), and refers to an envious attack on connectedness that can also take place. This moment in the group seemed to be an example of this, and Alison's immediate countertransference feelings were of uselessness. Steven was able to point out the connection that he had experienced between the group members which enabled her to think 'in role' again. Alison felt great relief that Steven was sharing the responsibility of defending the musical activity. As Holmes (2002, p.60) writes, 'it is all too easy to become sucked into the inner world of the depressive, in which the capacity to think, and so rise above pain, has been abandoned'. Steven's realistic perspective that despite the group members' lack of skill music could still be made helped Alison to maintain a thinking, therapeutic stance. She was then able to point out that half the group had been playing melodies whilst the others had supported them with rhythms – everyone had made a valid contribution.

Steven's nursing role gave his relationship with the patients a particular quality, which was distinct from Alison's. He frequently took the role of modelling how someone without musical training might engage in free improvisation. He was able to provide a containing function; sometimes this took the form of encouraging patients to play, challenging their sense of extreme hopelessness or demonstrating musical play in which he was energetic and lively in his self-expression.

The co-working relationship was a vital component in enabling music therapy to be an integral part of the ward treatment programme. This was particularly necessary given the very part-time nature of this post, all too common in music therapy employment. In these cases, the process of establishing a role and place for music therapy is particularly challenging.

The final example describes a collaboration between a music therapist and a dramatherapist as a response to a situation where creative engagement and making links can be subject to attack. Difficulties with linking the two modalities are overcome by the two therapists learning more about each other's approaches, building on common ground in terms of theoretical stance and thinking together at length. A non-judgemental response to each other's engagement with both media and a shared interest in group members' communications through their free use of the setting allows a creative space to open up for the therapists and consequently for the patients.

INTEGRATING TWO DIFFERENT DISCIPLINES: A MUSIC AND DRAMATHERAPY GROUP

Claire Miller (Music Therapist) and Mario Guarnieri (Dramatherapist)

This example describes the experience of a music therapist and a dramatherapist co-working a group using both modalities.

We will outline our rationale for this transdisciplinary initiative and our process of developing an approach that patients could find useful. We will then summarise our own experiences of this collaboration, highlighting the challenges and advantages.

Rationale

Our starting point for this description is the client group as we found that we shaped our approach and integrated the two disciplines in a way that responded to group members' needs.

The work took place on a secure ward within a forensic psychiatric service. Patients in the hospital have been diagnosed with mental illness and/or personality disorder. The requirement for security is due to patients either having a formal criminal conviction or being deemed to be a severe risk to others or themselves. In this setting all therapy groups are co-facilitated.

The group was part of a service to a rehabilitation ward for longer-stay patients. Most of the people on the ward have a diagnosis of schizophrenia and a history of non-engagement with a therapy programme despite access to interventions structured around individual needs and goals. Any engagement that does take place can be short-lived or inconsistent. Patients can be very isolated, finding it difficult to tolerate contact with others.

As therapists we both have in common an interest in understanding psychoses from a psychoanalytic perspective, in particular in terms of the primitive destructive impulses that can be a central aspect of psychotic functioning (Klein 1997). We have often experienced how any links the patient may make (with others, with their own internal world or in the form of coherent thoughts), and links the therapist makes with the patient, can be subject to destructive attacks (Bion 1967).

Patients may be extremely dependent on hospital care, although often are strongly defended against consciously acknowledging their degree of need. It can also seem as if the reality of 'life outside' has been lost to the imagination. Progress and the prospect of discharge (e.g. to a community supported hostel) can often precipitate a deterioration in mental state or a sabotaging of the plans. Inherent to this type of psychic functioning is an attack on resources and creativity. This may be evidenced by patients remaining in bed, having a bath, having a cigarette or using leave (i.e. going out) at the time of therapy sessions. Often, the offer of a creative space cannot readily be taken up. This prevailing psychic picture can leave the multidisciplinary team struggling with feelings of hopelessness: endurance is required from staff left with the task of holding the hope.

In planning our group we recognised the potential for feeling deskilled and resourceless, as is the experience of many of the people on this ward. We responded with efforts to keep our capacity for thinking and being creative intact. This included holding onto our own respective media and professional identities. We felt this would also foster an equal sense of ownership and expand the resources on offer. Thus, we decided to run a group that offered both our modalities rather than one.

We would like here to outline how we developed our collaboration by describing our experiences of the group in its early stages and how our approach then evolved in response. We will go on to give examples of how the sessions came to be used.

Developing an approach

The group aimed to help the most isolated patients begin to develop some contact with others. Patients were referred and there was a slow-open structure of membership. Numbers of attendees were often low and group composition was inconsistent. However, the patients who declined appeared to value our weekly presence on the ward and being asked to attend.

Sessions took place in a large designated dramatherapy room. There was a circle of chairs in the centre and musical instruments were set up in one corner. Dramatherapy objects such as miniature models of animals and people, hats, puppets and fabrics were arranged on shelves along one side of the room. Initially we aimed to introduce some music or dramatherapy structures to frame the session and also allow for undirected, patient-led time.

Clinical vignette 1   Group members come in and there is an invitation to sit together in the circle to begin the group. Some people, however, go straight to the instruments and choose one and some sit on the outskirts of the room, not in the circle. People start playing disparate, unconnected sounds. Shirley starts to talk to the music therapist whilst Margaret begins to bang the drum loudly with a smaller percussion instrument. Others seem to be accepting of this – for example, Stuart continues strumming the guitar quietly in the middle of it all, as if alone. Similarly, Shirley sustains her conversation with the therapist in competition with all the sound around. This music and talking continues for some time despite both therapists' suggestions offering some structure and ideas for bringing things together.

As can be seen by this vignette, during the initial sessions the music often expressed a sense of the fragmented experience of the people in the group. There was usually little or no verbal communication between group members. Talking only took place between patients and therapists or when therapists offered an interpretation or a lead with a structure. By playing loudly over them or simply ignoring them, the group communicated that these interventions and elements of direction, albeit very open ones, could not be used. For instance, invitations to pass an instrument around the group or dramatherapy processes such as the use of story in which a simple narrative is enacted could not be developed.

The majority of the time group members chose to use the musical instruments, mostly expressing their own ideas or physicality. Just occasionally a rhythm would emerge that people were able to take in and develop into shared play. Thus, there were transitory moments of contact in the music.

Reflection on the group process

Time to talk after each session and shared supervision were central to our process. After the early groups we discussed our approach and thought about how we could facilitate increased access to the drama, thereby integrating both mediums into the session more fully.

We thought about the different modalities of music and drama from a developmental perspective and felt that the group members' gravitation towards free musical expression and their difficulties with managing structure or more symbolic dramatic play was a communication about their needs. What felt important was recognising that patients were emotionally at a developmental stage where they needed to be 'held'. The group members' early histories confirmed that their experiences were of a lack of a 'good enough' 'facilitating environment', 'holding' (Winnicott 1965, 1971) or 'containing' (Bion 1962). We found ourselves returning to these concepts and Bion's formulations about the quality of 'maternal reverie', which increasingly came to represent a useful framework for our approach.

The concept of play became more central in our thoughts as a term that could link the music, the drama and the space. Goals and expectations could be suspended in the offering of a 'play space' in which group members' actions could be noticed, valued, digested and fed back. Music therapist Stewart talks of a therapeutic stance when working with a client group with similar needs. Amongst other things he highlights the importance of a 'soothing, benign presence', the 'availability and resilience of the therapist' and verbalising the 'what' of the group's experience a long time before the 'why' (1996, p.25). We developed a non-directive approach based on similar concepts which found a rhythm and flow of its own. We both took a watchful, reflective role, both using the music and observational comments to acknowledge and 'hold' individuals' contributions. The space and opportunity for play allowed us to witness and facilitate some liveliness and contact within the group.

Clinical vignette 2   Shirley comes in hungrily munching a large apple, in a way that seems to express something of her neediness. She uses the free space to talk, wishing to draw the female therapist's attention away from the group as a whole and into comparisons of clothes and jewellery. Ray finds it difficult to focus and talks excitedly over others' music/comments.

Shirley falls into a rather distant silence for several minutes then suddenly gets up to begin drumming – beating loudly in her own time and singing forcefully, disregarding others' input. She then apologises, fearing that she has been overwhelming for others, and returns to sitting non-participatively.

Ray is drawn to the dramatherapy objects. He speaks in an over-awed way about the costliness of the models, which he vastly inflates. This seems to represent a world of riches, which can serve as a manic defence against experiencing a sense of an impoverished personal world. Then, however, he likens himself to a model of an elderly woman with a walking frame. He quickly moves on to don a black hat and becomes a singing showman with a rendition of 'When You're Smiling'. Whilst he laughs and jokes, the experience is a poignant and painful one for us with whom he has deposited a sense of unease and disorientation through his earlier pressured monologue. We acknowledge Ray's rapid shifts through different ideas and states, attempting to hold onto and digest some of the material that has seemed unmanageable to him.

Later, Shirley talks about her loud drumming. She seems to us to be anxious about her aggressive feelings and about her difficulties with relationships. Shirley responds to our reflections about her worries, seeming a little relieved, and begins to make links between her actions and her underlying feelings. She then abruptly 'kills them off' by asserting her tiredness and a wish to leave the session. With encouragement she stays, picks up the guitar and sings a gospel tune.

Reflection on the group process
The vignettes aim to show how we developed a joint approach within the sessions which allowed the patients to use the space freely. The mediums of music and drama were available for use but a structure or agenda was not set; instead we used our shared theoretical approach to offer a potential space for play.

The examples reflect that we were working with a disparate set of people who were not able to come together as a 'group'. We needed to tolerate the anxiety and chaotic feelings that were engendered in us due to a lack of unifying structures or focus and not being able to use our mediums in our usual ways. We were able to do this due to our shared theoretical understanding that allowed us to essentially offer a space, observe and think. It seemed that this was more significant than sharing a discipline and we ended up developing an approach where the two mediums could be brought together in a way that didn't feel forced. Although the emphasis was mostly on the music as this was where the patients usually led us, the availability of the dramatherapy enriched the material significantly.

Conclusion: reflection on the collaborative process

We began this collaboration as a response to the very real difficulties patients had with making links with others and engaging in creative processes. In order to engage patients helpfully we felt we needed to find ways of managing countertransference feelings of hopelessness and resourcelessness. The process involved us exploring our own difficulties with linking up or integrating: this meant being prepared to be flexible, not being wedded to ways of working and not being precious or protective about our mediums. This was particularly true for the dramatherapist whose usual model involved more of an active directive element. We alleviated anxieties about having to impress each other or feeling competitive or judged early on through discussion, and tried to harness and support the curiosity we each felt about the other's medium. Our joint working brought energy, as it left neither one of us carrying the lead role. Our regular discussions, our shared theoretical language and the very open approach we evolved facilitated a space for our minds which mitigated against feelings of fragmentation or disconnection and fostered a creative experience of working together.

We hope that despite the group members' difficulties with sharing much contact the group provided a space where people could tolerate being together – something that they rarely did. Their engagement in the group gave us valuable opportunities to assess needs and think about each person's internal world.

CONCLUDING THOUGHTS

The authors of the case studies amplify points made earlier in the chapter about the value and challenges of collaborative and transdisciplinary working. They provide examples of the intricate web of conscious and unconscious dynamics within collaborations and the ways in which these may reflect the internal experiences of the client group. They demonstrate how building links across professional boundaries and fostering reflective connections between disciplines can open up creative spaces. Within this, differences can bring greater understanding.

All authors highlight the importance of good communication, shared ownership and joint thinking in order to provide services that are integrated and effective. Such practice can be seen to provide fertile ground and rich experiences.

Through these examples, the value of developing mutual understanding and respect across the different disciplines becomes apparent. Shared forums and collaborations can enable preconceptions and fantasies about each other's roles to be explored, diminish opportunities for splitting and allow common understandings of service users' needs and treatment aims to be developed.

GUIDELINES FOR GOOD PRACTICE

- Place service users' needs at the centre of collaborative initiatives.

- Develop opportunities and a language for communicating about your discipline to the wider team and service users.

- Participate in regular contact with the multidisciplinary team or co-workers and in developing shared goals.

- Participate in supportive/reflective opportunities to share experiences of or anxieties about the joint/collaborative working.

- There is value in a sense of belonging (for example, to a profession, team, co-working pair). Consider how to manage divided loyalties.

- There are creative possibilities in a flexible approach.

- Supervision and reflection are indispensable. An under-standing of psychodynamic principles is one way of reflecting on work: an alertness to the unconscious com-munications within mental healthcare settings can bring good use of team dynamics and help minimise any negative impact of defences.

- Develop opportunities for enhancing shared responsibility and ownership of collaborative endeavours.

- Explore the benefits of the differences/distinct roles offered by colleagues and co-workers within collaborative working. Acknowledge the different boundaries and the scope of distinct roles.

- Explore opportunities for learning about other disciplines.

NOTE

1 At the time of writing new ways of working and different models of practice are being developed (e.g. DoH 2005a).

Chapter 4

Team Working to Meet Complex Needs in Adults with Acquired Neurological Conditions

Wendy L. Magee

OUTLINE OF CLIENT GROUP

'Neuro-disability' is an umbrella term for a wide range of disabilities stemming from long-term neurological conditions which cause damage to the brain and nervous system. The predominant focus of this chapter is work with adults who have neuro-disability stemming from acquired conditions. Categories of the most common diagnoses a music therapist might come across when working with people with neuro-disabilities are listed below.

Sudden onset conditions

- Traumatic brain injury
- Anoxic brain damage caused by heart attacks, respiratory failure or anaesthetic accidents
- Stroke
- Subarachnoid haemorrhage
- Brain damage stemming from infection (e.g. encephalitis)
- Toxic brain damage (drugs, liver or renal failure)
- Vascular damage
- Guillain Barré Syndrome
- Locked-in Syndrome.

Progressive or degenerative conditions

- Multiple Sclerosis
- Huntington's Disease
- Motor Neurone Disease
- Parkinson's Disease
- Brain tumour
- Creutzfeldt-Jakob Disease and New Variant CJD.

Some of these conditions have a sudden onset, such as stroke, traumatic brain injury or Locked-in Syndrome, and after the initial onset of the condition the person's health and functioning may remain relatively static for many years. Other conditions are progressive, such as Parkinson's Disease, Huntington's Disease and Multiple Sclerosis. A person with one of these conditions is most likely to experience degenerative changes over time, which can sometimes be many years. The length of time someone lives with a neurological condition varies widely between conditions. For example, the average time between diagnosis and death for someone with Motor Neurone Disease is only 14 months, whereas someone with Multiple Sclerosis may live for many decades after diagnosis (DoH 2005b). All of the conditions listed above result in different symptoms; however, most neuro-disabilities affect motor, communication and cognitive abilities. All of them result in profound changes to many aspects of the individual's life, and therefore the social and emotional consequences are highly significant.

Without a doubt, one of the most challenging symptoms of neuro-disability for the music therapist is the range of movement disorders with which people present to differing degrees of severity, depending on which parts of the brain have been damaged. In some cases, such as with Motor Neurone Disease, Huntington's Disease, Multiple Sclerosis and Locked-in Syndrome, movement disorders can render the person completely dependent for all personal activities of daily living and managing their environment in any way. The consequences for people living with Huntington's Disease are most usually the large, uncontrolled 'choreic' movements involving the arms, legs, fingers, trunk, neck, head and face. Sometimes the disease results in movements which are slow and rigid. Both types of movement disorders make it difficult for the person to control their movements and engage in activities. People living with conditions such as Motor Neurone Disease and

Multiple Sclerosis experience problems such as weakness and extreme fatigue which can affect their physical participation. Muscle spasms causing pain are common for people with Multiple Sclerosis and after traumatic brain injury and stroke. Ataxia, which can affect people with Multiple Sclerosis or traumatic brain injury, is a movement disorder resulting in a lack of coordination while performing voluntary movements. Paralysis in one, two, three or all limbs is common for people with traumatic brain injury and stroke. In some conditions such as Locked-in Syndrome, active purposeful movement can be reduced to upward eye movements only. No matter what the types of physical problems the therapist meets in their client with neuro-disability, it will be frustrating for the client and greatly challenging for the music therapist. Finding instruments which are appropriate, safe, aesthetically pleasing and also responsive is no easy task. Therapists working with clients with such severe problems have described great ingenuity and creativity in their choice of tools, including calling on more unusual musical tools such as those which incorporate electronic technologies (Lindeck 2005; Millman and Jefferson 2000; Nagler 1998).

Difficulties with motor functioning can affect verbal communication. When people are no longer able to use speech to express their needs and wishes, they will likely have some other means to communicate through the use of augmentative and alternative communication aids. Such devices may be low or high technology. For example, 'listener scanning' is a low technology alternative communication aid. This requires the communication partner to speak the alphabet out loud whilst the client selects letters through eye blinks, spelling out the words of their intended message letter by letter. High technology alternative communication aids usually involve electronic aids and computer software. However, usually the use of alternative communication aids involves dependence on another person to act as a communication partner or setting up the system and enabling the client access.

Many neuro-disabilities result in some degree of cognitive impairment, although individuals with Locked-in Syndrome and Motor Neurone Disease are spared from cognitive changes. Cognitive changes in memory, attention, executive functioning, insight and disinhibition can affect an individual's capacity to take care of themselves, and these cognitive changes can also result in behavioural problems as well (DoH 2005b). Motor and cognitive problems can combine to cause communication disorders, meaning the person might have difficulty producing language or understanding others. Sensory functioning may be affected, in particular vision, hearing and pain sensation. The person with acquired neuro-disability encounters enormous changes in every aspect of their life affecting relationships, career prospects, income and expectations for the future (DoH 2005b). Significant emotional effects include stress, depression and loss of self-image and the individual and their family is affected in one way or another for the rest of their life (DoH 2005b). The emotional impact of acquiring such profound disabilities would seem obvious. However, in the months following acquired conditions, care is likely to focus on making the individual safe and medically stable with emotional needs taking a lower priority in care.

THE TREATMENT TEAM

The members of the treatment team will differ slightly between the different settings in which a music therapist might be working with a person with neuro-disability, depending on whether this is rehabilitation or a continuing care setting. In neuro-rehabilitation settings, the team is likely to include nurses, physiotherapists, occupational therapists, speech and language therapists, psychologists and doctors. Other disciplines who might be involved on the team include social workers, dieticians and wheelchair seating specialists. Whether the team defines itself as multi-, inter- or transdisciplinary depends on the philosophy of the setting and reflects the working practice of the team. Multidisciplinary and interdisciplinary are terms which tend to be used more commonly in neuro-rehabilitation settings. Multidisciplinary indicates that the team members have discrete roles in terms of the treatment they provide and each goal is usually the responsibility of one particular discipline. The boundaries for delivering interventions are clearly defined. In this case, each discipline is likely to set its own particular goals and offer treatment on a unidisciplinary basis. For example, speech and language therapists will prioritise improving the patient's communication and swallowing and set goals around improving lip closure within specific oro-motor activities. Music therapy might also set goals around lip closure and plan singing activities which will encourage this. Although the same goal is being addressed, treatment is not necessarily planned or offered jointly, and the two disciplines will feed back on progress within team meetings. Working in this way is common where part-time employment does not enable opportunities for the team to come together.

Interdisciplinary working suggests that goals are set between team members and treatment is delivered jointly, although particular goals may be assigned as the responsibility of one discipline or one subgroup of the broader team. Taking our existing example, speech and language therapy will highlight that lip closure needs to be improved, and then speech and language therapy and music therapy, as a subgroup, might plan together oro-motor activities within singing and vocalising tasks. The two disciplines then work together to address this goal. Treatment is likely to take place within joint music therapy and speech and language therapy sessions if staffing resources allow. In the situation where it is not possible to undertake all the sessions together, the two disciplines will plan the activities together and liaise regularly about the patient's progress in the different settings. There might be the opportunity for occasional joint sessions with regular discussion in between sessions about the patient's progress. This then allows the goals to be updated and the interventions revised accordingly.

Transdisciplinary working suggests that goals are set as a team, and all disciplines are responsible for delivering intervention which addresses all goals. In our working example, all members of the team will be introducing activities to address lip closure and working together within treatment sessions. For example, physiotherapy and speech and language therapy will come together within hydrotherapy sessions to focus on lip closure; nursing staff and family members might rehearse lip closure activities during social interactions with the patient; and occupational therapy and speech and language therapy might introduce specific activities during feeding and other personal activities of daily living.

WHY IS COLLABORATIVE WORKING IMPORTANT?

Working with people with acquired brain injury from stroke, trauma or illness can be one of the most challenging of clinical areas for music therapists. Because this is a relatively new clinical area for the profession at the current time, there are limited opportunities during training for learning about the theoretical or clinical applications of music therapy with people living with neuro-disability. This is in contrast with our allied health colleagues from other disciplines who include neurology placements as part of their student clinical rotations and core clinical subjects. Joint working therefore offers music therapists a chance to acquire essential skills and knowledge base specific to the clinical area that they may not learn during training. Colleagues may have a greater theoretical understanding of neuro-logical principles and experience working with these types of clients.

However, it is not only the music therapist's existing skill base which is a challenge, as the complex combination of disabilities with which clients can present is a far greater challenge still for all the team. Working to help a client improve in any one area of functioning usually requires addressing other aspects as well. For example, it is difficult to work on any activity unless the client is well positioned physically. Gaining the client's cooperation to work on physical positioning is best achieved if the client is able to communicate with staff. Assessing whether the client is able to communicate requires knowing something about their cognitive functioning. However, a client cannot be given the best chance for cognitive assessment unless they are well positioned. In this way, it can be seen that the client's best chance for getting the treatment most suited to their needs requires seamless, cooperative working from the team.

One more factor promotes the philosophy of team working with this population. Neurological conditions are common in the UK with approxi-mately ten million in the population (DoH 2005b). However, each individ-ual condition is relatively rare. This means that health professionals may work with very few people with a specific condition (e.g. Motor Neurone Disease). Therefore, it is difficult for professionals to become skilled in treating a specific condition as they may treat only one or two people with those specific needs over many years. Thus, working as a team provides opportunities to share the divergent skills, knowledge and experience which individuals can bring together.

The settings in which a music therapist is likely to work with people with acquired neuro-disabilities include both long-term care settings such as nursing home and young disabled units, as well as in neuro-rehabilitation units in hospital settings. The philosophy of care and models used differ in these different settings which is important to understand.

MODELS OF WORKING AND THE IMPACT ON COLLABORATIONS

The aim of rehabilitation is to increase the client's independence as quickly as possible, often providing opportunities only for short-term work which is essentially goal-oriented in focus. These two factors are the greatest challenge for clinicians who use solely psychodynamic models, which is the model emphasised by most music therapy trainings in the UK at the current time of writing. Psychoanalytically informed frameworks do not translate easily into rehabilitation settings as these frameworks lean to longer-term process-oriented work in which feelings of dependence are explored. Although working psychodynamically may not feel a comfortable fit within team working, drawing on such thinking can help to inform the work for the individual therapist as they reflect on their clinical work. However, it is important to understand that others in the team may not understand these principles nor feel that they are important in rehabilitating the client. Jochims discusses the conflict between the two models in greater detail, suggesting that the conflict may be one between 'deficit-oriented approaches' versus 'resource-oriented' approaches, with music therapy identifying with the latter category (Jochims 2004, p.165). She proposes that we need to be flexible enough to switch between 'experience-oriented therapy' and 'exercise-oriented therapy' as the patient's progress requires.

Rehabilitation models may also challenge a clinician's existing understanding on how music therapy can meet a client's needs. Often, music therapists place priority on the emotional needs of a client. Without a doubt, there can be considerable emotional adjustment required when living with acquired neuro-disability. However, assisting with emotional adjustment may not be a priority need for that individual at all times. Going home or getting out of hospital is most usually a person's most pressing aim and the one by which they are most motivated. For people whose only barrier to achieving this is their inability to do a standing transfer from their wheelchair, emotional needs are unlikely to be experienced as a priority. At that time, their greatest motivation will be in improving their standing balance which will enable them to achieve a standing transfer. In such cases, the music therapist might find that planning treatment which will help the client to rehearse physical movements may be more motivating and engaging for the client. Once more, working closely with other team members can provide support for the music therapist in planning and providing appropriate treatment.

Undoubtedly setting goals is one of the most difficult things for a music therapist new to rehabilitation models of working. Many rehabilitation settings require the team to set 'SMART' goals, which are specific, measurable, attainable, relevant and time-related (Maidment and Merry 2002). Once more, colleagues from the rest of the team can assist in learning these skills, particularly when setting collaborative goals.

In order to best meet the client's needs, it is essential that the music therapist is able to work as an integral part of the treatment team. This means being able to communicate to the rest of the team how music therapy is helping the client to reach their goals. If the therapist is not able to communicate in language which the rest of the team can understand, then he or she risks not integrating with team working. This demands particular skills in communicating with others and learning to set goals which are relevant to the client's priority health needs.

People living with chronic conditions are more likely to be living in community residential settings, including their own home, nursing homes or young disabled units. The team is likely to be quite different in these sorts of settings, involving the family or carers, nursing staff and recreational officers or volunteers. There might also be peripheral team members such as an occupational therapist, a physiotherapist or a speech and language therapist. However, staff resources are most likely to be part-time, making the possibility for joint working or even meeting other allied health professionals involved in care to be highly unlikely. This means that the music therapist is at risk of missing information from other perspectives which is relevant to holistic care.

Furthermore, the model of care in such settings is likely to be a social and recreational model rather than a rehabilitation model. Although this can free the therapist from having to work to SMART goals, it can, however, bring other challenges. Music therapy can easily be misunderstood within such models to be music recreation. Family, carers, recreation officers and the clients themselves may have little interest in the therapist's focus on relationship development and process. In these settings it is helpful to gain an understanding from the team (including the client) as to what they are hoping to gain from music therapy at the outset, planning the approach accordingly. Finding a common language to communicate meaningful information about the client's progress applies in this setting as well.

EXAMPLES OF COLLABORATIONS

Music therapy has a particular role in assisting the whole team in work involving complex cases. Claeys *et al.* (1989) provided a landmark description of working with people emerging from coma. In this account, the reader learns that music therapy can work within the team to address reality orientation, exercise routines, communication and in family therapy. A particular role for music therapy as part of collaborative work with this population where diagnosis is complicated has been identified (Magee 2005). This writing offers extensive suggestions of disciplinary groupings that music therapists may team up with to address very specific problems. For example, the use of musical activities carefully planned by the music therapist can provide alternative types of stimulation which enable occupational therapy and psychology to make their assessments of awareness. In reality, when presented with complex cases, the team is trying to piece together the jigsaw of responses with which such patients often present. Kennelly *et al.* (2001) describe joint physiotherapy, occupational therapy, speech and language therapy and music therapy sessions to meet widely varying rehabilitative needs in a complex case. Treatment then progresses towards more focused intervention involving music therapy and speech and language therapy pairing as the patient recovers. Speech and language therapists working with people emerging from coma have also described how music therapy provides a medium to assess the communicative intent of non-verbal vocalisations, which current speech and language therapy assessment tools are not sensitive enough to do (Finlay *et al.* 2001).

One of the most creative descriptions of how music therapy can integrate into functional rehabilitation is provided by Gervin (1991). Her patients with brain injury were unresponsive to traditional occupational therapy dressing techniques due to cognitive problems with initiation, sequencing, neglect and motor planning. However, the combination of music therapy and occupational therapy promoted independence in dressing when prompts were sung within simple song structures. Following this example, Soeterik, Roshier and Quinn (2005) used similar principles in collaborative work with occupational therapy and psychology to improve the ability of one man with neurobehavioural disorders following severe brain damage to brush his teeth. These might sound like minor achievements. However, for individuals fighting to relearn the most basic of personal care routines, such achievements can promote dignity and independence.

Increasingly, when integrated into physical rehabilitation, music therapy is seen to have the potential to address gross and fine motor skills, muscle strengthening, and sitting and standing balance (Paul and Ramsey 2000). Lucia (1987) stresses that 'the role of music therapist crosses departmental boundaries, with adjunctive programming offered interdisciplinarily' with occupational therapy, physiotherapy and speech and language therapy (p.38). Others provide support for this, highlighting that combined goals can improve movement strength, range of motion, balance, communication and cognition (Paul and Ramsey 2000). In particular, these authors suggest that collaborative working between music therapy and occupational therapy can eliminate the obstacles caused by movement disorders to enable a patient access to instruments, as described in this first case study.

This case study discusses some of the issues faced by Rachel Millman, a music therapist working within a multidisciplinary team, in a neuro-rehabilitation setting. It focuses on joint work with Richard Jefferson, an occupational therapist, which incorporates music technology and discusses the setting of joint goals and aims. Some of the benefits and difficulties encountered by this practice are discussed.

MUSIC THERAPY WITHIN THE MULTIDISCIPLINARY TEAM: DIFFERENT APPROACHES – SHARED GOALS

Rachel Millman (Music Therapist)

Music therapy is an established part of the nursing and therapy team on the brain injury rehabilitation ward where this work took place. On admission patients are individually assessed. As part of the assessment, the team establish common goals for each patient according to their particular needs and problems. Goals are set within all aspects of the patient's care as appropriate, and categorised in groups such as nutrition, communication and expression, physical status and activities of daily living. There is often an overlap between some of the multidisciplinary team and music therapy goals. Within this overlap, multidisciplinary team goals relating to communication, cognition or physical status, for example, may be directly or indirectly addressed in music therapy sessions. Observations from sessions and assessment results are discussed at regular goal planning meetings and patient reviews, attended by the whole team.

Liz, the young woman in this case study, was transferred to the hospital approximately one year after sustaining a traumatic brain injury. Her sessions began following an internal transfer once she had moved from the Brain Injury Assessment Unit to the neuro-rehabilitation ward. It was also noted that she had a background as a talented amateur musician.

A primary factor contributing to joint work came from Richard, the occupational therapist, wanting to see whether a different approach, such as using music, would affect Liz's participation. It was felt she had regained some physical and cognitive ability but that her motivation was affecting her general participation. Joint sessions were also felt to be the most appropriate method of working due to Liz's physical status. She was initially unable to access instruments independently and would be dependent on someone to support her physically. It was important to facilitate and reinforce responses that were beneficial to her movement, rather than detrimental, and to monitor any associated reactions leading to possible increase in muscle tone. A joint setting would provide a space for her to practise developing functional skills creatively. This, it was hoped, would lead to her achieving the highest level of control within music therapy and also translate to other areas of her life.

Richard had been working with Liz for several months prior to music therapy which meant he was familiar with her needs and developing abilities. This allowed me to present instruments, and grade activities at a level that ensured success rather than failure. In addition, I initially relied on Richard's understanding of Liz's behavioural responses, for example as to whether they were associative reactions, typical patterns of behaviour or spontaneous or different in any way within the music therapy environment.

The initial aims for joint input on the rehabilitation unit were to investigate whether music would be a motivating factor for the initiation of activity and to encourage functional use of the right upper limb in activity. Longer-term goals would then be to increase opportunities for meaningful, active and creative participation and to facilitate and increase independence of non-verbal expression. In addition, music therapy would offer a creative environment and a musical relationship within which physical changes and gaining abilities could be practised and explored, outside of a functional setting.

Together we aimed to identify suitable instruments for Liz to use spontaneously and as independently as possible and to maximise opportunities for choice-making in order to facilitate control and self-expression, for example by presenting choices relating to mood or tempo of music. We also monitored Liz's use of musical components such as pitch, dynamics and any initiation and imitation of these. From the start Liz was motivated to participate once instruments were positioned. The guitar, wind chimes, computer with music software and a single switch (Midigrid[1]), electric keyboard and later Soundbeam[2] were all trialled. Within the first few sessions Liz would often respond by mouthing 'no' when combinations of these instruments were offered. However, her physical behaviour was contradictory to this and she would move her arm towards the instruments, engage in playing (with support) and smile. Within other therapies she was also communicating by mouthing 'no' – but there she was not participating. Given Liz's limited opportunities for communication and control, this was a very powerful response, and something which could be addressed through the music.

Sessions followed an outlined structure, beginning with an opening activity which was initially a sung greeting. Instruments or sounds were then presented for choice making. A choice was offered in order to facilitate Liz's sense of control. Initially this was a choice of two instruments. However, these choices and options were increased and choices were later offered around the type of activity (turn-taking or playing together) and mood or style for the improvisations. Instrumental activities allowed Liz to explore the impact she could make within a musical environment and explore the potential of chosen instruments.

During the first few months, in order for Liz to be able to access the instruments, it was necessary for Richard, the occupational therapist, to support her right arm at the elbow. He could feel her initiating some movement to explore the instruments. She was therefore responding spontaneously (in contrast to other sessions), attempting to play different strings on the guitar and move her hand to press neighbouring notes on the keyboard. In order to increase her independence and examine her initiation, Midigrid was incorporated into sessions. Liz quickly developed a sense of how to use this and, when it was offered as an activity, she would consistently choose violin sounds. Her responses were intentional, appropriate in relation to the musical stimuli, and of meaning and significance since she had been a string player.

It was possible to introduce a mobile arm support around four months into the sessions which enabled Liz to access instruments without Richard supporting her arm. On experiencing the feedback she could get using this to play the guitar, she was highly motivated to use it. This reduced her reliance on Richard considerably and, as this dependency shifted in one relationship, so our musical relationship also altered. Liz's increasing independence within a musical environment increased the level of her interactive responses with me. It also opened up a new level in musical expression and she began to explore musical dynamics, now within her control. As she became more independent Liz started to explore her increased control. This included playing short phrases, playing whilst instruments were being positioned or after I had stopped playing. In this way Liz was exerting her character and presence. Control was something she could experience within the context of a musical interaction, as well as within a musical environment.

Gaining increased control of movement led to increased interaction, exploration of her environment and empowerment. Within our improvisations

Liz's responses were becoming more spontaneous and varied as her move-ments became more controlled and independent. This meant she was able to play a more equal role musically within improvisations and the joint setting was now providing a forum in which Liz could share her gaining abilities with her occupational therapist observing. For this particular individual an observer aided her motivation. Perhaps this had something to do with her musical background, and her familiarity with performing for others? In addition, Richard being, in his words, a musical 'non-expert' meant there was an inequality in ability and knowledge. Thinking of this in terms of the future is important too. Experiencing a relationship becoming more equal over time is relevant in terms of transferring to new relationships, for example with carers.

Once Liz was more independent within the musical environment, music and sound – initially a means of establishing a connection and encouraging her to explore – became a vehicle for a musical relationship to develop. In these later sessions music therapy stopped being a joint session with occupational therapy, and we started to work on a one-to-one basis. Music was allowing Liz to experience a more able physical self, and also facilitated an emotional experience. She demonstrated different emotional responses in relation to music, such as tearfulness, and sessions also enabled her to experience difficult emotions. When using Soundbeam, she began to develop enhanced control of fine movement, using small, expressive gestures as well as gross motor movement. This led to increased expressive, creative and interactive responses, and to Liz developing unique and varied ways of playing Soundbeam. These are all of significant importance in terms of developing a sense of self and identity and for increasing morale.

In conclusion, working with another discipline really supported the work. Initially, the existing relationship with Richard the occupational therapist enabled me as a music therapist to develop a relationship with Liz, based on ability. It also meant I was free to support musically, rather than physically, whatever Liz brought into the musical environment. Working alongside an occupational therapist also provided valuable insights and understanding around motivational issues. From Richard's observations and involvement he could determine that, within these joint sessions, Liz was approximately two weeks ahead regarding initiation, in contrast to all other activities.

As roles and boundaries were established within the joint work before it started, we as therapists were able to pre-empt any pitfalls. It was important to ensure the musical relationship was not sullied in any way by a joint approach. Richard was careful not to reflect on the music or refer to Liz's progress during their daily one-to-one occupational therapy sessions. We felt it was important that any reflections or reference to the music or instruments were made within the context of the joint sessions in order to respect the musical relationship.

As seen, Liz's independence within musical activities created a shift in Richard's role as occupational therapist. From initially needing to support instruments for her and facilitate her playing by supporting her arm, he became more of a 'prop' or 'guitar stand' (to use his own words!) and eventually became redundant altogether. Throughout the sessions this meant Liz was able to experience a sense of achievement and increasing control – gaining empowerment not only within musical activities, but also within the context of a relationship. As she became more active so Richard was able to become more passive. This led to a more interactive and immediate musical relationship with me and slowly more emotional and expressive needs emerged and could be explored. Liz's music therapy stopped once she was able to be discharged from the hospital but her involvement in music did not. Liz has continued to enjoy and benefit from her musical independence and is actively participating in music workshops run by the Drake Music Project. Her independence is complete – she no longer needs a music therapist or occupational therapist.

MUSIC THERAPY AND SPEECH AND LANGUAGE THERAPY

Of all the clinical areas in neuro-disability, music therapy and speech and language therapy appear to be the most comfortably paired in collaborative working. However, whilst there are many descriptive and research papers now available about speech and language outcomes following music therapy (see www.rhn.org.uk/institute/neurocommunicationdisorders), very few of these have been written collaboratively. It would seem that, whilst music therapists are producing accounts and research of communication outcomes following music therapy, there are fewer accounts offering both disciplines' perspectives. Speech and language therapists have described that working collaboratively with music therapists can help to promote a relaxed atmosphere, social interaction and opportunities for success as well as reducing the monotony of carrying out repetitive exercises when working with people with complex neuro-communication disorders (Crozier and Hamill 1988; Magee *et al.* 2006). Kennelly *et al.* (2001) illustrate the different things that conjoint and unidisciplinary sessions can bring. They suggest that joint sessions can address common communication goals relating to specific speech and language difficulties and non-verbal communication strategies, whilst unidisciplinary sessions can work towards other goals, such as emotional support (music therapy) and language skills (speech and language therapy).

Hobson (2006a) examines collaborations between music therapy and speech and language therapy from a variety of perspectives, outlining that the speech and language therapist's role in collaborative working with people with neurogenic communication disorders is key in assessing the type of communication disorders. Following this, music can be used as a therapeutic tool. In a successive paper, Hobson (2006b) also highlights that the use of different vocabularies may challenge collaborative working. Also, the two disciplines may assess risk differently, resulting in the abandonment of psychosocial goals and further differences. For example, assessing that the patient is at risk of choking due to dysphagia will always take priority by the speech and language therapist over assessing the risks caused by communication difficulties which the music therapist may be working towards. Understanding the different skills and knowledge that each brings can strengthen collaborative working and make it more effective.

In this second case study, Jackie Lindeck and Amy Pundole describe a collaborative group work project between speech and language therapy and music therapy, working with head-injured adults.

EXPRESS YOURSELF!

Jackie Lindeck (Music Therapist) and Amy Pundole (Speech and Language Therapist)

Setting

The therapists work at the Royal Hospital for Neuro-disability (RHN) in Putney, London. This is a national medical charity which provides rehabilitation and care for adults with profound disability resulting from brain injury or neurological illness. The therapists work on one of the brain injury unit wards providing rehabilitation as part of a multidisciplinary team.

The multidisciplinary team on the ward where the therapists work consists of physiotherapy, occupational therapy, speech and language therapy, music therapy, psychology and social work, as well as medical, nursing and dietetics. The Royal Hospital also provides social and recreational services for the patients. The team works closely together to provide a coordinated treatment approach to address common goals that are patient-centred, needs based and responsive. Individuals with neuro-disability have complex needs; these are best met through close collaborative working between different professionals.

The music therapist contributes to internal and external case reviews and funding reports. Music therapy assessment and intervention on the unit is activated through multidisciplinary referral. The responsibilities of the music therapy service on the ward are:

- to assist with psycho-socio-emotio-adjustment to acquired disabilities
- to provide a forum which addresses broader functional goals in a creative and responsive therapeutic environment in order to promote well-being
- to assist with the development of guidelines which contribute to maximising function in environments post-discharge.

(Music Therapy Department, RHN 2006)

Speech and language therapists are responsible for the assessment, diagnosis and management of the communication disorders arising from complex neuro-disability. They are skilled at taking into account all factors that could impact on communication in order to facilitate optimal participation by working either at an impairment level or within the wider social context.

Patients attend the hospital as in-patients for an initial three-month period of assessment and intervention, but may stay for up to 12 months or longer. After a period of assessment, intensive impairment-based therapy is provided where appropriate, by different professionals. As rehabilitation progresses, the focus often shifts from an impairment-based medical model to a social model of intervention, to provide opportunities to carry over those skills worked on in rehabilitation and to prepare for discharge (highlighted in *The National Service Framework for Long-term Conditions*, Quality Requirement Four (DoH 2005b)). Following a review of patient needs on the ward, the therapists set out to facilitate this change of focus in a collaborative project involving speech and language therapy and music therapy.

Theoretical background
The social model emphasises how people with disabilities often become socially isolated and are excluded from participating in many aspects of life.

Byng and Duchan argue that therapies should provide experiences that are engaging so that participants feel their contribution is worthwhile and valued by themselves and others: 'The end product of therapy for most people needs to be that they feel more equipped to exchange opinions, negotiate, express affection, express needs, and so on – the real life purposes to which most of us put our communication' (2005, p.917).

Group work provides the opportunity for individuals to socialise with peers who have had similar experiences and can help participants to recognise and accept deficits in themselves (Feinstein-Whittaker and O'Connell-Goodfellow 1989). This insight is important to the rehabilitation process as reduced awareness of the impact of injury can influence the use of strategies and the return to functional activities (Port, Willmott and Charlton 2002).

It was decided that collaborative working between the music therapist and the speech and language therapist would best meet the needs of the patients in the group. This would optimise service provision, promote the carrying over of previously practised skills, provide a more motivating forum and maximise use of preserved neuro-pathways. As the patients identified to take part in the group had different skills, it was agreed that the use of music and drama techniques would provide opportunities for each patient to participate to the best of their abilities.

The group: Express Yourself!

The therapists decided to run a 12-week group called 'Express Yourself!' The aims of the group were to provide a forum to practise work from individual sessions that had focused on voice, speech and social interaction skills; facilitate self-expression in a creative environment using music and drama; and improve confidence in communication. The focus of the group was participation and identity rather than impairment. Close working between music therapy and speech and language therapy enabled the therapists to devise tasks that would enable creative expression but also encourage the carrying over of previous impairment-based speech work.

Prior to the programme the therapists met several times to identify suitable patients, to brainstorm activities and to prepare resources. This meant that the week-to-week running of the group did not need extra preparation. An evaluation sheet was developed which identified group and individual goals and provided a concise means of documenting individual progress after each session. By having an extensive list of potential procedures that had been identified in the planning stage, the therapists were able to draw on this pool of ideas each week, allowing the group to evolve at its own pace. Once the group was under way it was found that some of the procedures lent themselves to further development on a weekly basis. For example, the warm-up activity was extended each week to contain more information (see Box 4.1). While it was identified in advance that the speech and language therapist would lead the voice warm-up, and the music therapist would provide musical accompaniment as needed, the role of each therapist within the group was largely interchangeable, and specific activities were not allocated to a particular therapist. This enabled spontaneity within the group as either therapist could lead tasks.

Four patients were identified who had all received intensive one-to-one input for voice and/or speech and who were coming to the end of their stay in hospital. They were all enthusiastic about participating. It was a small but mixed group with a range of gender, ages and nationalities, although all had fluent English premorbidly. Three of the four had moderate to mild cognitive impairment affecting memory or flexibility of thinking. Cause of brain injury was varied and included stroke and meningitis.

Each participant had individual goals. Some related to previous interventions, for example turn taking. Most goals were common to each participant, for example A will respond to a prompt from other group members to speak more clearly and B will interact with each member of the group. Goals were based on communication and participation but the use of creative tasks to achieve these goals reflected close collaborative working between music therapy and speech and language therapy.

As this was the first group of its kind in our setting, the therapists chose a theme to run through each session. The theme of the sea was chosen as the therapists felt it would lend itself to using music and movement for expression and would be a concept to which all participants could relate. An occupational therapy art technician was invited to three sessions and the group made sea creatures and a collage of characters to use during activities. This encouraged project-based collaborative working.

Outcome measures and analysis

Three different outcome measures were used to record change at the start and end of the 12 weeks. Both therapists were involved in administering these measures. The first outcome measure was a standardised visual analogue self-esteem scale (VASES) (Brumfitt and Sheeran 1999). Second was the non-sexist blob tree (Wilson 1985). This is a picture of characters in a tree representing different levels of confidence and feelings. Patients are

---

Box 4.1 Typical group activities

Review group guidelines (that were generated by participants).

Voice warm-up including face, head and neck exercises (most participants had altered tone that would impact on head and neck).

Warm-up activity passing names/personal information round to a drum beat.

Passing movements and sounds of sea creatures from person to person using mime, voice and instruments.

Movement to music using a sheet of lycra to represent the sea and create waves.

Recording instruments making the sound of a calm and stormy sea and using this to make the lycra 'sea' move appropriately.

Choosing and developing a character: type of creature, sound and movement and generating a group story.

Singing 'Yellow Submarine' with word and picture prompts.

---

asked to choose the character that best represents how they feel about any given situation. In this case each patient was asked to indicate feelings about different communication scenarios. Third, sociograms were generated from sections of videotaped sessions to record group interaction patterns.

O'Callaghan, Powell and Oyebode (2006) found that being with others with the same problems helps to normalise and validate experiences and reduces anxiety. All participants came from the same ward and saw each other every day; however, the sociogram from week three showed little interaction between group members and all interactions involved a therapist. By the end of the twelfth week participants demonstrated a reduced reliance on therapists to facilitate interactions and an increased confidence in communicating independently amongst themselves. Carry-over of these skills was also informally observed, as other members of the team reported an increase in spontaneous interactions between group members when on the ward. This suggests that providing engaging experiences and broadening the range of communication partners, within a social model of intervention, helps to reduce reliance on specific people and provides opportunities to practise real-life communication skills.

Head-injured patients often have to experience a situation to increase insight into their impairments and O'Callaghan *et al.* (2006) surmise that the most direct way of realising the effectiveness of their communication is feedback from others. This was directly facilitated in the group, as members were encouraged to ask others to clarify if they had not understood and each had a goal to respond to the requests of others to speak more clearly. Participants responded well to this and one person in particular was very vocal in giving positive feedback to others as well as seeking clarification when required.

Reflections and future ideas

The speech and language therapist reflected that the creative focus of the group enabled participants to access skills that were not usually the focus of more formal impairment-based sessions. For example, as an extension of working at an impairment level on speech, participants had the opportunity to extend the range of sounds used through song and the creation of characters. The group also provided a risk-free environment in which to experiment with different methods of communication via movement and music.

The music therapist reflected that participation in a shared group song could promote a sense of group identity. In addition, the use of musical elements such as pulse and rhythm created a structure for group activities within which each patient could practise and extend both verbal and non-verbal communication skills. The use of shared creative techniques encouraged freedom of self-expression that might be challenging within a more formal environment.

The feedback from group members was extremely positive. They reported that they had enjoyed the group and 'had a laugh'. This is a realistic function of communication and is something that is perhaps difficult to facilitate in the rehabilitation setting.

In future similar groups, the therapists would like both to involve participants more closely with the choice of theme and to work more specifically on concepts such as self-esteem and preparation for discharge using creative activities such as role-plays with masks or puppets. This would enable participants to explicitly practise communication scenarios they may face in the wider community.

Both therapists felt that through running the group together they had learnt more about each other's role with head-injured adults. Joint working allowed both therapists to work in a more spontaneous and holistic way, and to be involved in activities that would not fit in to a unidisciplinary approach. This was facilitated by thorough and effective collaborative planning and by the flexibility of the individual therapists in responding to the different approaches taken by speech and language therapists and music therapists in general.

CONCLUDING THOUGHTS

Team working in neurological settings is essential for optimal care. The music therapist brings a medium for motivating the client and offering the client opportunities to rehearse functional tasks and experience success. Regardless of the models adopted by the music therapist or the team, it is essential for a common language to be found for the team to communicate about goal-setting and the client's progress. Ultimately, this will improve the client's overall care. Jochims (2004) proposes that music therapy may be considered by medical staff as the link between different approaches to medical and psychological treatments.

The literature covered in this overview has focused primarily on clinical descriptions of collaborative working to address different functional goals. However, it should be stressed that there are many additional research publications from interdisciplinary collaborations that have not been included here. In determining best practice, these publications should also be consulted, particularly in the current absence of profession-specific guidelines for best practice in interdisciplinary working.

Bringing diverse skills and experience to a team improves the whole team's understanding of a client's global needs. Working as part of the team means meeting with others to discuss the client's needs, setting goals and aims together, planning treatment together and most likely providing that treatment together. There is a strong argument for ensuring that music therapy is integrated within treatment teams in neuro-disability, optimising its contribution to the client's treatment (Magee and Andrews 2007). In some settings it may also mean contributing to team reports and meetings for updating funders on the client's progress. Working as part of the team in these ways will provide the best possible care for the client.

GUIDELINES FOR GOOD PRACTICE

- Find a common language to communicate with colleagues about the aims and outcomes of your work.

- Set goals and aims together with colleagues, and plan and deliver treatment together if possible.

- Ascertain what different forums exist at which you could usefully contribute (for example, multidisciplinary clinical meetings, funding meetings).

- Be open to learning from colleagues who may have a greater theoretical understanding of neurological principles and experience working with these types of clients.

- Ensure that you are aware of best practice in this clinical area, and keep up to date with research and literature relating to interdisciplinary working.

- Be flexible in your approach and consider how you can combine different approaches to provide optimum thera-peutic opportunities. This will often include working on functional skills as well as in the area of emotional devel-opment.

- Collaboration can provide a creative setting in which a client can develop and practise his or her returning func-tional skills. Therefore, collaborations with speech and language therapy, occupational therapy and physiotherapy might be particularly fruitful for the client and for your multidisciplinary colleagues.

- Establish roles and boundaries within any collaboration prior to starting work in order that differences in practice are understood and discussed.

- Consider carefully your choice of instruments for clients who have movement disorders. The use of electronic tech-nologies may enable clients to access instruments.

NOTES

1   Midigrid is a computer-based performance instrument which allows players to use a computer mouse (or various other electric instruments) to play notes, chords and sequences. The name is derived from the grid of boxes which appears on the computer screen and the MIDI method of sound production which uses commercial synthesisers and samplers to make the sound (Hunt and Kirk 1997).

2   Soundbeam is a distance-to-MIDI device which converts physical movements into sound by using information from interruptions of ultrasonic pulses emitted from a sensor (see www.soundbeam.co.uk).

Part 3

Collaborative Work
with the Elderly

Chapter 5

The Elderly

Adrienne Freeman

Two are better than one, because they have a good return for their work.
(Ecclesiastes 49)

INTRODUCTION

This chapter explores collaborative approaches used by music therapists
working with older client groups. The chapter opens with reflections on
attitudes towards ageing, followed by an exploration of the benefits and
challenges of collaborative work. Subsequently, UK client groups, clinical
settings and multidisciplinary team formations are described, followed by an
overview of collaborative practice as seen in Britain, including a literature
review. Topics including collaboration with relatives/carers, multi-cultural
awareness and spirituality are addressed in turn, and illustrated with case
studies. Tools to enable professionals engaged in this type of work are then
offered to the reader before the chapter concludes with guidelines for good
practice.

Elderly people are held in different levels of regard according to the
society in which they are placed. Western society, with its idolisation of
youth, beauty and high productivity, perhaps holds older people in less high
regard than other cultures whose respect for and care of their elders we can
learn much from. Goodman challenges our attitude towards ageing:

> What is the dominant model or image we have of ageing? All too often,
> the associations that spring to mind are of decrepitude and senility, of
> nursing homes whose occupants are seen as redundant and useless to
> society. These negative models may act as destructive, self-fulfilling
> prophecies. They are, according to...rabbi Zalman Schachter-Shalomi,

part of a paradigm of ageing that needs to be reshaped and trans-
formed. The whole ageing process, he says, needs healing. (Goodman
1999, p.65)

Negative attitudes can insidiously pervade the institutions in which we work
as therapists: work with the elderly is perhaps sometimes regarded as
without worth or hope of a 'cure'. Garner (2004) and Ardern (2004) each
describe the presence of negative ageism, at both unconscious and conscious
levels, brought into our work as clinicians. 'We want our patients to get
better, to be cured. Unconscious determinants of our chosen healthcare profession may not be satisfied by patients whose condition is chronic, even
deteriorating' (Garner 2004, p.221). It can be hard for professionals within a
team to bear in mind the positive outcomes of working with this client
group. Nockolds beautifully describes her feelings of inadequacy as she
approached music therapy sessions with older clients:

> I felt intimidated by the fact that they were my grandparents' genera-
> tion, people with all their wisdom – and who was I to come in and offer
> anything? I felt inadequate, not ready to take this step. I was so caught
> up in my personal experience of old people, and my own fears of my
> own mortality…and I thought, I never want to become senile like this,
> I never want to be in a home like this, be treated like this…I never want
> to lose so much of my life like this. With those negative feelings I was
> never going to value the people…for who they were and how they
> could be…I forgot that there is always the music. (Nockolds 1999,
> p.129)

Our elderly clients bring with them the wisdom of their years. This may be
the wisdom of life-long illness, as in the case of learning disabilities or
enduring functional mental health problems, often accompanied by strained,
if not broken, family networks. In comparison, our clients may have led a relatively normal life and faced major illness only in their later years, as in the
case of physical/terminal illness or dementia. In these cases, family relationships are more often intact and family members may be anxious to be
involved in sessions, or at least informed as to the nature of the therapy that
their loved one is receiving. The grieving process is present for all concerned
in such scenarios and needs to be given full consideration in approaching
therapy.

Collaborative working, at its best, brings a reciprocal wisdom to
working clinically with older people. Two minds, harnessed to the task of

providing therapy together, can provide a fuller richness and enlightenment to the therapeutic process.

BENEFITS AND CHALLENGES

The benefits of collaborative working are numerous. A recent survey of the membership of the Association of Professional Music Therapists (APMT) ascertains trends in working with the elderly and levels of collaborative working (Freeman 2007). Respondents indicated various positive outcomes with the most highly rated being the increased benefit to the client. The following list of benefits gives a descending order of priority, as depicted by respondents to the survey:

- greater benefit to client, including better coordination of care package
- greater awareness of multidisciplinary team as to what music therapy can offer
- greater awareness of relatives/carers
- greater involvement of relatives/carers in music therapy treatment
- enhanced evidence base for practice of music therapy
- establishment of new funding for further clinical work in this area
- establishment of stronger links between the different collaborating disciplines
- enhanced learning, both for therapists involved and for training other disciplines.

Conversely, there are a number of challenges to good collaborative working. Supervision may be lacking or inadequate and the collaborative process can then become disabled. For various reasons, there may be a lack of cohesion between disciplines or a history of negative relating – this will be counter-productive to effective transdisciplinary practice. The busy culture of many clinical settings leads to a lack of time for vital preparation and feedback with colleagues – effective communication is necessary in order for the collaborative process to be established, developed, understood and successfully enacted by all parties involved. Lack of resources is also attributed as a reason for not co-working, rather than lack of will. Possibilities for transdisciplinary working may be constrained by budgets, but this is at great cost to our clients.

CLIENT GROUPS

British music therapists work with elderly people within a broad range of client groups, indicated as follows by survey responses:

- mental health – functional illness
- mental health – dementia
- learning disabilities
- palliative care
- medicine
- physical/emotional difficulties
- rehabilitation.

The survey ascertained that work within the mental health category was most prevalent, with the majority of respondents working in these two areas. It was noted that many individual music therapists work with several of the above client groups and in a number of different clinical settings. Although not shown by the survey, it is probable that a small number of music therapists work with elderly clients in other settings such as forensic or prison services.

Music therapists see their clients in a diverse range of clinical settings as listed below. Whilst the majority work within community settings it is interesting to consider the variety of other settings in which music therapists work with elderly clients:

- community setting
- continuing care ward
- day hospital
- acute ward
- residential retirement/care/nursing home
- hospice

- client's own home
- rehabilitation ward
- private practice
- day centre.

THE MULTIDISCIPLINARY TEAM

Collaboration with fellow professionals takes place within the context of the multidisciplinary team and can be on both a formal and an informal basis. It may take the shape of liaising with fellow team members outside clinical sessions or can involve collaboration within clinical sessions where trans-disciplinary working is undertaken. Multidisciplinary team members will come from a range of professions. A team might include medical and nursing staff, working alongside therapists (e.g. arts therapists, occupational therapists, speech and language therapists, physiotherapists and psychologists/counsellors). Other key professions are dieticians, social workers and bereavement support staff. There may also be a spiritual care team (including chaplains), complementary therapists (such as aromatherapists) and activities coordinators (including artists). All these staff are supported by carers and care staff, and strong management of such a diverse team will be essential.

Respondents to the survey indicated that music therapists collaborate most often with nurses, family members, other arts therapists, doctors, occupational therapists and psychologists. Chaplains and social workers were also frequently involved in collaborative work with music therapists.

It is significant that proportionally more collaboration takes place with nurses and the family of the client: representative of those people with whom our clients perhaps spend the larger amount of their time. Those who spend the most time with our clients are likely to know them best: investing our time in collaborating with these people will be fruitful.

OVERVIEW OF COLLABORATIVE WORK

Much collaborative work between music therapists and other disciplines takes place outside clinical sessions. The nature of such collaborations is broad and may range through formal and informal liaison with team members about client interventions; to communicating with relatives; to training staff; to co-working in sessions.

The majority of collaboration takes place on an ongoing basis although specific projects are often more likely to be time-limited to various periods, from eight weeks and upwards in duration.

Despite the amount of collaborative work that has taken place, there is a dearth of British material published on the subject. Powell (2004) describes her work in a community setting for clients with dementia, using a range of approaches covering the spectrum from music therapy to community music. She focuses on making connections and shares the powerful experience of performing *A Dream Wedding* with her clients and their community. Her work is open to the varied encounters she has with clients, staff and relatives: she develops many different kinds of appropriate collaborative responses and incorporates these into her work with this community. She offers music therapy in individual sessions and closed and open groups (the latter will also receive staff, family and friends). She additionally provides spontaneous groups as appropriate together with the occasional planned performance. Spontaneous groups appear to offer a particularly unique form of collaboration as:

> They happen all over the place – in corridors, in the lobby areas, outside residents' rooms or out of doors on sunny days. Residents and staff appear from other parts of the building when they hear the music (on one occasion there is dancing in the car park). These groups are visible and audible to others in the building, and are inclusive, linking people in the building. (Powell 2004, p.176)

Powell's work conveys a strong sense of being flexible and responsive to opportunities for input as they present themselves. She demonstrates an appropriate range of responses along a continuum from therapy to performance. Such responsiveness requires acute awareness of and attunement to the presenting needs of clients together with interpretation of what will be appropriate.

Gale and Matthews portray their short-term collaborative project, involving the disciplines of music, drama and art therapies in the field of learning disabilities. This involved an assessment group for a mix of ages, with approximately half the group members being elderly. Each discipline led two sessions in turn, with the other therapists adopting a supporting role. The focus of the project thus conveys a comparative feel, but there is a strong sense of shared thinking. There were six sessions in total, after which the authors note 'a very clear distinction between assessment and therapy, although the principles of working in therapy very much underlay it' (1998, p.182). In planning for this project, disciplines involved spent considerable time furthering their understanding of each other's work:

> We considered our ideas about how the other two therapies were practised; in which way they were effective; and how this differed from – or perhaps even contradicted – our own theory and practice. The issue of working alongside colleagues inspired some anxiety. Our work as therapists normally takes place in a private space. There was a difference for each of us between discussing something in supervision and having work with clients observed by other therapists in the room. This was welcomed in principle but we felt wary about it in practice. In particular, we needed to consider the roles we would play in relation to one another. (Gale and Matthews 1998, p.173)

Such collaboration requires vulnerability and openness between disciplines but results in deeper understanding of each other's approaches and thinking. This is conducive to forming stronger team alliances, ultimately only of benefit to the client.

Odell-Miller presents her research with the elderly mentally ill, comparing levels of engagement of clients in music therapy and reminiscence therapy. Clients had a mix of functional and organic illness, with a prevalence of dementia. The overall sense of this project is comparative rather than collaborative, particularly as the music therapist led both types of session. Odell-Miller finds that 'relationships between therapist, assistants and group members built up over a period of time help to achieve benefits for elderly mentally ill people' (1995b, p.103). It is noteworthy that successful relationships cannot be built in haste – all collaboration requires time and attentive commitment.

An example of collaboration outside sessions is seen in the current author's writing about Fay (Freeman 2003). Collaboration with nurses around sessions is described: all those concerned struggled as they attempted to supply Fay's needs in her final days – here, in the face of not knowing what would be best, team members tried to work out together what they could realistically attempt and were able to share some of the surprising outcomes.

The author has also had experience of working jointly within clinical sessions (usually for time-limited projects) with various disciplines at different times, including nursing, occupational therapy, speech and language therapy and drama therapy. Collaboration with nurses led to their adoption of a co-therapist role within music therapy sessions. In work with other disciplines, more of a blend of approaches occurred. In all cases, it was vital to have enough time for preparation and feedback around sessions in order for differing roles and approaches to be understood and integrated. The joint approach thus required more planning and could be less spontaneously enacted than work on one's own. It was interesting that the coming together of two disciplines within sessions meant that one was no longer offering 'pure' music therapy. Notably, when presented with combined drama therapy and music therapy, clients could choose to engage in either drama or music or both. This meant that if a client disliked using one art form they could choose to use only the other. Both art forms were offered simultaneously for much of the time but in combination (involving forms of story-telling) so that each enhanced the other.

Bryant describes her collaboration with a music therapist from the occupational therapist's perspective. Here, a blended approach was also adopted. Bryant finds that 'the roles of the two therapists evolved so that their respective skills were combined equally'. Examples are given of sounds that were 'used to emphasise the movement of objects' and music made by 'throwing a ball onto a large drum' (1991, p.189). The resultant interaction is highlighted: however, such examples also demonstrate the integration of diverse approaches.

Other music therapists may collaborate with colleagues in order to train and educate staff about approaching the client in alternative ways, thereby aiming to positively impact on overall client care. Such projects focus on enabling other disciplines by coming together to increase professionals' understanding of clients. In addition, they can raise team awareness of what collaborating professions offer. Undoubtedly, participation in collaboration establishes stronger links between the disciplines involved.

COLLABORATING WITH RELATIVES/CARERS

When considering collaboration, it is vital not to overlook the family and carers of our clients. Illness and hospitalisation of loved ones is frequently an overwhelming and disempowering experience for those closest to the client. Kitwood speaks of the isolation and burden of carers:

> Those who have this role take on, almost single-handed, a colossal task. The weight of evidence from anthropology is that no individual was ever 'designed' for such an onerous commitment; human beings emerged through evolution as a highly social species, where burdens are carried by a group. (Kitwood 1997, p.41)

The possibilities of collaboration with relatives and carers are varied. Outside clinical sessions, collaboration may take place informally when one encounters relatives on the unit. More formal contact may take place in the setting of the ward round or case conference. Either location requires the music therapist to communicate professionally yet in a supportive and empathic manner. At times, relatives will be extremely distressed at the losses their loved ones have undergone. This can be difficult to respond to, especially if such distress is expressed in the presence of the client. Here, one needs much tact and sensitivity. It may be useful to give brief examples of some of the positive events that have taken place within music therapy sessions whilst of course holding the confidentiality of the work.

Collaboration within sessions needs careful management as there is the possibility that the client who was originally referred for music therapy could be overwhelmed by the presence of a relative/carer. At the point of commencing collaborative work with a family member, the music therapist would need to have built an understanding of the type of relationship held by the client and the relative in question. Here, a detailed personal history is useful. Where the relative's presence is thought to be in the best interests of the client, it would be deemed beneficial to embark on collaborative work. It is important to monitor the ongoing benefits and negotiate the shifts in the levels of involvement of client and relative, with the aid of ongoing clinical supervision.

Weber describes her work in Germany in a hospice context where she includes families in her approach. She notices that, after severed relationships, family members return to their dying relative: 'sitting in the room together and listening to the music at least allows them to be together peacefully and is often a decisive step to forgiveness and reconciliation' (2000, p.193). Such outcomes represent some of the spiritual tasks associated with end of life.

Clair writes of her work in America, with couples where one partner is suffering from dementia. As a response to the deterioration in the quality of interaction between the couple, she uses music therapy to teach a range of input, including dancing and singing (drawing on repertoire significant to the couple involved), before withdrawing. The study concludes that 'music therapy applications are effective in increasing mutual engagement in caregiving and care receiving couples with dementia, and that caregivers can effectively facilitate the engagement using music' (2002, p.286). This work aims to recover the loss of 'satisfying reciprocity' between the couple and to enhance the quality of relating.

The following case study illustrates how involvement in music therapy of a close family member, in this case the partner, achieves richer and more informed clinical work. Joyce's husband was able to bring his wife's and indeed their shared history into the sessions. In a situation of grief and loss he was able to bring a positive contribution with which the music therapist could work, enabling life review and perhaps some form of closure.

MUSIC THERAPY WITH AN ELDERLY COUPLE

Rachel Darnley-Smith (Music Therapist)

The following is a case study[1] of work undertaken within a large inner city hospital, which provided healthcare to people of all ages with mental health problems. The music therapy department, consisting of eight part-time music therapists, was one of a group of departments which worked closely together in a specially designed centre complete with a music room. The other professional departments included occupational therapy, art therapy and physiotherapy. The music therapists were employed in a wide range of multidisciplinary teams, working both on the hospital site in the therapies centre, on in-patient wards and in the community, for example in day centres.

Rachel, the music therapist whose work this case study describes, worked part-time for the hospital and was also responsible for the overall management of the music therapy department. The impact of these responsibilities meant that time for clinical practice was scarce and she therefore chose to concentrate her work on the in-patient services for older adults with dementia. Such scarcity of time meant that taking a full part in the life of a multidisciplinary team was impossible. Rachel found that actively seeking co-working relationships in some form or other was essential in order that she might receive referrals or make contributions to case conferences through reports. If her presence was in name only, the service was liable to be underused.

Co-working frequently took the form of developing close collaborations with occupational therapists and old-age psychiatrists, using lunchtime meetings to discuss freely and think about particular patients from as broad a perspective as possible, including their practical, emotional and therapeutic needs.

Another form of co-working was the gathering of informal referrals from nursing staff on the continuing care wards where patients with severe dementia lived. Rachel usually made sure she had enough time to talk to staff working on a ward before she started sessions, sometimes by attending the formal handover meetings at the change of nursing shift, or simply by sitting down in the busy office and joining in whatever conversation was taking place. Frequently, little information was available about a patient's life prior to being admitted to hospital but the nurses who cared for them had often come to know about their musical responses and preferences simply through spending long days in their presence with the television or radio on in the background. It was upon the basis of such knowledge that live music was often sought for patients with dementia or a referral was made for music therapy. Music therapy could offer the possibility of emotional and social connection and the opportunity for some expressive engagement with others, where memory and language might have deteriorated. This was especially pertinent where, as was frequently the case, patients seemed isolated and appeared to have few friends or relatives.

In this case, however, the situation was different as the referral came from a relative rather than another professional. It should be stressed that usually there was no structure from within which families could refer their relatives to particular services and so this situation was most unusual. It was also rare for a relative to become so directly involved in their spouse's care and for such a collaborative working relationship to develop.

Joyce had been living on the continuing care ward for nearly seven years when her husband, Henry, wrote to the new consultant in old-age psychiatry to enquire about the possibility of her being referred for music therapy. The idea was welcomed by both consultant and nursing staff. Joyce had taken part in a music therapy group in the past and also had been seen individually by a music therapy student. Now, in the late stages of Alzheimer's disease, she had withdrawn into her own world, becoming very isolated, and in this particular instance Henry was concerned that she was not receiving sufficient musical stimulation. It was his level of concern and commitment to her that enabled this unusual working collaboration to unfold.

Joyce had a lifelong attachment to music. As a young woman, during the 1939–45 world war, she had served as a nurse in the Army, and immediately afterwards trained as a singer at a London conservatoire of music. She had spent the rest of her working life singing and conducting choirs. Joyce and Henry had met whilst at college, having grown up in the same city in the South of England.

Henry lived near the hospital and would visit most days on a regular basis. He had provided Joyce with a personal stereo cassette player and he frequently brought her tapes of music from their extensive collection of recordings. Rachel met with Henry and heard about his concerns for his wife and his wish for her to have some access to musical experiences.

At this point it did not occur to Rachel that Henry might be involved in the actual sessions; she simply assumed they would talk and keep in touch over the work. Subsequently she began to work with Joyce individually, on a weekly basis. Joyce could walk a little at first, from the sitting room area of the ward to a side room, but she seemed to retain little memory of their sessions together from week to week. She took no interest in the simple percussion instruments which Rachel offered to her, probably because she did not understand what they were. She did, however, make vocal 'calling' sounds, often from the back of her throat, with the pitch rising up and down. She also looked momentarily interested in the instruments when Rachel played, but it soon became clear that what she responded to most was the therapist's singing. Rachel began to sing songs which came into her head quite spontaneously. Joyce would either smile and nod or she would join in, vocalising freely. Rachel also began to improvise vocally, matching her pitches, and sometimes providing some musical structure from two simple chords played on the guitar.

Although it was unlikely that Joyce remembered her weekly visits, it felt to Rachel as though some familiarity was being established between them. *Rachel* remembered *her*, and what she responded to musically, and it was possible that Joyce sensed that she was known, and certainly that through music they had something in common. It was quite hard for Rachel to hold on to this idea all the time as Joyce might fall asleep, or barely respond for entire sessions.

As there were so many unknowns Rachel decided to arrange another meeting with Henry. Henry was very positive in response to her account of the sessions and full of suggestions, so much so that Rachel felt from their meeting there might be mutual benefit in Henry joining the sessions too. The three of them, Rachel and Joyce and Henry, subsequently worked together for ten months, up to the week of Joyce's death.

Henry immediately began to bring songs that they had sung together in younger days. These were mostly British folk songs, which he brought with the words carefully written out for Rachel to sing. Sometimes he brought music from Joyce's own collection of sheet music. As the months progressed Henry began to bring other personal items, for example the hand-written manuscripts of songs which Joyce had arranged for choir. He began to talk about their married life together, the concerts they had attended, and the premieres of works by well-known composers, conducted by the famous conductors of the time. He also began to talk about how Joyce had first become ill, and how the person he had known for so long had begun to lose her patience, her trust in others (including him), as well as her memory. Joyce would take part in these sessions to varying degrees.

It astonished Rachel that the sessions lasted an hour, a length of time she would normally consider far too long in such circumstances. Sometimes Joyce would fall asleep, which at first seemed to embarrass Henry, until he realised that Rachel did not feel that they were 'wasting her time' if she 'didn't respond'. Occasionally Joyce would say something, a short phrase, such as 'lovely, lovely, lovely'; often though the only sound from her would be the grinding of her teeth. Rachel encouraged Henry to sing to Joyce and she in turn would occasionally give a bemused smile or vocalise with the songs. Rachel sometimes responded to her sounds as before with free improvisation, using the guitar as an accompaniment. She would also sing songs as they occurred to her spontaneously, and would move freely between songs and improvised music, in addition to helping Henry to choose songs from the song sheets he had brought. Gradually, they built up a repertoire of musical possibilities, both pre-composed and improvised.

The atmosphere changed over the months, with both Rachel and Henry becoming more relaxed in their therapeutic trio, where one member was increasingly absent. Whilst Henry always focused upon the needs of Joyce, when she slept during the sessions he gradually began to talk more about himself and his current life outside the hospital.

Over the ten months, Joyce's responses did not change very much except during the last two weeks when she slept through most of the sessions. In the final session, Joyce hardly seemed aware of what was happening around her. Rachel and Henry, however, improvised and sung their repertoire of songs, and as usual left spaces for her response. At one moment she woke up and vocalised loudly whilst they were singing, before falling asleep again.

The following week Henry phoned Rachel to tell her of his wife's death, saying how kind everyone had been. They arranged to meet a few weeks later as a way of saying goodbye and finishing the work. During the session Henry talked about his wife and her long time spent in the hospital; he also told Rachel about the hymns he had chosen for her funeral. This was the last time they met as Henry made it quite clear that he did not feel the need or wish for any further contact. He suggested that he would probably see Rachel again when he came to visit staff and patients on the ward as he intended to do on a regular basis.

It was here that this unusual and most creative collaboration ended, a collaboration facilitated by two crucial factors: first Joyce, as an elderly woman with almost no speech or other means of effective communication, had an advocate, her husband Henry. Henry not only knew the music which was important to her, he also knew what it *meant* to her, and in turn what it meant to him. Second, Henry was also in need. He visited the ward most days and was gradually losing the means of active communication with his wife. It was becoming increasingly difficult to know just how to be with his wife, how to pass the long hours. It could be said his motivation was key to the entire process.

In conclusion Rachel felt strongly that the music therapy sessions had created a particular opportunity for the couple to be together during the last months of Joyce's life in a way that could reflect some of the earlier times they had shared together, making and listening to music.

MULTICULTURAL AWARENESS

Older clients of other ethnicities may be less westernised than their younger counterparts, especially if they immigrated later in life. There may be problems of language (together with other difficulties such as refugee status) which lead to these clients feeling excluded and alien from the culture around them. In the context of music therapy, the universal language of music is a great advantage as clients of diverse ethnicity can together share the experience of corporate music making. Music transcends verbal language barriers and offers clients a means of connection at a non-verbal level. Music's power to transcend diverse and at times opposing cultures is beauti-fully demonstrated in the realm of orchestral performance. Mayne writes of watching a Prom concert given by

> a remarkable orchestra, the West-Eastern Divan Orchestra, founded by Daniel Barenboim, a Jew, and the late Edward Said, a Palestinian, and made up of young Jews and Arabs to prove that music, with a power far

beyond that of language, has the power to heal and reconcile and speak across all barriers of prejudice and frozen history. (Mayne 2006, p.85)

However, despite the power of music to overcome barriers of verbal language, it is important to address our clients' need for reciprocal verbal understanding. In such circumstances, music therapists may use an interpreter as co-therapist. The co-therapist may be a colleague of another discipline who is also able to speak the specific language, or it may be necessary to utilise the skills of an interpreter (who would be likely to require training for the task). Working with an interpreter represents a unique form of collaboration that facilitates clients' access to therapy. For those clients to whom the English language is unfamiliar, this situation eases what could have been an uncomfortable experience into something much more accessible, incorporating the familiar aspect of native tongues.

Unwittingly, we as professionals can display negative attitudes towards our clients. The Macpherson Report on the Stephen Lawrence inquiry offers a useful exploration as to causes of such attitudes.

Unwitting racism can arise because of lack of understanding, ignorance or mistaken beliefs. It can arise from well intentioned but patronising words or actions. It can arise from unfamiliarity with the behaviour or cultural traditions of people or families from minority ethnic communities. (Macpherson 1999, p.22)

Garner (2005) led Psychiatry of Old Age teams at Chase Farm Hospital to produce guidelines and reflections on avoidance of institutional abuse, offering practical considerations for action in the face of encountering abuse. This publication offers potential use as a training tool.

It is important to invest time in learning about our clients' culture and traditions and to allow our understanding to inform our work. Collaboration with relatives will be productive in this regard. It is useful for music therapists to gather musical material (e.g. songs) relevant to the cultures with which they are working. Where possible, it is important to gain experience (and perhaps training) in playing music in the style of the diverse cultures represented, rather than remaining enmeshed in western classical tradition.

Hoskyns (2007) reflects on her work in New Zealand, where she is incorporating aspects of Maori tradition into her bi-cultural teaching of music therapy students. She emphasises the importance of consultation and respect, both of which require time. One interesting and challenging outcome of her consultation is that she finds she should not improvise with

Maori songs. In order to negotiate such a cross-cultural transition, openness, flexibility and the readiness to change are required. Hoskyns finds that 'consultation builds communication and trust…everyone benefits' (2007). It is striking that one could possibly substitute the word 'consultation' with 'collaboration'.

SPIRITUALITY

Older clients are perhaps more likely to bring matters of spirituality into clinical work. As they are usually chronologically more likely to be nearer the end of their lives than younger clients, they will, whether consciously or unconsciously, be addressing matters such as the imminence of death and all that this raises. It is particularly important for all professionals to consider the spiritual needs of clients, especially those who are facing the end of life.

Wilson suggests that 'to maintain a sense of wholeness the needs of the body, mind and spirit must be taken into account' (1999, p.108). It is useful to define spirituality as broader than religion: one way of making a distinction between the two is to regard spirituality as the 'umbrella' under which religion is one of various ways of expressing spirituality. Wensley poses this distinction: 'while religious life and experience are a significant part of one's spirituality, other parts must not be overlooked, particularly those that search for meaning, hope or love' (Wensley 1995, p.19). In addition, Murray and Zenter suggest that spirituality is:

> A quality that goes beyond religious affiliation, that strives for inspiration, reverence, awe, meaning and purpose, even in those who do not believe in any god. The spiritual dimension tries to be in harmony with the universe, strives for answers about the infinite and comes into focus when a person faces emotional stress, physical illness and death.
> (Murray and Zenter 1989, p.259)

Therefore, spirituality is a framework within which can be found peace and hope (together with other aspects of transcendence), each vitally important but especially so for those who find themselves both aged and in ill health. Facilitating clients' spirituality is a task that can unexpectedly arise for professionals in their clinical practice and it is necessary for one to stand apart from one's own personal faith position in order to maintain boundaries in the correct manner. The lens is on the client's spirituality rather than on that of the therapist.

The following case study illustrates how the music therapist can encounter the sudden emergence of acute spiritual need and is then impelled to act, drawing on all the resources afforded by the multidisciplinary team. In this case, resources beyond the immediate team were also utilised, creating the effect of a collaborative web or network.

GROUPWORK, THE TEAM AND SPIRITUALITY
Adrienne Freeman (Music Therapist)

The setting

Primrose Court is a NHS residential continuing care ward for older people with severe and enduring functional mental health problems. It is set in the community, away from the main general hospital site.

The multidisciplinary team comprises a consultant psychiatrist and associate specialist doctor, art therapist, music therapist and occupational therapists, all of whom hold regular sessions on the unit. Other disciplines such as chaplain, physiotherapist, psychologist, social worker and speech therapist attend the unit as required. Most multidisciplinary team members visit the unit on a peripatetic basis, whilst nursing staff provide continuous cover on a shift basis.

Music therapy is well established on the unit after many years of input. The music therapist provides a closed group session on a weekly basis, on which this case study is based. In addition individual sessions are provided as appropriate.

In order to be as well integrated with the team as possible, the music therapist meets with the nurse-in-charge for a handover when she arrives on the unit. After clinical sessions, any significant issues are discussed with the associate specialist who is present on the unit at that time. Further conversation takes place between the music therapist and nursing staff about how clients have been in music therapy that day. This occurs whilst writing up client notes, physically present within the nursing team at handover for the change of shift. Liaison with other disciplines may take place elsewhere, both by face-to-face contact and via e-mail.

The music therapy group has space for six clients, all of whom usually attend on a regular basis. These clients have endured many years and even decades of hospitalisation and have suffered much loss in their lives. The music therapy group aims to provide them with a safe space where they can bring pertinent issues from their lives, share the experience of making music together and reflect on the material this may raise. Within this context, clients can voice deeply felt issues and experience being responded to. The work is frequently expressive of pain and difficulty, perhaps linked to the fact that there are seldom any discharges from the unit. This, together with other losses, often engenders hopelessness, whether at a conscious or unconscious level. These clients lead profoundly disconnected lives and within music therapy are able to experience connection on a number of different levels. One visitor to this group (a nurse on induction) commented that it was the 'most real' group they had ever experienced. Another visitor (a trainee psychotherapist) commented that the clients were 'survivors'.

The format of each session falls into three parts:

1.   an opening greeting, where each client is sung to and encouraged to share their news

2.   free group improvisations, followed by related discussion

3.   closing songs, usually selected by clients and often holding powerful symbolism.

The group consists of equal numbers of male and female clients. These clients are all in their 60s and 70s, with a mix of diagnoses which include bi-polar affective disorder, schizophrenia, schizoaffective disorder, paranoia and depression. One group member also has an additional diagnosis of Parkinson's Disease.

The session

This case study focuses on one session and the subsequent collaboration with a number of different team members, and with religious communities in the area. The session took place shortly before Christmas, and unusually, only men were present. One woman came in and out a number of times, a normal feature due to restlessness. The men, Colin, Ian and Felix, commented that it felt different without the women. Ian thought that it made a difference to the group's music, that the women made it lighter and gave it more 'top notes'.

In the free group improvisations, Ian played the cimbala (small harp) and Colin played bongos. Felix chose the metallophone but was less engaged in the improvisation as he was preoccupied with his two pairs of glasses. The music therapist played the piano to support the men, whose music was very connected – they watched each other as they played and Colin timed his rhythms to fit with Ian's. The music had a purposeful quality and incorporated marching rhythms. Afterwards, Colin spoke of the music conveying an image of animals holding each other's tails, symbolising connection. In further discussion of images conveyed by the music, it was likened to a procession to church (an image of connection with the outside world perhaps). Colin and Felix both said that they liked going to church but had not been able to do so for a long time.

This led into a discussion on attending places of worship. It was clear that people had the desire to attend rather than receive a visit from a religious representative. Attendance would certainly be more 'normalising' and would maintain people's links with their own faith communities. Colin expressed the view that 'they are too short-staffed to take us'. The men commented that they had not seen the Roman Catholic representative, who for a long time used to bring Mass to Primrose Court. Ian spoke of his desire to attend a synagogue, naming the particular place he would like to attend. He said that it made him feel peaceful to go and pray with others in the synagogue. The music therapist, feeling that it was vital for clients' spiritual needs to be met, said she would raise the issue with staff.

Colin had brought the words of a song to the group and read this out at the end. *The First Mercy*, by Peter Warlock (1927), tells the story of the Christmas Nativity from the perspective of several small creatures in the stable. They marvel at the unfolding events, describing the arrival of peace and love in the midst of their fear. The symbolism of being small and afraid might be representative of how clients feel at times. The human search for peace and love is common, especially in such difficult circumstances as terminal illness and long-term mental health problems.

The group frequently receives offerings such as songs, poems, letters, cards and sometimes photographs from its members. Items brought may have a powerful connection with family members or a link with a significant life event. Words to songs usually hold strongly symbolic imagery. It is an important function of the music therapy group that people are able to bring, and have received, such aspects of themselves that reflect their lives and beliefs: who they are as people rather than clients with problems. In the context of the unit being the clients' home, and indeed in any clinical setting, it is vitally important that each individual remains seen as a whole and unique person.

After the session

During the course of their usual post-session informal feedback, the music therapist and associate specialist decided to raise the matter with nursing staff. Together they spoke with the nursing staff during the subsequent handover at change of shift. The nurses confirmed that the Roman Catholic representative no longer visited and thought that in rare instances clients' relatives could take them to their regular place of worship when they had weekend leave (very few clients are able to take weekend leave either due to the intensity of their mental health problem or to their having no family). Nurses also stated that it was difficult to access places of worship due to clients' physical limitations requiring the use of wheelchairs, frames, etc. The music therapist referred to legislation that obliges public buildings to provide disabled access (HMSO 2005) and thought that places of worship could work out a practical means of access if contacted.

Later that week, the music therapist and occupational therapy colleagues informally discussed how very important it was to meet clients' spiritual needs, especially in the case of terminal illness. They decided that the music therapist should contact both the consultant psychiatrist and the hospital chaplain (an Anglican priest) in order to progress matters at Primrose Court. The music therapist described the situation to the psychiatrist and the chaplain and offered the view that the experience of clients going out to places of worship would maintain their fragile connection with the outside world. However, if this were not possible, the visits of religious representatives to the unit would be the next best option.

The consultant psychiatrist had previously been able to draw in appropriate representatives in the context of the Jewish faith and now thought that the Jewish chaplain, a rabbi, would perhaps visit the client. Alternatively, the client's key nurse could contact the chosen synagogue who might provide someone to take the client there as family members were unable to do so.

The hospital chaplain offered to help facilitate spiritual needs in any way he could and suggested visiting the unit to discuss with clients how their spiritual needs might be best met. He also provided the contact details of the Jewish chaplain. He and the music therapist together worked to set up a meeting with the ward manager, who was supportive of the idea, to further progress this matter.

The outcome was that the Jewish client received a visit from a representative of his faith. The contact details of the rabbi were placed in the ward diary as a resource to draw on when required. The client changed his mind about visiting the synagogue, but the option would now be more possible in future, should he change his mind again, due to the established contact. Over the Christmas period, other clients were able to attend a service at the local church.

Reflections

There was a heightened awareness within the team about sensitivity to the spiritual needs of clients. All team members require attunement, flexibility and resourcefulness on an ongoing rather than a one-off basis in order to provide for these needs. This case study provides an example of an instance when one may need to act as an advocate for one's clients in the face of their feelings of resignation and disempowerment. It is important to be constantly alert for when this might be required of us as professionals of any discipline. This case study illustrates collaboration both within the multidisciplinary team, but also in the wider context of the community.

This experience of collaboration made the music therapist realise that sometimes a wider than usual view is needed when liaising. Here, the liaison extended through and beyond the immediate multidisciplinary team. It was encouraging that those contacted responded with willing reciprocity and brought to mind the *ripple effect* (or chain reaction) of a positive and cohesive team. It was salutary that perhaps opportunities for our clients can be missed due to our lack of thought or perseverance on their behalf, often through time constraints. The fact that such an issue arose in a music therapy session was significant, increasing general awareness that this treatment offers a potential space for clients to express matters of great importance.

REFLECTION FROM THE CONSULTANT PSYCHIATRIST

This work illustrates the importance of music therapy as a means of understanding and working with often very disabled individuals in a therapeutic and sustained way.

REFLECTION FROM THE CHAPLAIN

Music can touch people profoundly at what might be described as a spiritual level. This applies not only to music from a particular religious tradition or faith group but also to any piece of music that connects with someone's soul.

Creating or making music can enable people to express their spirituality; hearing music can enable people to access their spirituality. When a client is unable to create or make music, and struggles with expression more generally, observing their reaction upon hearing different kinds of music can give vital clues about their spirituality.

A great strength of the practice set out in this case study is the proactive approach of the music therapist in acting on what she observes, to foster spiritual expression and to involve others who can ensure that spiritual needs are met holistically.

Conclusion

It is fitting to conclude with the thought that both music and spirituality offer connection in very profound ways: in this case, the connection of the multidisciplinary team was able to facilitate the clients' spiritual needs; however, it could easily have been another type of need. This demonstrates just how vital it is for team members to operate closely together at all times in order for clients' best interests to be achieved.

SUPERVISION

In order to achieve best practice, it is vital for collaborating parties to receive good supervision. It may be necessary to seek supervision from a profession other than music therapy, so that the professionals involved receive support appropriate to their collaboration. Psychotherapists and psychoanalysts are identified as appropriate supervisors and often there is a need for specialist one-off supervision for unfamiliar methods (to music therapy) that are present within collaborations. Group supervision is also a useful tool. Roberts and Bull (2005) recommend joint supervision as enabling professionals to cope with challenges to the co-relationship and to remain strongly paired. They point out that a pair of therapists is more able to contain the work, but this advantage is offset by greater enactment of transference. Where there are two therapists, phenomena such as splitting, transference and countertransference present themselves with magnified power and complexity. Garner (2004), in considering challenges within therapy for those with dementia, suggests the following:

> Due to the particular countertransferential feelings evoked by this type of work, the therapist requires good support and supervision. The patient will almost inevitably be older, maybe much older, and may represent a close elderly relative or the therapist's imagined self in old age while at the same time expressing infantile needs and dependency on the therapist. (Garner 2004, p.221)

These thoughts are also relevant to work with older clients with other diagnoses. Transference and countertransference issues are also emphasised by Ardern (2004) who alludes to the importance of adequate supervision to prevent unwitting abuse of clients. Although practically difficult to achieve, joint supervision of collaborating pairs enables greater transparency and awareness around these powerful issues.

CONCLUDING THOUGHTS

This chapter has described a rich diversity of collaborative practice, embracing a broad range of professions and clinical contexts. Investment in collaboration has been highlighted as ultimately being of great benefit to our clients and worth the necessary time and resources. This chapter has shown that effective collaboration requires flexibility and breadth of approach, supported by good supervision.

This chapter holds the following refrain: the recommendation to invest time in building good collaboration. The benefits of giving time and attention to clients, relatives/carers and colleagues have been demonstrated, as have the benefits of developing understanding of spirituality, race and culture. Investment in thinking time is imperative and can only lead to positive outcome. Time is required to navigate what the author refers to as the *collaborative map*. There is a broad range of possibility as to with whom the music therapist might need to liaise, both within and outside sessions. It can be helpful to ask of oneself: with whom, when and how do I need to collaborate in order to navigate this next section of the clinical path?

Collaboration brings a great richness of thinking and experience to clinical work, ultimately only of benefit to the client. It would seem a great shame were cost-cutting and time-pressure implications to reduce the opportunity to work in such enriching ways as this chapter has explored.

GUIDELINES FOR GOOD PRACTICE

The following list provides good practice guidelines for collaborative work in this clinical area.

- Make time to understand each other's disciplines and approaches.
- Use training tools such as handouts/workshops to familiarise other disciplines with expectations within music therapy.
- Be willing to take on expectations of other disciplines with whom you collaborate.

- Be prepared to adapt and perhaps work in new ways in order to develop a collaborative blend – flexibility is essential.

- Be open to communicating difficulties to collaborating colleagues.

- Be aware of stronger manifestations of splitting, transference and countertransference.

- Seek joint supervision if at all possible.

- Supervision may be required from a profession other than music therapy, dependent on the discipline(s) represented in the collaboration.

- Beware of unwitting abuse of clients.

- Compile personal histories of clients for team use, to foster understanding of clients as individual and unique persons.

- Invest in corporate thinking time.

- Plan, prepare and feed back adequately.

- Celebrate new achievements made by the collaborators.

- Present and write up your work – it will help others.

NOTE

1   This case study originally appeared in Darnley-Smith and Patey (2003) *Music Therapy*. London: Sage Publications. This revised version is included here by kind permission of the publishers.

Chapter 6

Collaboration
The Bigger Picture

Alison Barrington

Priestley writes: 'the multidisciplinary team – I loved it and hated it, but we music therapists could not and cannot do without it, so the more young music therapists have time to get to know and work with its members, the better' (1993, p.27). As she suggests, team work is not without its challenges, but it is absolutely necessary for music therapists to engage with the process. The issues raised in this book highlight some of the reasons why music therapists might love and hate team work.

This chapter considers two main areas. First it explores the broader context within which team work exists and includes some of the historical factors that have made it difficult for some professionals to relinquish autonomy and become active members of multidisciplinary teams. This chapter notes that sometimes professions have been in competition with each other and this has been detrimental for the care of patients. In recent years the government has encouraged the public to become more vocal about health care provision and this development has helped health care professionals to re-focus their work.

The second main area that is reviewed in this chapter is the way in which the music therapy profession has engaged with the concept of team work. The music therapy profession in the UK has developed at the end of the twentieth century when the expectation of collaboration is firmly established. As such it has not struggled with the concept of collaborative work at varying levels. Instead, being such a small discipline, it has struggled hard to find its place in an already over-crowded market. Thus this chapter explores some of the difficulties that clinicians have had to raise the profile of music therapy.

This chapter focuses closely on team work within the NHS primarily because the Association of Professional Music Therapists in the UK has spent much time collaborating with the NHS. The term 'interagency' is used collectively to include collaborative team work at multi-, inter- and trans-disciplinary levels. It is hoped that this chapter offers enough insight into interdisciplinary issues to be applicable to all practitioners, whether employed by the NHS, working for another organisation or self-employed. Thus this chapter will explore both clinical and political implications involved in team work.

COLLABORATION BETWEEN CLINICIANS AND MANAGERS: A CAUTIOUS RELATIONSHIP

Interagency work is complex. It involves so many different strands, not only the different members of the team itself but also the many organisations and agencies that surround it. Perhaps most influential is the organisation within which a team functions. It may have been the driving force that created the team in the first place. It may have expectations of what the team might achieve, producing demanding terms and conditions, all of which can put pressure on teams.

Much has been written about the NHS and the way it has established interagency teams. It is an organisation which has developed a divide between management and clinicians and this itself raises many questions. How do collaborative teams that are made up of different disciplines work within the NHS? Recently the government has encouraged the public to be more vocal about what it wants from the health service. Can patients become involved in the collaboration between government and professions? Music therapy is a relatively small, new profession within the health service. How can it survive within such a large and competitive marketplace? Are clinicians happy to collaborate with each other? What are the potential pitfalls and what are the advantages to interagency work?

Anna Cohen suggests that communication is a problem between clinicians and management primarily because of the different experiences and knowledge that each party brings to the situation (Cohen 1995). Studies into the NHS workforce have shown that the majority of clinicians are women whereas most managers are men, which is perceived to be a contributing factor (Owens and Petch 1995). Clinicians distrust the decisions made by management as they consider they are more interested in the financial implications of their work. Clinicians also note that general management are removed from the 'coal-face' of the work (that is, working with patients) which does not help to foster feelings of respect towards managers (Cohen 1995). Overall there is a sense that managers and clinicians have different focuses – managers concentrate on the broader issues regarding service provision whilst practitioners focus on the needs of individual service-users (Owens and Petch 1995).

Helen Odell-Miller offered a good example of collaborative work where the two parties involved had different agendas regarding the provision of health care and yet the negotiations between the two proved satisfactory for all concerned. The music therapy service in the community for adults with mental health problems in the Cambridge area was hoping to focus on long-term treatment procedures because of the perceived benefits to the patients. Concerned that this form of treatment may be seen as financially prohibitive, Odell-Miller approached the Director of the Purchasing Team for the local mental health service, to explain the issues involved. The Director was enthusiastic about this use of the music therapy service, not for clinical reasons, but because he was hoping that music therapy could fill a perceived gap in the service and cope with patients who 'might otherwise have slipped through the net'. Odell-Miller explained, 'his priorities and ours as therapists, whilst at first seemingly based at opposite ends of the spectrum of health care priorities, are closer than we might first have thought' (Odell-Miller 1995a, p.8). The music therapy service was reacting to the needs of the clients whilst the Director of the Purchasing Team was keen to demonstrate that gaps in the service were being covered. Thus, whilst the motivating factors might have been different, the service was approved.

The difficulties in establishing effective collaboration within the field of medicine can be traced back to the nineteenth century when doctors had enormous amounts of autonomy and their affairs were conducted with little intrusion from the government. It was felt distasteful to intrude in the affairs of medics who hailed from the gentry and this laissez faire attitude suited both parties: the doctors enjoyed their freedom, and the government was spared the effort of having to get involved in what was considered private patient–doctor relationships.

However, by the end of the nineteenth century there was a movement towards greater governmental involvement in the affairs of the professions (Etzioni 1964; Larkin 1995). Basic changes in the structure of society such as state education and the growth of urbanisation meant that the professions were carrying out the work of the state and this forced the government to pay more attention to the active role which professions were taking in society (Larson 1977; Rueschemeyer 1983). The founding of the NHS in 1948 provided the government with a clear opportunity to manage actively the national provision for health. Levels of management have increased significantly since the 1980s, causing tension between the management and clinical sides. The management side is seen to be more focused on cost effectiveness which has caused clinicians to compete with each other for financial security. How has this affected interdisciplinary team work?

COLLABORATION BETWEEN CLINICIANS: A COMPETITIVE SITUATION?

Since the government introduced service purchasers and providers within the NHS in the 1980s each department has been required to provide evidence of the most cost-effective and clinically effective treatments with the most effective winning the contracts. This can thwart attempts at productive team work because each department is competing for work. It is the antithesis of healthy interagency collaboration and it has encouraged an atmosphere within the NHS in which the various professions have become more focused on their own needs rather than the needs of the patients. The introduction of the internal market, at its worst, has established power struggles *between* different services within the NHS.

Despite this rather gloomy view of inter-professional competitiveness the government has been keen for interagency teams to flourish. As early as 1968 primary health care teams introduced community nursing staff across different local authorities. In the 1980s the government noted that inter-professional work would profit patients but divisions between professionals were hindering both the health and social care service (Carrier and Kendall 1995). Establishing links between different professions is not simple:

> It should come as no surprise that calls for interprofessional collaboration have proved to be more an aspiration than an easily achieved reality. Such collaboration implies the sharing of knowledge; respect for individual autonomy of different professional groups and administrators; the surrender of professional territory where necessary; and a shared set of values concerning appropriate responses to shared definitions of need. Professions, whether defined in terms of either altruistic

service-ideals or conspiratorial power-seeking, are likely to find this an
ambitious and demanding agenda. (Carrier and Kendall 1995, p.18)

The notion of conspiratorial power-seeking professionals can lead to hostile,
in-house competitiveness which is counter-productive to healthy collaboration. Recognising this problem in the 1990s the new government felt that
patients also had the right to voice their opinions regarding their own health
care. Thus the focus shifted at the end of the twentieth century to promote
the needs and choice of the patients themselves. Despite continuing bureaucratic wrangling, this does, at least, offer patients some opportunities to
contribute their views.

As a result patients have become more interested in exploring different
types of treatment procedures and the marketplace is full of professions
attempting to promote themselves. Since the 1960s and 1970s unsuccessful
or controversial drug trials have caused the public to question the safety of
the pharmaceutical services as well as the perceived authoritarian attitude of
medics. Thus professions such as the arts therapies have taken the opportunity to establish and maintain themselves more firmly as credible alternatives
(Cant and Sharma 1996). As Morag McGrath wrote:

> It is possible that the traditional supremacy of doctors is being chal-
> lenged as the newer professions, such as social work and nursing, gain
> confidence and as their professional roles develop. Team work and
> multi-disciplinary working has been given more prominence in profes-
> sional training in recent years so that barriers may be more easily
> overcome among younger professionals. (McGrath 1991, p.48)

Despite the fact that interagency work is not a new phenomenon, doctors
still tend to be reluctant to join in with team work, preferring to remain
autonomous (Miller et al. 2001). All interagency teams will have representatives from a variety of different professions bringing with them contrasting
training backgrounds, value systems and expectations. The newer professions have incorporated the notion of collaborative work at an earlier stage in
their development than, for example, doctors. However, the problems of collaboration are not just between management and clinicians; clinicians themselves struggle to accept the notion of team work.

HEALTHY COLLABORATION INCLUDES PATIENTS

For most of the time the notion of interagency collaboration describes inter-professional teams. However, I want to introduce another kind of collaboration. In the 1990s the government invited patients to take a more pro-active role in the health service, which can be represented as a triangular diagram (Johnson 1972) (see Figure 6.1).

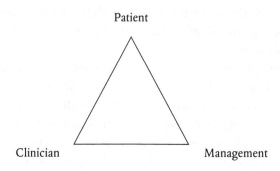

Figure 6.1 Johnson's depiction of a three-way collaboration

I am suggesting that these are the three parties that are involved in the provision of health care in the UK at the beginning of the twenty-first century. Collaboration ought to focus on the needs of the patients and this will be achieved more successfully if the patients themselves are included at the negotiating table.

This triangle offers a clear and simple diagram but perhaps it doesn't quite tell the whole story. Collaboration is based upon careful balancing between the needs and demands of each party in quite a precarious manner. I have already hinted that interagency and inter-departmental teams can be fraught with power struggles and tensions because every member has different expectations. Clinicians and managers can be motivated by different agendas. If there are disputes *between* professionals the danger is that a team's focus will turn away from the patients' needs. In an ideal world collaboration should encourage an attitude where all parties are working productively for the good of the patients (Hugman 1991). The art therapist Diane Waller suggested that the professionals are involved in political games aiming to enhance their own needs. This is really the antithesis of the core values of arts therapies. As she wrote,

> Why [do] art therapists want to [become involved with political games] when it appears so much at odds with the attitude of an art therapist to encourage honesty, openness and integrity for self and clients? Why is it necessary? When the art therapist has so often identified with the 'outsiders' in our society what is to be achieved and what lost in the process? (Waller 2001, p.246)

If the patients' needs are lost within bureaucratic wrangling the work becomes pointless. Therefore, it is advantageous for patients to have their voices heard in order for the professionals to be reminded of their prime responsibilities.

The responsible way to achieve healthy collaboration is through transparent partnership. Employers require clear levels of accountability, through research, auditing and codes of conduct. The process needs to be *seen* to be transparent and the management needs to be *seen* to be impartial. Similarly, clinicians need to be *seen* to be providing accurate and honest information. This will demonstrate both the clinical and management sides are acting responsibly. The Association of Professional Music Therapists in the UK has sought to achieve this by seeking governmental approval. The public will tend to trust a profession if it has government backing. The government hopes to gain public respect because it is seen to be working for the good of the public by monitoring the music therapy service. It is hoped the public are able to monitor the collaboration between the management and clinical sides and feel content that they have been included in the process.

Michel Foucault understood the complexity of these interagency teams when he wrote about the relationship between the professions and the government. He suggested that professions are not separate from the government. Rather, professions come under the umbrella of the governmental organisation (Johnson 1995). Clinicians and managers need to recognise a sense of inter-dependency in order to function most effectively.

MUSIC THERAPISTS' APPROACHES TO INTERAGENCY COLLABORATION

The complex interrelations between different teams can provide challenges and opportunities for music therapists. Whilst some practitioners are employed by the NHS others work more independently. Leslie Bunt explained that some practitioners have set up 'peripatetic services, following their clients out into the community. Others [have become] part of community-based teams, linking with other creative therapists or local para-medical services' (Bunt 2004, p.269). How music therapists are integrated into teams can have a significant impact on the way in which clinical services can be delivered.

The Arts Therapies Department within Cambridge Mental Health Trust has explored the advantages and disadvantages of working either within or outside the NHS (Arts Therapies Discussion Group 1997). By working outside the NHS a professional can offer an independent service which can be more autonomous and flexible. There can be less pressure on the practitioner to have to conform to NHS structures or other professions' terminology in order to 'conform' to in-house demands. Bunt's response to Care in the Community (The Community Care Act, DoH 1990) has been based on his desire to make music therapy as widely accessible as possible, which he stated could be achieved more effectively *outside*, and yet in conjunction with, the NHS. He has established the music therapy charity MusicSpace which aims to deliver a network of services within the community. Each project within the service is reactive to the particular needs of each client group and institution in which it works (Bunt 2004).

Music therapists who work within the NHS may have to cope with the imposition of strict, organisational regulations. Employers are in a powerful position because they impose regulations, financial restrictions and other limitations on resources and demand accountability. As such it would seem that this type of collaboration is based on an imbalanced relationship with the more powerful employer making exacting demands on the music therapists. And it also needs to be remembered that the NHS, like all other institutions is, in turn, accountable to the government.

Do music therapists who work in private practice have more autonomy? In the 1950s and 1960s pioneering music therapists such as Juliette Alvin, Paul Nordoff and Clive Robbins and Mary Priestley were able to focus their attention on their relationship with their patients without enormous levels of accountability imposed by external authorities. At the beginning of the twenty-first century accountability has become a significant issue for music therapists. Whether a music therapist is working in private practice, for a music therapy charity such as MusicSpace, a large institution such as the NHS or a smaller, community-based project, the practitioner will be engaged in collaborative work at some level. In fact, all arts therapists are accountable to the Health Professions Council which is the statutory body to which many professions allied to health belong. Thus collaborative work (in the broadest sense) is an inevitable part of all arts therapists' work.

ARTS THERAPIES: CHOOSING THE RIGHT BED-FELLOWS

Becoming a member of a team has both clinical and political implications. Although a practitioner may not have much choice as to which team to join, considering these implications is vital.

Simon Proctor raised a concern that patients' needs will be compromised if the music therapy profession forges inappropriate allegiances within professional teams. He is particularly worried that the music therapy profession has collaborated too closely with the orthodox medical profession for its own gains. He explains that

> [p]erhaps, as a profession, music therapy desires to bask in the respectability of medicalism, hence choosing to concentrate on issues such as state registration at the expense of the breadth of services available to users. Or perhaps individual music therapists are simply reluctant to abandon the status and authority that medicalism confers upon them... We must not merge entirely into a medicalised professional hierarchy: to empower and enable, wherever we work, we need hearing minds and radical hearts. And if that means being regarded as mavericks and naïve, then so be it. (Proctor 2002, pp.100 and 106)

Is Proctor more concerned that music therapy is becoming more medicalised or that the public will *perceive* it to be more medicalised?

Jaakko Erkkilä disagrees with this view, noting that the music therapy profession has

> had to fight for the status and approval of music therapy for years... It would be a professional suicide to change the track which links us with the other therapy professions. Psychiatry 'yes,' medical 'yes,' individual 'yes,' we must say. (Erkkilä 2003, p.3)

He states that the professional identity of the music therapist needs to remain within the medical realm and that it is not fully up to us as music therapists to define music therapy – unfortunately. When defining music therapy we must pay attention to the professional context (and culture) next to us. This context consists of psychiatry, psychology, psychotherapy, and medicine. (Erkkilä 2003, p.4)

Music therapy, like other fields, is not able to define itself completely independently (Bruscia 1987). Instead the identity or image of music therapy is co-constructed by both the professionals themselves and the public. Working within specific teams may help clarify a professional image of music therapy. To work closely with doctors suggests an allegiance to the medical profession. To work closely with teachers suggests a more educational slant. What are the political implications for the profession?

To become a member of a team requires careful consideration. Working within a team of diverse disciplines may require a music therapist to find a balance between offering a unique contribution and working in conjunction with the overall, corporate aims of the group.

One way of increasing the potential inclusion of music therapy within transagency collaboration has been to define and highlight the unique service that only music therapy can provide. An example of this has been offered by Connie Isenberg-Grzeda. She suggested that the creation of assessment procedures specific to music therapy practice is vital in providing opportunities for effective collaborative partnerships. This development could enhance the 'professional credibility of...music therapy...[because an]...insistence on the specialized capacities of the music therapist reinforces the concept of a unique contribution to the interdisciplinary team [and]...establishes a specific technology for music therapists' (Isenberg-Grzeda 1988, p.166). This is only one way in which music therapy may be able to stress the necessity of including the services of a music therapist into a team. More research is needed in order to promote the unique service of music therapy within collaborative situations.

CONCLUDING THOUGHTS

Whilst the notion of collaborative work has been developing within the NHS and other large social care organisations for a number of decades it is an ideal which has taken a long time to set up effectively. This seems to be due to the fact that, although not against the concept of team work, some clinicians have been reticent about relinquishing the amount of autonomy they believe they have. Collaboration has come more easily to some professions within the NHS than others.

Within music therapy there has been little dissent with regard to the development of collaborative work. However, there is some concern that the ethos of music therapy does not fit well with that of orthodox medical professions. Proctor is one of the most vocal practitioners to criticise any decisions to work alongside the bio-medical model. Erkkilä's response is a pragmatic one and I suggest that collaborative team work needs to be engaged with pragmatically. Collaborative work is not easy. It requires flexibility and respect for differences of opinion. It requires coordination, cooperation and communication (Øvretveit 1993). And it requires colleagues to recognise that they are 'different aspects, or profiles, of a single social phenomenon in the modern world' (Johnson 1995, p.13).

Is it more beneficial to work together? I believe it is. Time and energy taken to work independently from, or in a worse case scenario actively antagonistically against, other professions will be wasted when it could be spent providing a productive service for patients.

Chapter 7

Postscript

Karen Twyford and Tessa Watson

It is in the overlap where disciplines meet that practitioners really begin to be creative. (Goodyear, this volume, p.60)

This book has described in detail the importance and increasing prevalence of collaborative working at different levels within varied multidisciplinary teams. As confirmed by all our authors, the multidisciplinary team, however constructed, can be of great value to the music therapist, allowing rich and beneficial collaborative opportunities to be offered to service users. Throughout the chapters of this book, a number of key messages have emerged which illustrate the core themes and benefits of collaborative work.

COLLABORATION AND PROFESSIONAL IDENTITY: CONSOLIDATING OUR ROLES

To become a member of a team requires careful consideration. Working within a team of diverse disciplines may require a music therapist to find a balance between offering a unique contribution and working in conjunction with the overall, corporate aims of the group. (Barrington, this volume, p.212)

Since the beginnings of the profession in the UK, music therapists have worked hard to establish their role in relation to the multidisciplinary team. This has meant clarifying the purpose and boundaries of the role, and informing other professions about the specific role of the music therapist and the way in which the therapy works. For many, it has been necessary to protect key facets of the work. Hedderly confirms this, stating: 'Historically, there has been a need for music therapists and other arts therapists to maintain clear boundaries around our practice in order to establish and preserve the value and authenticity of our clinical work.' (this volume, p.140).

Taking a team approach involves addressing issues such as professional protectionism and rivalry amongst staff and professionals. In her chapter, Miller describes the way in which 'envy and rivalry can play a part in professional relationships, and are often related to fantasies and misunderstandings about each other's role and function. The full range of skills and abilities of each discipline are infrequently recognised by the whole team' (this volume, p.133). Team work, therefore, may not be easy and requires open discussion and honesty between colleagues.

Despite these challenges, working collaboratively within teams has been effective in accomplishing a consolidated role for music therapists, as described by numerous authors within this book. Perhaps because music therapists now feel more confident within a more widely established profession, they are frequently seeking partnership and collaboration with colleagues, finding that this can be a different way of clarifying the roles and boundaries of the different professions within a team. Tyas illustrates this when she states that:

> I have always sought out transdisciplinary working, initially due to working in isolation and increasingly as I have seen its value to clients and to mutual understanding amongst professionals. The process of merging skills, ways of working, insight and experience has sometimes felt like a journey fro m separate parts into one entity and has been well worth the effort. (This volume, p.117)

This book has sought to document and celebrate this development in the profession; the case studies in each chapter show how collaboration can be a fruitful way to convey the importance and efficacy of our work. Music therapists will continue to negotiate their level of collaboration in discussion with their colleagues, finding, inevitably, that the service user's needs will dictate how the team can most usefully collaborate together.

Rationale to collaborate

In order to best meet the client's needs, it is essential that the music therapist is able to work as an integral part of the treatment team. (Magee, this volume, p.161)

In the quotation above Magee identifies the fundamental reason for collaboration. Bringing different areas of expertise together allows skills and perspectives to be combined in order to meet clients' needs more effectively and comprehensively. This may particularly be so where a client has significant difficulties or impairments. These thoughts are validated by Twyford, Parkhouse and Murphy in their collaborative assessment work:

> In working together we felt that our approaches became inextricably linked. We obtained experiential insight into ways of working with complex children which we believe would have been more difficult had we undertaken the assessments separately. Working collaboratively revealed the potential of each child and informed future planning not only for those of us directly involved but also other professionals involved with the child. (This volume, p.53)

This quotation also highlights another rationale for collaboration: the rich learning experience that takes place between colleagues. Talking about her work with a speech and language therapist, with adults with learning disabilities, Tessa Watson explains how:

> I felt as though we quickly found a way to work together; this seemed to be partly because we were very respectful of each other's knowledge and experience, and we listened carefully to the reasons why we might each do something in a particular way, rather than being defensive about our own ways of working. I remember the challenge of needing to explain clearly my rationale for practice; this really helped me to clarify my thoughts! (This volume, p.116)

Here we can see how each collaborating partner learns not only about their colleague's role, skills and attitudes, but is also challenged to review and critique their own practice. This is deep learning indeed, and valuable to continuing professional development.

Additionally collaborative working is valuable in enabling support between colleagues. O'Neill describes how joint working provides 'the emotional support needed in order to work with children and families who are coping with the challenges of life-threatening conditions' (this volume, p.73). Where teams are working with clients who are facing great challenges, in the form of illnesses and disabilities, the team can be helped greatly in their work if they are able to support each other, sharing difficulties and challenges through collaboration. This theme is highlighted time and again in the case studies in this book.

WHO ARE OUR COLLABORATIVE PARTNERS?

> *Working as music therapists within a multi-professional team can at times be difficult and isolating. We have found it crucial and extremely beneficial to embrace input, advice and support from other disciplines. (Fearn and O'Connor, this volume, p.60)*

We have seen in this book that collaboration occurs with a wide variety of different professionals. This is determined by the needs of the client, and the type of team in which music therapists are employed. The case studies in this book have described music therapists working with speech and language therapists, physiotherapists, occupational therapists, dramatherapists, dance movement therapists, play specialists, teachers, psychologists, consultant psychiatrists, nurses, chaplains and family members. However, this list is not exhaustive and we acknowledge that music therapists are working within increasingly unique partnerships with a variety of different colleagues and co-workers.

Close work with relatives and carers is becoming more prevalent in providing effective care. In her chapter, Freeman advises that it 'is vital not to overlook the family and carers of our clients… The possibilities of collaboration with relatives and carers are varied' (this volume, pp.186–7). Freeman stresses the importance of family and carers in enabling greater understanding of issues relating to culture, ethnicity and spirituality. Woodward believes that work with families creates 'opportunities for joint thinking, and for both of us to see things from a different perspective' (this volume, p.85).

Thus we can see that the net of collaboration has been cast widely and creatively by our contributors. The authors hope that this will inspire other music therapists to look around them and consider the network of collaboration that could be built in their working practice.

THE GOVERNMENT: BEST PRACTICE AND COLLABORATION

The government has called for professionals to consider joint working practices, suggesting that this is best practice, and will help to provide high quality and coordinated services. While for many collaborative approaches have always been essential, the government's more recent directives have given guidance to encourage workers to utilise the team to achieve comprehensive care in which all professionals, the client and their family and carers are considered. However, in her chapter, Barrington strikes a note of warning when she states that '[c]linicians and managers need to recognise a sense of inter-dependency in order to function most effectively' and that '[t]he responsible way to achieve healthy collaboration is through transparent partnership' (this volume, p.209). Clinicians and managers may sometimes work in an uneasy partnership, but Barrington's message is clear: they can and should learn from each other.

CREATIVITY, ENERGY AND LEARNING

Our joint working brought energy, as it left neither one of us carrying the lead role. Our regular discussions, our shared theoretical language and the very open approach we evolved facilitated a space for our minds which mitigated against feelings of fragmentation or disconnection and fostered a creative experience of working together. (Miller and Guarnieri, this volume, p.151)

This quotation summarises the benefits of collaborative work for music therapists. As well as providing a rich and multi-skilled therapeutic environment for the client, it brings energy, creativity and learning for all workers involved. Collaborative working demands both personal commitment and professional skill from practitioners. Significant self-reflection is required in order to ensure that workers can collaborate without defensiveness and competitiveness. Ultimately, openness to change and honesty about one's own practice is required by all involved.

Those case study authors who have embarked on collaborations show that the benefits of new energy, creativity and learning are the exciting rewards for working through the challenges.

Over time, collaborating partners may feel the need to develop or change their practice. Supervision and continuing professional development is essential in supporting the development of practice. In addition there are many ongoing considerations that must be addressed in order to achieve effective partnership practice. The guidelines for good practice found at the end of each chapter include practical points for practitioners to consider and draw on as a useful reference within their collaborative work.

CONCLUDING THOUGHTS

In the pages of this book, a comprehensive picture of collaborative and transdisciplinary practices is provided. As the book concludes the authors hope that the reader has gained a deeper understanding of the potential of collaborative and transdisciplinary approaches. We hope that the reader will feel inspired by the insights offered in such ways that they may embark on some collaborative working of their own, or reflect and develop their own practice, taking into account some of the key themes and guidelines from the text. Inevitably, it is not possible to include all the clinical areas in which this type of work takes place (we are aware of the omission of children's and adults' hospice work and early years work). We hope that there will be an opportunity in the future to provide a second volume of the book in which the evolution and development of collaborative and transdisciplinary approaches can be explored further.

References

Aasgard, T. (2000) 'A suspiciously cheerful lady: a study of a song's life in the paediatric oncology ward, and beyond…' *British Journal of Music Therapy 14*, 2, 70–82.

Abad, V. and Edwards, J. (2004) 'Strengthening families: a role for music therapy in contributing to family centred care.' *The Australian Journal of Music Therapy 15*, 3–17.

Abad, V. and Williams, K. (2006) 'Early intervention music therapy for adolescent mothers and their children.' *British Journal of Music Therapy 20*, 1, 31–38.

Agazarian, Y. and Peters, R. (1995) *The Visible and Invisible Group.* London: Karnac. (Original work published 1981).

Agrotou, A. (1999) *Sounds and Meaning: Group Music Therapy with People with Profound Learning Difficulties and their Carers.* London: Lumiere.

Ahonen-Eerikainen, H. (2003) 'Musical Dialogue and Other Working Methods of Music Therapists and Forms of Music Therapy for Children.' in L. Kossolapow, S. Scobie and D. Waller (eds) *Arts-Therapies-Communication: On the Way to a Regional European Arts Therapy, Volume 2.* New Brunswick: Transaction Publishers.

Allen, N.J. and Hecht, T.D. (2004) 'The "romance of teams": toward an understanding of its psychological underpinnings and implications.' *Journal of Occupational and Organizational Psychology 77*, 439–461.

Allgood, N. (2005) 'Parents' perceptions of family-based group music therapy for children with ASD.' *Music Therapy Perspectives 23*, 2, 92–99.

American Psychiatric Association (1994) *Diagnostic and Statistical Manual of Mental Disorders: DSM IV.* Washington, DC: American Psychiatric Association.

Anthony, T. (2003) *TDPB Evaluation and the Young Child who is Deafblind: Assessing Orientation and Mobility Skills.* Available at www.tsbvi.edu/Education/om-tdpb.htm, accessed 26 January 2007.

Ardern, M. (2004) 'Ethical Aspects of Psychotherapy and Clinical Work with Older Adults.' In S. Evans and J. Garner (eds) *Talking Over the Years: A Handbook of Dynamic Psychotherapy with Older Adults.* Hove: Brunner-Routledge.

Arts Therapies Discussion Group (1997) *Potentials for Growth of Arts' Therapies Department.* Minutes of a meeting of the Arts Therapies Department within the Cambridge Mental Health Trust (unpublished, 25 September).

Association of Professional Music Therapists (APMT) (2004) *Re: Current Music Therapy Statistics.* Personal communication (27 March).

Bang, C. (1996) 'Musical Voice: Treatment and Speech Therapy with Deaf Children.' In I. Pedersen and L. Bonde (eds) *Music Therapy within Multidisciplinary Teams – Proceedings of the 3rd European Music Therapy Conference.* Aalborg: Aalborg University.

Bannerman-Haig, S. (1999) 'Dance Movement Therapy: A Case Study.' In A. Cattanach (ed.) *Process in the Arts Therapies.* London: Jessica Kingsley Publishers.

Barrington, A. (2003) *Multi-professional Teamwork.* Unpublished paper.

Bateman, A. and Fonagy, P. (1999) 'Effectiveness of partial hospitalization in the treatment of borderline personality disorder: a randomized controlled trial.' *American Journal of Psychiatry 156*, 10, 1563–1569.

Bateman, A. and Holmes, J. (1995) *Introduction to Psychoanalysis: Contemporary Theory and Practice.* London and New York: Routledge.

Bertolami, M. and Martino, L. (2002) 'Music therapy in a private school for visually impaired and multiply handicapped children.' *Voices: A World Forum for Music Therapy.* Available at www.voices.no/mainissues/Voices2(1)Bertolami.html, accessed 26 January 2007.

Best, P. (2000) 'Theoretical diversity and clinical collaboration: reflections by a dance/ movement therapist.' *The Arts in Psychotherapy 27*, 3, 197–211.

Bion, W.R. (1962) *Learning from Experience.* London: Heinemann.

Bion, W.R. (1967) *Second Thoughts.* London: Heinemann.

Bonny, H. (1997) 'The state of the art of music therapy.' *The Arts in Psychotherapy 24*, 1, 65–73.

Booth, R. (2004) 'Current practice and understanding of music therapy in Victorian special education.' *Australian Journal of Music Therapy 15*, 64–75.

Brightman, A. and Ridlington-White, H. (2005) 'Co-therapy within arts therapy: splits and opposites – the healing journey.' *BSMT/APMT Annual Conference Proceedings.* London: BSMT Publications.

Brill, N.I. (1976) *Teamwork: Working Together in the Human Services.* Philadelphia: J.B. Lippincott Company.

Brown, D. (2000) 'Self Development through Subjective Interaction: A Fresh Look at "Ego Training in Action".' In D. Brown and L. Zinkin (eds) *The Psyche and the Social World: Developments in Group Analytic Theory.* London: Jessica Kingsley Publishers. (Original work published 1994.)

Brown, S. (1999) 'Some thoughts on music, therapy, and music therapy.' *British Journal of Music Therapy 13*, 2, 63–71.

Brumfitt, S. and Sheeran, P. (1999) *Visual Analogue Self Esteem Scale.* Winslow: Bicester.

Bruscia, K. (1987) 'Professional Identity Issues in Music Therapy Education.' In C. Dileo-Maranto and K. Bruscia (eds) *Perspectives on Music Therapy Education and Training.* Philadelphia: Temple University, Esther Boyer College of Music.

Bryant, W. (1991) 'Creative group work with confused elderly people: a development of sensory integration therapy.' *British Journal of Occupational Therapy 54*, 5, 187–192.

Bunt, L. (1994) *Music Therapy: An Art Beyond Words.* London: Routledge.

Bunt, L. (2004) 'Music, Space and Health: The Story of MusicSpace.' In M. Pavlicevic and G. Ansdell (eds) *Community Music Therapy.* London: Jessica Kingsley Publishers.

Burns, T. and Lloyd, H. (2004) 'Is a team approach based on staff meetings cost-effective in the delivery of mental health care?' *Current Opinion in Psychiatry 17*, 4, 311–314.

Byng, S. and Duchan, J. (2005) 'Social model philosophies and principles: their applications to therapies for aphasia.' *Aphasiology 19*, 10/11, 906–922.

Canadian Institutes of Health Research (2003) 'Definition of Transdisciplinary'. Available at www.cihr-irsc.gc.ca, accessed 26 March 2008.

Cant, S. and Sharma, U. (eds) (1996) *Complementary and Alternative Medicines: Knowledge in Practice.* London: Free Association Publishers.

Cardone, L., Marengo, J. and Calisch, A. (1982) 'Conjoint use of art and verbal techniques for the intensification of the psychotherapeutic group experience.' *The Arts in Psychotherapy 9*, 263–268.

Carrier, J. and Kendall, I. (1995) 'Professionalism and Interprofessionalism in Health and Community Care: Some Theoretical Issues.' In P. Owens, J. Carrier and J. Horder (eds) *Interprofessional Issues in Community and Primary Health Care.* Basingstoke: Macmillan Press.

Carter, E. (2002) 'Playing Our Part: The Role of a Music Therapy Group as an Aid to Diagnosis.' In J. Fachner and D. Aldridge (eds) *Dialogue and Debate* – Conference Proceedings of the 10th World Congress on Music Therapy. Available at www.musictherapyworld.net/modules/ wfmt/stuff/oxford2002.pdf, accessed 25 January 2007.

Claeys, M.S., Miller, A.C., Dalloul-Rampersad, R. and Kollar, M. (1989) 'The role of music and music therapy in the rehabilitation of traumatically brain injured clients.' *Music Therapy Perspectives 6*, 71–77.

Clair, A. (2002) 'The effects of music therapy on engagement in family caregiver and care receiver couples with dementia.' *American Journal of Alzheimer's Disease and Other Dementias 17*, 5, 286–290.

Cohen, A. (1995) 'The Market and Professional Frameworks.' In P. Owens, J. Carrier and J. Horder (eds) *Interprofessional Issues in Community and Primary Health Care.* Basingstoke: Macmillan Press.

Cohen, B. (1983) 'Combined art and movement therapy group: isomorphic responses.' *The Arts in Psychotherapy 10*, 229–232.

Cordess, C. (1998) 'The Multi-disciplinary Team: Introduction.' In C. Cordess and M. Cox (eds) *Forensic Psychotherapy, Crime, Psychodynamics and the Offender Patient.* London: Jessica Kingsley Publishers. (Original work published 1996.)

Crozier, E. and Hamill, R. (1988) 'The benefits of combining speech and music therapy.' *Speech Therapy in Practice*, November, 9–10.

Darnley-Smith, R. and Patey, H. (2003) *Music Therapy.* London: Sage.

Davies, A. and Richards, E. (1998) 'Music therapy in acute psychiatry: our experience of working as co-therapists with a group for patients from two neighbouring wards.' *British Journal of Music Therapy 12*, 2, 53–59.

Department for Education and Skills (DfES) (2003) *Every Child Matters.* London: The Stationery Office.

Department for Education and Skills (DfES) (2004) *Every Child Matters: Change for Children.* London: HMSO.

Department of Health (DoH) (1990) *National Health Service and Care in the Community 1990 Elizabeth II*, Chapter 19. London: Department of Health.

Department of Health (DoH) (1997) *The New NHS.* London: Department of Health.

Department of Health (DoH) (1999) *The National Service Framework for Mental Health (NSFMH).* London: Department of Health.

Department of Health (DoH) (2000) *The NHS Plan.* London: Department of Health.

Department of Health (DoH) (2001) *Valuing People: A New Strategy for Learning Disability for the 21st Century.* London: Department of Health.

Department of Health (DoH) (2003) *Getting the Right Start: National Service Framework for Children, Young People and Maternity Services: Standard for Hospital Services.* London: Department of Health.

Department of Health (DoH) (2004a) *The National Service Framework for Children, Young People and Maternity Services.* London: Department of Health.

Department of Health (DoH) (2004b) *The Ten Essential Shared Capabilities – A Framework for the Whole of the Mental Health Workforce.* London: Department of Health/NHSU/Sainsbury Centre/National Institute for Mental Health in England.

Department of Health (DoH) (2005a) *New Ways of Working for Psychiatrists: Enhancing Effective, Person-Centred Services Through New Ways of Working in Multidisciplinary and Multi-Agency Contexts.* London: Department of Health. Final report from the National Steering Group, co-chaired by National Institute for Mental Health in England and Royal College of Psychiatrists.

Department of Health (DoH) (2005b) *The National Service Framework for Long-term Conditions.* London: Department of Health.

Durham, C. (2002) 'Music therapy and neurology.' In L. Bunt and S. Hoskyns (eds) *The Handbook of Music Therapy.* London: Brunner-Routledge.

Edwards, J. (1999) 'Music therapy with children hospitalised for severe injury or illness.' *British Journal of Music Therapy 13*, 1, 21–27.

Edwards, J. (2002) 'Using the evidence based medicine framework to support music therapy posts in healthcare settings.' *British Journal of Music Therapy 16*, 1, 29–34.

Edwards, J. and Kennelly, J. (2004) 'Music therapy in paediatric rehabilitation.' *Nordic Journal of Music Therapy 13*, 2, 112–126.

Eisler, J. (1993) 'Stretto – music therapy in the context of the multidisciplinary team: establishing a place in the multidisciplinary team.' *Journal of British Music Therapy 7*, 1, 23–24.

Elefant, C. and Lotan, M. (1998) 'Rett syndromes: a transdisciplinary approach. Music and physical therapy intervention.' *Music Therapy – A Dialogue: Proceedings of the 4th European Music Therapy Congress.* Available at www.musictherapyworld.net, accessed 28 October 2006.

Elefant, C. and Lotan, M. (2004) 'Rett syndrome: dual intervention – music and physical therapy.' *Nordic Journal of Music Therapy 13*, 2, 172–182.

Emerson, E., Hatton, C., Felce, D. and Murphy, G. (2001) *Learning Disabilities: The Fundamental Facts.* London: The Foundation for People with Learning Disabilities.

Erkkilä, J. (2003) 'Review: *Contemporary Voices in Music Therapy. Communication, Culture and Community.* C. Kenny and B. Stige (eds). Oslo: Unipubforlag.' Available at www.njmt.no/bookreview_2003029.html, accessed 25 February 2003.

Etzioni, A. (1964) *Modern Organizations.* Englewood Cliffs: Prentice-Hall Foundations of Modern Sociology Series.

Farmakopoulou, N. (2002) 'Using an integrated theoretical framework for understanding inter-agency collaboration in the special educational needs field.' *European Journal of Special Needs Education 17*, 1, 49–59.

Farnan, L. (2003) 'Music therapy at Central Wisconsin Center for the Developmentally Disabled.' *Voices: A World Forum for Music Therapy.* Available at www.voices.no/mainissues/mi40003000121.html, accessed 26 January 2007.

Fearn, M. and O'Connor, R. (2003) 'The whole is greater than the sum of its parts: experiences of co-working as music therapists.' *British Journal of Music Therapy 17*, 2, 67–75.

Fearn, M. and O'Connor, R. (2004) 'Music and attuned movement therapy: a therapeutic approach developed at the Cheyne Day Centre, London.' *BSMT/APMT Annual Conference Proceedings. Changes: Exploring Clinical, Professional and Global Perspectives.* London: BSMT Publications.

Feinstein-Whittaker, M. and O'Connell-Goodfellow, E. (1989) *Group Treatment for Head Injury: A Linguistic and Cognitive Approach.* Arizona: Communication Skills Builders Inc.

Figlure Alder, R. and Fisher, P. (1984) 'My self...through music, movement and art.' *The Arts in Psychotherapy 11*, 203–208.

Finlay, C., Bruce, H., Magee, W.L., Farrelly, S. and McKenzie, S. (2001) 'How I use music in therapy.' *Speech Therapy in Practice*, Autumn, 30–35.

Fonagy, P., Gergely, G., Jurist, E.L. and Target, M. (2004) *Affect Regulation, Mentalization, and the Development of the Self.* London: Karnac. (Original work published 2002.)

Freeman, A. (2003) 'Following the path: how two cases finally ended.' *Community, Relationship and Spirit: Continuing the Dialogue and Debate.* Papers from the BSMT/APMT Annual Conference. London: BSMT Publications.

Freeman, A. (2007) *Collaborative Working with Elderly Clients.* Unpublished survey of Association of Professional Music Therapists' database.

Gale, C. and Matthews, R. (1998) 'Journey in Joint Working: Some Reflections on an Experience of Arts Therapies Collaboration.' In M. Rees (ed.) *Drawing on Difference: Art Therapy with People who have Learning Difficulties.* London: Routledge.

Galvin, S. and McCarthy, S. (1994) 'Multi-disciplinary community teams: clinging to the wreckage.' *Journal of Mental Health 3*, 157–166.

Garner, J. (2004) 'Dementia.' In S. Evans and J. Garner (eds) *Talking Over the Years: A Handbook of Dynamic Psychotherapy with Older Adults.* Hove: Brunner-Routledge.

Garner, J. (ed.) (2005) *Understanding Institutional Abuse of Older Patients: Some Reflections.* Barnet, Enfield and Haringey Mental Health NHS Trust.

Gersie, A. (1992) *Earth Tales: Storytelling in Times of Change.* London: The Merlin Press.

Gervin, A.P. (1991) 'Music therapy compensatory technique utilizing song lyrics during dressing to promote independence in a patient with brain injury.' *Music Therapy Perspectives 9*, 87–90.

Glyn, J. (2002) 'Drummed out of Mind: A Music Therapy Group with Forensic Patients.' In A. Davies and E. Richards (eds) *Music Therapy and Group Work: Sound Company.* London: Jessica Kingsley Publishers.

Glyn, J. (in press) 'Two's Company, Three's A Crowd: Hatred of Triangulation in Music Therapy, and its Supervision in a Forensic Setting.' In E. Richards and H. Odell-Miller (eds) (as yet untitled).

Goodman, J. (1999) 'Harvesting a Lifetime.' In A. Jewell (ed.) *Spirituality and Ageing.* London: Jessica Kingsley Publishers.

Grasso, M., Allison, D.J., Button, B.M. and Sawyer, S.M. (1999) 'Music and Physiotherapy: Evaluation of a Program Developed for Caregivers of Infants and Toddlers with Cystic Fibrosis.' in R. Rebollo Pratt and D. Erdonmez Grocke (eds) *MusicMedicine 3 – MusicMedicine and Music Therapy: Expanding Horizons.* Parkville: Faculty of Music, The University of Melbourne.

Grocke, D. and Wigram, T. (2007) *Receptive Methods in Music Therapy: Techniques and Clinical Applications for Music Therapy Clinicians, Educators and Students.* London: Jessica Kingsley Publishers.

Halton, W. (1994) 'Some Unconscious Aspects of Organizational Life: Contributions from Psychoanalysis.' In A. Obholzer and V. Zagier Roberts (eds) *The Unconscious at Work: Individual and Organizational Stress in the Human Services.* London: Routledge.

Hattersley, J. (1995) 'The Survival of Collaboration and Cooperation.' In N. Malin (ed.) *Services for People with Learning Disabilities.* London: Routledge.

Her Majesty's Stationery Office (HMSO) (2005) *Explanatory Memorandum to the Disability Discrimination Act.* London: The Stationery Office.

Hill, C. (2005) *Bridge Over Troubled Waters? A Study of Music Therapy and Speech and Language Therapy in Combined Practice.* Unpublished Masters dissertation: MMT thesis. Nordoff-Robbins Music Therapy Centre. London: City University.

Hills, B., Norman, I. and Forster, L. (2000) 'A study of burnout and multidisciplinary team-working amongst professional music therapists.' *British Journal of Music Therapy 14,* 1, 32–40.

Hobson, M.R. (2006a) 'The collaboration of music therapy and speech-language pathology in the treatment of neurogenic communication disorders: part I – diagnosis, therapist roles, and rationale for music.' *Music Therapy Perspectives 24,* 2, 58–65.

Hobson, M.R. (2006b) 'The collaboration of music therapy and speech-language pathology in the treatment of neurogenic communication disorders: part II – collaborative strategies and scope of practice.' *Music Therapy Perspectives 24,* 2, 66–72.

Holmes, J. (2002) *Depression.* Cambridge: Icon Books.

Hooper, J. and Lindsay, B. (1990) 'Music and the mentally handicapped: the effect of music on anxiety.' *Journal of British Music Therapy 4,* 2, 18–26.

Hooper, J., McManus, A. and McIntyre, A. (2004) 'Exploring the link between music therapy and sensory integration: an individual case study.' *British Journal of Music Therapy 18,* 1, 15–23.

Hoskyns, S. (2007) 'New night sky: renewing my music therapy culture.' *Voices: A World Forum for Music Therapy.* Available at www.voices.no/columnist/colHoskyns070507.php, accessed 25 May 2007.

Hudson, B. (1995) 'Is a Coordinated Service Attainable?' In N. Malin (ed.) *Services for People with Learning Disabilities.* London: Routledge.

Hugman, R. (1991) *Power in Caring Professions.* Basingstoke: Macmillan Press.

Humpal, M. (2004) 'Reflections on Orff music therapy.' *Voices: A World Forum for Music Therapy.* Available at www.voices.no/discussions/discm29_01.html, accessed 26 January 2007.

Hunt, A. and Kirk, R. (1997) 'Technology and music: incompatible subjects?' *British Journal of Music Education 14,* 2, 151–161.

Iles, P. and Auluck, R. (1990) 'From organizational to interorganizational development in nursing practice: improving the effectiveness of interdisciplinary teamwork and interagency collaboration.' *Journal of Advanced Nursing 15,* 50–58.

Isenberg-Grzeda, C. (1988) 'Music therapy assessment: a reflection of professional identity.' *Journal of Music Therapy 25,* 3, 156–169.

Jacobs, A. (2000) *An Investigation into the Perception of Music Therapy in a Service for Adults with Learning Disabilities – The Way Forward.* Unpublished Masters Dissertation: MMT thesis. Anglia Ruskin University: Cambridge.

Jacobs, A. and Lincoln, S. (2003) *Swimming against the Flow: What is the Role of the Arts Therapies in Multidisciplinary Teamworking?* Paper presented at Nordic Music Therapy Conference in Bergen, May 2003.

Jeffcote, N. and Travers, R. (2004) 'Thinking about the Needs of Women in Secure Settings.' In N. Jeffcote and T. Watson (eds) *Working Therapeutically with Women in Secure Mental Health Settings.* London: Jessica Kingsley Publishers.

Jeffcote, N. and Watson, T. (eds) (2004) *Working Therapeutically with Women in Secure Mental Health Settings.* London: Jessica Kingsley Publishers.

Jochims, S. (2004) 'Music therapy in the area of conflict between functional and psychotherapeutic approach within the field of neurology/neurorehabilitation.' *Nordic Journal of Music Therapy 13*, 2, 16.

Johnson, T. (1972) *Professions and Power.* London: Macmillan Press.

Johnson, T. (1995) 'Governmentality and the Institutionalization of Expertise.' In T. Johnson, G. Larkin and M. Saks (eds) *Health Professions and the State in Europe.* London: Routledge.

Jones, L. and Cardinal, D. (1998) 'A descriptive analysis of music therapists' perceptions of delivering services in inclusive settings: a challenge to the field.' *Journal of Music Therapy 35*, 1, 34–48.

Kennelly, J., Hamilton, L. and Cross, J. (2001) 'The interface of music therapy and speech pathology in the rehabilitation of children with acquired brain injury.' *Australian Journal of Music Therapy 12*, 13–20.

Kitwood, T. (1997) *Dementia Reconsidered: The Person Comes First.* Maidenhead: Open University Press.

Klein, M. (1997) 'Notes on Some Schizoid Mechanisms.' In M. Klein (ed.) *Envy and Gratitude and Other Works 1946–1963.* London: Vintage. (Original work published 1946.)

Krout, R. (2004) 'A synerdisciplinary music therapy treatment team approach for hospice and palliative care.' *The Australian Journal of Music Therapy 15*, 33–45.

Lacey, P. (1998) 'Meeting Complex Needs through Collaborative Multidisciplinary Teamwork.' In P. Lacey and C. Ouvry (eds) *People with Profound and Multiple Learning Disabilities: A Collaborative Approach to Meeting Complex Needs.* London: David Fulton.

Larkin, G. (1995) 'State Control and the Health Professions in the UK: Historical Perspectives.' In T. Johnson, G. Larkin and M. Saks (eds) *Health Professions and the State in Europe.* London: Routledge.

Larson, M. (1977) *The Rise of Professionalism: A Sociological Analysis.* California: University of California Press.

Leaning, B. and Watson, T. (2006) 'From the inside looking out – an intensive interaction group for people with profound and multiple learning disabilities.' *British Journal of Learning Disabilities 34*, 103–109.

Lee, K. and Baker, F. (1997) 'Towards integrating a holistic rehabilitation system: the implications for music therapy.' *The Australian Journal of Music Therapy 8*, 30–37.

Lindeck, J. (2005) 'Music technology – a tool for clinician and community.' Abstract in *Handbook and Abstracts 11th World Congress of Music Therapy: From Lullaby to Lament, Brisbane 2005*, 98.

Loth, H. (1994) 'Music therapy and forensic psychiatry – choice, denial and the law.' *Journal of British Music Therapy 8*, 2, 10–18.

Lucia, C.M. (1987) 'Toward developing a model of music therapy intervention in the rehabilitation of head trauma patients.' *Music Therapy Perspectives 4*, 34–39.

Macadam, M. and Rodgers, J. (1997) 'The Multi-disciplinary and Multi-agency Approach.' In J. O'Hara and A. Sperlinger (eds) *Adults with Learning Disabilities: A Practical Approach for Health Professionals.* Somerset: John Wiley and Sons.

McCracken, W. (2002) *Multiple Disability and Multi-professional Working.* Available at www.deafnessatbirth.org.uk/content2/practice/multi/01, accessed 9 November 2005.

McGauley, G. (1997) 'A Delinquent in the Therapeutic Community: Actions Speak Louder than Words.' In E.V. Welldon and C.V. Velsen (eds) *A Practical Guide to Forensic Psychotherapy.* London: Jessica Kingsley Publishers.

McGrath, M. (1991) *Multi-Disciplinary Teamwork.* Aldershot: Avebury Studies of Care in the Community Publication.

Macpherson, W. (1999) *The Stephen Lawrence Inquiry: Report of an Inquiry by Sir William Macpherson of Cluny.* London: Stationery Office.

Magee, W.L. (2005) 'Music therapy with patients in low awareness states: assessment and treatment approaches in multidisciplinary care.' *Neuropsychological Rehabilitation 15*, 3–4, 522–536.

Magee, W.L. and Andrews, K. (2007) 'Multi-disciplinary perceptions of music therapy in complex neuro-rehabilitation.' *International Journal of Therapy and Rehabilitation 14*, 2, 70–75.

Magee, W.L., Brumfitt, S.M., Freeman, M. and Davidson, J.W. (2006) 'The role of music therapy in an interdisciplinary approach to address functional communication in complex neuro-communication disorders: a case report.' *Disability and Rehabilitation 28*, 19, 1221–1229.

Maidment, A. and Merry, L. (2002) 'Smart Goal Setting.' In *Proceedings of the Resna 98 Annual Conference: The State of the Arts and Science.* Oxford: Oxford Brookes University, School of Health Care.

Maranto, C.D. (1993) *Music Therapy: International Perspectives.* Pennsylvania: Jeffrey Books.

Maratos, A. (2004) 'Whatever Next! Community Music Therapy for the Institution.' In M. Pavlicevic and G. Ansdell (eds) *Community Music Therapy.* London: Jessica Kingsley Publishers.

Mayne, M. (2006) *The Enduring Melody.* London: Darton, Longman and Todd.

Meadows, A. (1997) 'Music therapy for children with severe and profound multiple disabilities: a review of literature.' *The Australian Journal of Music Therapy 8*, 3–17.

Meadows, A. (2002) 'Approaches to music and movement for children with severe and profound multiple disabilities.' *The Australian Journal of Music Therapy 13*, 17–27.

Meisels, S. and Atkins-Burnett, S. (1999) 'Assessing intellectual and affective development before age three: a perspective on changing practices.' *Food and Nutrition Bulletin 20*, 1. Available at www.unu.edu/unupress/food/V201e/ch04.htm, accessed 26 January 2007.

Menzies-Lyth, I. (1988) *Containing Anxiety in Institutions: Selected Essays, Volume 1.* London: Free Association Books.

Miller, C., Freeman, C.M. and Ross, N. (2001) *Interprofessional Practice in Health and Social Care: Challenging the Shared Learning Agenda.* London: Arnold Press.

Millman, R. and Jefferson, R. (2000) *Music Therapy within the Multi-disciplinary Team: Different Approaches – Shared Goals.* Paper presented at the Annual Conference, British Society for Music Therapy and Association of Professional Music Therapists, 2000.

Molyneux, C. (2002) *Short Term Music Therapy within a Child and Adolescent Mental Health Service – A Description of a Developing Service.* Unpublished MA dissertation. Cambridge: Anglia Polytechnic University.

Molyneux, C. (2005) 'Music therapy as a short term intervention with individuals and families in a child and adolescent mental health service.' *British Journal of Music Therapy 19*, 2, 59–66.

Money, D.F. and Thurman, S.C. (1994) 'Talkabout: a teaching course.' *Bulletin of the College of Speech and Language Therapists 504*, 12–13.

Moss, H. (1999) 'Creating a new music therapy post: an evidence-based research project.' *British Journal of Music Therapy 13*, 2, 49–58.

Murray, R. and Zenter, J. (1989) *Nursing Concepts for Health Promotion.* London: Prentice-Hall.

Music Therapy Department, Royal Hospital for Neuro-disability (RHN) (2006) *Music Therapy Service Standards for Clifden Ward.* Unpublished document.

Nagler, J. (1998) 'Digital Music Technology in Music Therapy Practice.' In C. Tomaino (ed.), *Clinical Applications of Music in Neurologic Rehabilitation.* St Louis: Magnamusic-Baton.

Newbigging, K. (2004) 'Multidisciplinary Teamworking and the Roles of Members.' In T. Ryan and J. Pritchard (eds) *Good Practice in Adult Mental Health.* London: Jessica Kingsley Publishers.

Nitsun, M. (2003) *The Anti-Group: Destructive Forces in the Group and their Creative Potential.* East Sussex: Brunner-Routledge. (Original work published 1996.)

Nockolds, J. (1999) 'Olive and Jim: Senility and Wisdom.' In M. Pavlicevic (ed.) *Music Therapy: Intimate Notes.* London: Jessica Kingsley Publishers.

O'Callaghan, C., Powell, T. and Oyebode, J. (2006) 'An exploration of the experience of gaining awareness of deficit in people who have suffered a traumatic brain injury.' *Neuropsychological Rehabilitation 16*, 5, 579–593.

O'Gorman, S. (2006) 'The infant's mother: facilitating an experience of infant-directed singing with the mother in mind.' *British Journal of Music Therapy 20*, 1, 22–30.

O'Hagan, S., Allen, D., Bennett, M., Bridgman, A., Lumsden, K. and Wallace, L. (2004) 'Transdisciplinary teamwork improves care: five disciplines combine skills to assist people with intellectual disabilities.' *Annual Journal of the New Zealand Society for Music Therapy 2*, 50–57.

Obholzer, A. and Zagier Roberts, V. (eds) (1994) *The Unconscious at Work: Individual and Organisational Stress in the Human Services.* London: Routledge.

Odell, H. (1979) 'Music therapy in SSN hospitals: report of BSMT meeting.' *British Journal of Music Therapy 10*, 4, 12–15.

Odell-Miller, H. (1993) 'Stretto – music therapy in the context of the multidisciplinary team: working with a multidisciplinary team.' *Journal of British Music Therapy 7*, 1, 24–25.

Odell-Miller, H. (1995a) 'Why provide music therapy in the community for adults with mental health problems?' *British Journal of Music Therapy 9*, 1, 4–10.

Odell-Miller, H. (1995b) 'Approaches to Music Therapy in Psychiatry with Specific Emphasis upon a Research Project with the Elderly Mentally Ill.' In T. Wigram, B. Saperson and R. West (eds) *The Art and Science of Music Therapy: A Handbook.* Chur, Switzerland: Harwood Academic Publishers.

Odell-Miller, H. (2001) 'Music Therapy and Its Relationship to Psychoanalysis.' In Y. Searle and I. Streng (eds) *Where Analysis Meets the Arts: The Integration of the Arts Therapies with Psychoanalytic Theory.* London: Karnac Books.

Odell-Miller, H. (2002) 'Musical Narratives in Music Therapy Treatment for Dementia.' In L. Bunt and S. Hoskyns (eds) *The Handbook of Music Therapy.* London: Brunner-Routledge.

Oldfield, A. (1993) 'Music Therapy with Families.' In M. Heal and T. Wigram (eds) *Music Therapy in Health and Education.* London: Jessica Kingsley Publishers.

Oldfield, A. (2000) 'Music Therapy as a Contribution to the Diagnosis Made by the Staff Team in Child and Family Psychiatry – An Initial Description of a Methodology that is Still Emerging through Clinical Practice.' In T. Wigram (ed.) *Assessment and Evaluation in the Arts Therapies.* St Albans: Harper House Publications.

Oldfield, A. (2001) 'Music therapy with young children with autism and their parents: developing communication through playful musical interactions specific to each child.' *Music Therapy in Europe – Proceedings of the Vth European Music Therapy Congress, Naples.* Available at www.musictherapyworld.net, accessed 20 January 2007.

Oldfield, A. (2006) *Interactive Music Therapy in Child and Family Psychiatry: Clinical Practice, Research and Training.* London: Jessica Kingsley Publishers.

Oldfield, A. and Bunce, L. (2001) 'Mummy can play too...: short term music therapy with mothers and young children.' *British Journal of Music Therapy 15*, 1, 27–36.

Oldfield, A., Adams, M. and Bunce, L. (2003) 'An investigation into short-term music therapy with mothers and young children.' *British Journal of Music Therapy 17*, 1, 26–45.

Onyett, S. (1999) 'Community mental health team working as a socially valued enterprise.' *Journal of Mental Health 8*, 3, 245–251.

Øvretveit, J. (1993) *Coordinating Community Care: Multidisciplinary Teams and Care Management.* Buckingham: Oxford University Press.

Owens, P. and Petch, H. (1995) 'Professionals and Management.' In P. Owens, J. Carrier and J. Horder (eds) *Interprofessional Issues in Community and Primary Health Care.* Basingstoke: Macmillan Press.

Owens, P., Carrier, J. and Horder, J. (eds) (1995) *Interprofessional Issues in Community and Primary Health Care.* Basingstoke: Macmillan Press.

Papousek, H. and Papousek, M. (1979) 'The Infant's Fundamental Adaptive Response System in Social Interaction.' In E.B. Thoman (ed.) *Origins of the Infant's Social Responsiveness.* Hillsdale, NJ: Lawrence Erlbaum.

Papousek, H. and Papousek, M. (1981) 'Musical Elements in Infants' Vocalisation: Their Significance for Communication, Cognition and Creativity.' In L.P. Lipsitt (ed.) *Advances in Infancy Research, Volume 1.* Norwood, NJ: Ablex.

Paul, S. and Ramsey, D. (2000) 'Music therapy in physical medicine and rehabilitation.' *Australian Occupational Therapy Journal 47*, 111–118.

Petersen, E. (2005) 'Music therapy and oncology at the National Institute of Cancer.' *Voices: A World Forum for Music Therapy*. Available at www.voices.no/mainissues/ mi40005000195.html, accessed 26 January 2007.

Pines, M. (2000) 'The Group-as-a-Whole.' In D. Brown and L. Zinkin (eds) *The Psyche and the Social World: Developments in Group Analytic Theory*. London: Jessica Kingsley Publishers. (Original work published 1994.)

Port, A., Willmott, C. and Charlton, J. (2002) 'Self-awareness following traumatic brain injury and implications for rehabilitation.' *Brain Injury 16*, 4, 277–289.

Powell, H. (2004) 'A Dream Wedding: From Community Music to Music Therapy with a Community.' In M. Pavlicevic and G. Ansdell (eds) *Community Music Therapy*. London: Jessica Kingsley Publishers.

Priestley, M. (1993) 'Stretto – music therapy in the context of the multidisciplinary team: music therapy in the multidisciplinary team.' *Journal of British Music Therapy 7*, 1, 26–27.

Proctor, S. (2002) 'Empowering and Enabling – Music Therapy in Non-medical Mental Health Provision.' In C. Kenny and B. Stige (eds) *Contemporary Voices in Music Therapy: Communication, Culture and Community*. Oslo: Unipubforlag.

Proctor, S. (2005) 'Parents, children and their therapists: a collaborative research project examining therapist–parent interactions in a music therapy clinic.' *British Journal of Music Therapy 19*, 2, 45–58.

Read Johnson, D. (1985) 'Perspectives – envisioning the link among the creative arts therapies.' *The Arts in Psychotherapy 12*, 233–238.

Register, D. (2002) 'Collaboration and consultation: a survey of board certified music therapists.' *Journal of Music Therapy 4*, 305–321.

Richards, E. and Hind, H. (2002) 'Finding a Place to Play: A Music Therapy Group for Adults with Learning Disabilities.' In A. Davies and E. Richards (eds) *Music Therapy and Group Work Sound Company*. London: Jessica Kingsley Publishers.

Ritchie, F. (1991) 'Behind closed doors: a case study.' *Journal of British Music Therapy 5*, 2, 4–10.

Ritchie, F. (1993a) 'Stretto: music therapy in the context of the multidisciplinary team.' *British Journal of Music Therapy 7*, 1, 25–26.

Ritchie, F. (1993b) 'Opening Doors: The Effects of Music Therapy with People who have Severe Learning Difficulties and Display Challenging Behaviour.' In M. Heal and T. Wigram (eds) *Music Therapy in Health and Education*. London: Jessica Kingsley Publishers.

Roberts, C. and Bull, R. (2005) 'The odd couple: an exploration of co-working with non-music therapists.' *No Man is an Island: Groups, Partnerships and Teams in Music Therapy*. Papers from the BSMT/APMT Annual Conference. London: BSMT Publications.

Royal Hospital for Neuro-disability. *Music Therapy in the Treatment of Neurocommunication Disorders*. Available at www.rhn.org.uk/institute/neurocommunicationdisorders, accessed 24 June 2007.

Rueschemeyer, D. (1983) 'Professional Autonomy and the Social Control of Expertise.' In R. Dingwall and P. Lewis (eds) *The Sociology of the Professions: Lawyers, Doctors and Others*. London: Macmillan Press.

Ryan, P. (2001) *The Devil's Bet: Shakespeare's Storybook*. Bath: Barefoot Books.

Sainsbury Centre for Mental Health (SCMH) (2001) *The Capable Practitioner: A Framework and List of the Practitioner Capabilities Required to Implement the National Service Framework for Mental Health*. London: Sainsbury Centre for Mental Health.

Sayers, K. (1993) 'Stretto: music therapy and its relationship with creative arts therapies.' *British Journal of Music Therapy 7*, 2, 23–25.

Schaffer, R. (1977) *Mothering: The Developing Child*. London: Fontana.

Schwarting, B. (2005) 'The Open Music Therapy Group Session.' In M. Pavlicevic (ed.) *Music Therapy in Children's Hospices: Jessie's Fund in Action*. London: Jessica Kingsley Publishers.

Seytter, A. (1998) 'Music therapy with mother and infant – sense and possibilities of a triangular setting.' *Music Therapy – A Dialogue: Proceedings of the 4th European Music Therapy Congress.* Available at www.musictherapyworld.net, accessed 28 October 2006.

Shaw, F. (2006) 'Triadic improvisations: developing communication skills.' *The New Zealand Journal of Music Therapy 4,* 46–63.

Shoemark, H. (1996) 'Family-centred early intervention: music therapy in the playgroup program.' *The Australian Journal of Music Therapy 7,* 3–15.

Sines, D. and Barr, O. (1998) 'Professions in Teams.' In T. Thompson and P. Mathias (eds) *Standards and Learning Disability.* Oxford: Bailliere Tindall.

Skewes, K. and Thompson, G. (1998) 'The use of musical interactions to develop social skills in early intervention.' *The Australian Journal of Music Therapy 9,* 35–44.

Skille, O., Wigram, T. and Weekes, L. (1989) 'Vibroacoustic therapy: the therapeutic effect of low frequency sound on specific physical disorders and disabilities.' *British Journal of Music Therapy 3,* 2, 6–10.

Sloboda, A. and Bolton, R. (2002) 'Music Therapy in Forensic Psychiatry: A Case Study with Musical Commentary.' In L. Bunt and S. Hoskyns (eds) *The Handbook of Music Therapy.* East Sussex: Brunner-Routledge.

Smitskamp, H. (2003) 'Image versus word? Communication between Creative Arts Therapists and Verbal Psychotherapists.' In L. Kossolapow, S. Scobie and D. Waller (eds) *Arts-Therapies-Communication: On the Way to a Regional European Arts Therapy, Volume 2.* New Brunswick: Transaction Publishers.

Soeterik, S., Roshier, H. and Quinn, L. (2005) *The Colgate Smile: The Use of Music as a Positive Programming Strategy in Skill Acquisition.* Poster session presented at the Institute of Applied Behaviour Analysis 3rd International Conference, Dublin, Eire.

Soundbeam. *Soundbeam.* Available at www.soundbeam.co.uk, accessed 24 June 2007.

Stern, D. (1985) *The Interpersonal World of the Infant.* New York: Basic Books, Inc.

Stewart, D. (1996) 'Chaos, noise and a wall of silence: working with primitive affects in psychodynamic group music therapy.' *British Journal of Music Therapy 10,* 2, 21–33.

Stewart, D. (2000) 'The state of the UK music therapy profession: personal qualities, working models, support networks and job satisfaction.' *British Journal of Music Therapy 14,* 1, 13–31.

Stewart, G. (2006) *Understanding Mental Illness.* London: Mind Publications.

Storey, J. (2005) 'The Development of a Schools Music Therapy Service with an Illustrative Case Study of Work with a Child with Autism.' In D. Aldridge, J. Fachner and J. Erkkilä (eds) *Many Faces of Music Therapy: Proceedings of the 6th European Music Therapy Congress, June 16–20, 2004, Jyvaskyla, Finland.* eBook at *MusicTherapyToday.com 6,* accessed 4 November 2005.

Strange, J. (1987) 'The role of the music therapist in special education.' *Journal of British Music Therapy 1,* 2, 28–31.

Styron, W. (1991) *Darkness Visible.* London: Jonathan Cape.

Summer, L. (1997) 'Considering the future of music therapy.' *The Arts in Psychotherapy 24,* 1, 75–80.

Sutton, J. (2002) 'Survival in the workplace: the strength and vulnerability of the music therapy practitioner.' *British Journal of Music Therapy 16,* 2, 62–64.

Sweeney-Brown, C. (2005) 'Music and Medicine: Music Therapy within a Medical Setting.' In M. Pavlicevic (ed.) *Music Therapy in Children's Hospices: Jessie's Fund in Action.* London: Jessica Kingsley Publishers.

Tollerfield, I. (2003) 'The process of collaboration within a special school setting: an exploration of the ways in which skills and knowledge are shared and barriers are overcome when a teacher and speech and language therapist collaborate.' *Child Language Teaching and Therapy 19,* 1, 67–84.

Toolan, P. and Coleman, S. (1995) 'Music therapy, a description of process: engagement and avoidance in five people with learning disabilities.' *British Journal of Music Therapy 9,* 1, 17–24.

Trevarthen, C. and Hubley, P. (1978) 'Secondary Intersubjectivity: Confidence, Confiding and Acts of Meaning in the First Year.' in A. Lock (ed.) *Action, Gesture and Symbol*. London: Academic Press.

Turnbull, D. and Robinson, M. (1990) 'Music and movement as therapy for primary language and learning disordered children.' *The Australian Journal of Music Therapy 1*, 45–49.

Twyford, K. (2004a) *New Directions: An Investigation into Music Therapy as Part of a Collaborative Multidisciplinary Approach*. Unpublished Masters dissertation. London: University of Surrey Roehampton.

Twyford, K. (2004b) 'From multidisciplinary to interdisciplinary: an investigation into collaborative approaches in music therapy practice.' Paper from the BSMT/APMT Annual Conference – Changes: Exploring Clinical, Professional and Global Perspectives. London: BSMT Publications.

Usher, J. (1998) 'Lighting up the mind: evolving a model of consciousness and its application to improvisation in music therapy.' *British Journal of Music Therapy 1*, 4–19.

Vaac, N. and Ritter, S. (1995) *Assessment of Preschool Children*. Available at www.ericdigests.org/1996-3/preschool.htm, accessed 26 January 2007.

Van der Drift, I. (2003) 'To Be or Not to Be: Creative Therapists Working in a Multi-disciplinary Team.' in L. Kossolapow, S. Scobie and D. Waller (eds) *Arts-Therapies-Communication: On the Way to a Regional European Arts Therapy, Volume 2*. New Brunswick: Transaction Publishers.

Voight, M. (2001) 'Promoting parent–child interaction through Orff music therapy.' *Music Therapy in Europe: Proceedings of the Vth European Music Therapy Congress, Naples*. Available at www.musictherapyworld.net, accessed 20 January 2007.

Waller, D. (2001) 'Come Back Professor Higgins – Arts Therapists Need You! The Importance of Clear Communication for Arts Therapists.' In L. Kossolapow, S. Scoble and D. Waller (eds) *Arts-Therapies-Communication: On the Way to a Communicative European Arts Therapy, Volume 1*. Münster: Lit Verlag.

Walsh Stewart, R. (2002) 'Combined Efforts: Increasing Social-emotional Communication with Children with Autistic Spectrum Disorder using Psychodynamic Music Therapy and Division TEACCH Communication Programme.' In A. Davies and E. Richards (eds) *Music Therapy and Group Work*. London: Jessica Kingsley Publishers.

Warlock, P. (1927) *The First Mercy*. London: Hawkes and Son.

Warwick, A. (1995) 'Music Therapy in the Education Service: Research with Autistic Children and their Mothers.' In T. Wigram, B. Saperston and R. West (eds) *The Art and Science of Music Therapy: A Handbook*. Chur, Switzerland: Harwood Academic Publishers.

Watson, T. (2002) 'Music Therapy with Adults with Learning Disabilities.' In L. Bunt and S. Hoskyns (eds) *The Handbook of Music Therapy*. London: Brunner-Routledge.

Watson, T. (2007) *Music Therapy with Adults with Learning Disabilities*. London: Routledge.

Watson, T. and Vickers, L. (2002) 'A Music and Art Therapy Group for People with Learning Disabilities.' In A. Davies and E. Richards (eds) *Music Therapy and Group Work*. London: Jessica Kingsley Publishers.

Watson, T., Bragg, A. and Jeffcote, N. (2004) 'Working Together: Integrated Multi-disciplinary Practice with Women.' In N. Jeffcote and T. Watson (eds) *Working Therapeutically with Women in Secure Mental Health Settings*. London: Jessica Kingsley Publishers.

Weber, S. (2000) 'Remembering and Forgiving.' in D. Aldridge (ed.) *Music Therapy in Dementia Care*. London: Jessica Kingsley Publishers.

Weinstein, J. (1998) 'The Professions and Their Interrelationships.' In T. Thompson and P. Mathias (eds) *Standards and Learning Disability*. London: Balliere Tindall.

Wells, N.F. and Stevens, T. (1984) 'Music as a stimulus for creative fantasy in group psychotherapy with young adolescents.' *The Arts in Psychotherapy 11*, 71–76.

Wensley, M. (1995) 'Spirituality in nursing.' *St. Vincent's Nursing Monograph 1995: Selected Works*. Available at www.ciap.health.nsw.gov.au/hospolic/stvincents/1995/a04.html, accessed 20 June 2007.

West, M. and Slater, J. (1996) *Teamworking in Primary Healthcare: A Review of its Effectiveness.* Sheffield: Health Education Authority Report.

Wheeler, B. (2003) *The Interdisciplinary Music Therapist.* Available at www.voices.no/columnist/colwheeler020603.html, accessed 16 August 2005.

Wigram, T. (1988) 'Music therapy – developments in mental handicap.' *Psychology of Music 16,* 1, 42–51.

Wigram, T. (1992) 'Aspects of music therapy relating to physical disability.' *The Australian Journal of Music Therapy 3,* 3–15.

Wigram, T. (1995) 'A Model of Assessment and Differential Diagnosis of Handicap in Children through the Medium of Music Therapy.' In T. Wigram, B. Saperston and R. West (eds) *The Art and Science of Music Therapy: A Handbook.* Chur, Switzerland: Harwood Academic Publishers.

Wigram, T. (2002) 'Indications in music therapy. Evidence from assessment that can identify the expectations of music therapy as treatment for autistic spectrum disorder (ASD): meeting the challenge of evidence based practice.' *British Journal of Music Therapy 16,* 1, 11–28.

Wigram, T. interviewed by Loth, H. (2000) 'Historical perspectives interview series.' *British Journal of Music Therapy 14,* 1, 5–12.

Wigram, T., Pedersen, I. and Bonde, L. (2002) *A Comprehensive Guide to Music Therapy.* London: Jessica Kingsley Publishers.

Wilson, B. and Smith, D. (2000) 'Music therapy assessment in school settings: a preliminary investigation.' *Journal of Music Therapy 37,* 2, 95–117.

Wilson, P. (1985) *Games without Frontiers.* Basingstoke: Marshall Pickering.

Wilson, P. (1999) 'Memory, Personhood and Faith.' In A. Jewell (ed.) *Spirituality and Ageing.* London: Jessica Kingsley Publishers.

Wilson, V. and Pirrie, A. (2000) 'Multidisciplinary teamworking indicators of good practice.' *Scottish Council for Research in Education Spotlights 77,* 1–4.

Winnicott, D.W. (1964) *The Child, the Family and the Outside World.* London: Penguin.

Winnicott, D.W. (1965) *The Maturational Processes and the Facilitating Environment.* London: Hogarth Press.

Winnicott, D.W. (1971) *Playing and Reality.* London: Tavistock Publications.

Winnicott, D.W. (1988) *Human Nature.* London: Free Association Books.

Woodward, A. (2004) 'Music therapy for autistic children and their families: a creative spectrum.' *British Journal of Music Therapy 18,* 1, 8–14.

World Health Organization (1992) *The ICD-10 Classification of Mental and Behavioural Disorders: Clinical Descriptions and Diagnostic Guidelines.* Geneva: World Health Organization.

Wrench, M. (1998) 'The Multi-Disciplinary Team: The Social Worker.' In C. Cordess and M. Cox (eds) *Forensic Psychotherapy, Crime, Psychodynamics and the Offender Patient.* London: Jessica Kingsley Publishers. (Original work published 1996.)

Zagelbaum, V.N. and Rubino, M.A. (1991) 'Combined dance/movement, art and music therapies with a developmentally delayed, psychiatric client in a day treatment setting.' *The Arts in Psychotherapy 18,* 139–148.

Zulueta, F. de (1997) 'Working on the Borderline: Can We Continue to Turn a Blind Eye?' In E.V. Welldon and C.V. Velsen (eds) *A Practical Guide to Forensic Psychotherapy.* London: Jessica Kingsley Publishers.

Zwarenstein, M., Reeves, S., Barr, H., Hammick, M. *et al.* (2000) 'Interprofessional education: effects on professional practice and health care outcomes (Cochrane Review).' *The Cochrane Library Issue 3.* New York: John Wiley and Sons.

Contributors

Karen Twyford trained as a music therapist at the University of Melbourne in Australia, graduating in 1992. The majority of her clinical experience was gained in the UK within the area of special education where her interests lay in the utilisation of the multidisciplinary team. In 2004 she completed an MA at the University of Surrey, Roehampton, where she researched the use of collaborative multidisciplinary approaches within music therapy practice in the UK. She relocated to Wellington, New Zealand, in 2006 where her current clinical work is with children with special educational needs included in mainstream school settings. Karen would like to thank **Charlotte Parkhouse** and **Joanne Murphy** for their contributions to the case studies.

Tessa Watson is a music therapist and music therapy trainer, currently Convenor for Arts and Play Therapies programmes at Roehampton University. She has experience of working within teams in a wide variety of clinical areas, and has a special interest in adults with learning disabilities, women in secure settings, group work, and learning, teaching and assessment in the arts therapies. Tessa would like to thank **Alison Germany** for her contribution to the case study.

Alison Barrington has been a music therapist for 16 years working primarily with children with special educational needs. More recently she has also worked with adults with palliative care needs. She completed her PhD from Durham University in 2005 which focused on the Professionalisation of Music Therapy in the UK. Her interest in interagency work has developed through both her clinical practice and research. She has taught in the music department at Durham University and currently lectures on the music therapy MA course at Guildhall School of Music and Drama.

Rachel Darnley-Smith is Senior Lecturer and Programme Coordinator for the MA in Music Therapy at Roehampton University. She is also conducting doctoral studies into the Aesthetics of Free Improvisation in the music department at the University of Durham. She has worked in NHS settings with elderly adults over many years and is co-author with Helen Patey of *Music Therapy*, published by Sage Publications in 2003.

Mary-Clare Fearn and **Rebecca O'Connor** shared a lead music therapy post at the Cheyne Child Development Service, Chelsea and Westminster Hospital, London, for 13 years. During this time they developed many different ways of collaborative working with a variety of professionals. Both Mary-Clare and Rebecca also have extensive teaching experience. The development of music and attuned movement therapy has only been possible due to the dedication and expertise of the team at the Cheyne Day Centre. Their openness towards this therapeutic approach and their invaluable insight and experience in working with children with profound disabilities has been integral to the success of this approach to collaborative working.

Adrienne Freeman trained as a music therapist at the Guildhall School of Music and Drama, qualifying in 1985. Her clinical experience lies chiefly within the area of adult and elderly mental health: she has worked in the Mental Health Unit at Chase Farm Hospital, Enfield, since 1988. She is an experienced supervisor of both qualified and student music therapists and is external examiner for music therapy trainees. She has a special interest in dementia and end-of-life work. Adrienne would like to acknowledge numerous clients and colleagues (together with her family) for their part in the formation of her chapter.

Paula Hedderly trained at the Guildhall School of Music and Drama, graduating in 2000. She initially worked in an educational setting with children with special educational needs, later developing her clinical work in mental health, in particular with adults suffering from psychosis or with a diagnosis of personality disorder. Paula has undertaken further training in group work and has a special interest in the collaborative working involved in treatment for people with personality disorders.

Jackie Lindeck is Senior 1 Music Therapist at the Royal Hospital for Neuro-disability (RHN) in London, UK. Jackie works both as part of a music therapy team and as part of a ward-based multidisciplinary team at the RHN. The clinical work described in the case study was undertaken jointly with **Amy Pundole**, specialist speech and language therapist, who also co-authored the case study. Jackie would like to acknowledge the support of the music therapy and speech and language therapy departments in preparing this work for publication.

Wendy L. Magee holds a post-doctoral fellowship at the Institute of Neuropalliative Rehabilitation in London and is Honorary Senior Research Fellow in the Department of Palliative Care, Policy and Rehabilitation at Kings College London. She has been a music therapy clinician, manager and researcher since 1988 in the field of adult neurology. She has published widely on research and clinical practice with people with complex disabilities stemming from head injuries, stroke, Huntington's Disease and Multiple Sclerosis and is recognised internationally as a specialist in the field. Specialist research interests include electronic music technologies and validating assessment tools.

Claire Miller studied music at university before completing a Masters degree in the psychology of music. She qualified as a music therapist from the Guildhall School of Music and Drama in 1997. Since then she has practised in the areas of learning disability, neuro-disability and, for the last nine years, adult mental health (forensic services). She currently holds a professional development lead post in a forensic mental health arts therapies service in London and is one of the Association of Professional Music Therapists Professional Development Officers. Acknowledgements and thanks go to **Mario Guarnieri**, dramatherapist, who contributed greatly to the writing of the third case study within the adult mental health chapter. Mario has worked within forensic mental health services for over ten years.

Rachel Millman worked as a music therapist in London with people with neurological disorders before moving to Dorset to set up a music therapy service. She now continues to work with adults with neuro-disabilities in addition to people with dementia and pre-school children. Acknowledgements and thanks go to the client and family featured in her case study for their consent, and to Dr Wendy Magee and Richard Jefferson.

Claire Molyneux trained as a music therapist in the UK. Since qualifying, she has worked in the fields of child and adolescent mental health and learning disabilities. Claire moved to Auckland, New Zealand, in 2005 where she is currently employed as Head of Clinical Services at the Raukatauri Music Therapy Centre. Claire would like to thank her colleagues Jeanette Allen, Ingrid Davidson and Ellisa Fisher who contributed to the case studies, the wider multidisciplinary team at CAMHS who were supportive in encouraging the development of music therapy within the service and the clients who have shared their journeys in music therapy.

Nicky O'Neill works as a music therapy clinician, tutor and manager at the Nordoff-Robbins Music Therapy Centre, London, from where she is also seconded to Great Ormond Street Hospital to work with children with life-threatening conditions. Her collaborative working started over ten years ago when she took up a position in a special needs nursery in Greenwich (she also works for Greenwich TPCT). The success and reward of such working led her to develop it into her other places of work. Nicky would like to thank Mercedes Pavlicevic for her support in writing the case study.

Maria Radoje studied music therapy at Roehampton Institute and qualified in 1999. She has experience in a wide variety of clinical settings. She currently works with the elderly for Hackney Social Services and with children and adults with learning disabilities at St Joseph's Pastoral Centre. Maria and her colleagues would like to thank Jim, and their client, supervisors Linda Batty (Lead Psychologist) and Rachel Darnley-Smith.

Ann Sloboda studied music at Oxford University. She qualified as a music therapist in 1985 from the Guildhall School of Music and Drama, London. She worked as a music therapist in the NHS for 20 years, in adult learning disability, eating disorders, general psychiatry and forensic psychiatry. A past chair of the Association of Professional Music Therapists, she was Head of Arts Therapies at West London Mental Health Trust for ten years. Her current post is Head of Music Therapy at the Guildhall School of Music and Drama. She also works as a clinical supervisor, in the NHS and privately.

Rosanne Tyas trained as a music therapist in 1982 at the Guildhall School of Music and Drama. She has worked with various client groups including children with emotional difficulties and developmental delay, adolescents with emotional needs, adults with mental health needs, adults with neurological damage and adults with learning disabilities and challenging needs. She is presently Head Music Therapist at a residential setting for adults with profound learning disabilities and manages a joint arts therapies project where she worked with Justine Souster and Chloe de Sousa. She also teaches on the introduction to music therapy course at the Royal College of Music.

Sally Watson qualified as a music therapist from the Roehampton Institute in 1996, and has worked in a wide variety of clinical settings. She chose to specialise in music therapy with people with learning disabilities in 2001, and also has a private supervision practice. Sally would like to thank all the staff and clients involved in the music and physio group. Her case study is in memory of one of her clients, Louise, who sadly died last year.

Tessa Watson is a music therapist and music therapy trainer, currently Convenor for Arts and Play Therapies programmes at Roehampton University. She has experience of working within teams in a wide variety of clinical areas, and has a special interest in adults with learning disabilities, women in secure settings, group work, and learning, teaching and assessment in the arts therapies. Tessa would like to thank **Alison Germany** for her contribution to the case study.

Ann Woodward read music at Cambridge University before training as a music therapist. Since qualifying, she has worked with children of all ages and abilities, in a variety of settings. She has a special interest in autism, and in working with parents and children together. Ann has recently moved to Cumbria where she divides her time between working with children with special needs and exploring the mountains.

Subject Index

Author Index